International Satellite Broadcasting in South Asia

Political, Economic and Cultural Implications

Editors
Srinivas R. Melkote
Peter Shields
Binod C. Agrawal

University Press of America,® Inc.
Lanham • New York • Oxford

Copyright © 1998
University Press of America,® Inc.
4720 Boston Way
Lanham, Maryland 20706

12 Hid's Copse Rd.
Cummor Hill, Oxford OX2 9JJ

Library of Congress Cataloging-in-Publication Data

International satellite broadcasting in South Asia : political,
economic, and cultural implications / editors Srinivas R. Melkote,
Peter Shields, Binod C. Agrawal.
p.   cm.
Includes index.
1. Direct broadcast satellite television—Social aspects—South
Asia. 2. Direct broadcast satellite television—Social aspects—India.
3. Doordarshan (Television station : New Delhi, India) I. Melkote,
Srinivas R. II. Shields, Peter.
HE8700.66.S64I58 1998   302.23'45'0954—dc21   98-26805 CIP

ISBN 0-7618-1201-6 (cloth: alk. ppr.)
ISBN 0-7618-1202-4 (pbk: alk. ppr.)

Contents

Part II: Critical Issues in the Asian Context

Foreword

Let me introduce this discussion of 'satellite broadcasting in south Asia' with some personal observations gleaned since 1964 during dozens of research stays in Asia and the Caribbean. I believe such reminisces will show how drastically the mediascapes have been altered.

Mediascape 1. Manila, 1964-65---the highly touted 'transistor revolution' was in its fifth year when I went to the Philippines in the summer of 1964. The Philippine radio, television, and film were accused of catering to a *bakya* (lowest common denominator fare) mentality, and television was not very prevalent with only 500 sets in all of the province of Davao. Where television existed, receivers were tuned to the dominating US programs such as *Bonanza, Amos Burke, the Man from U.N.C.L.E, Ed Sullivan Show, the Untouchables,* and others. Local television shows were labeled as photographed radio programs. The University of Philippines Institute of Mass Communication was being conceptualized for its eventual role in promoting development communication at a time when the philosophies of Americans such as Wilbur Schramm, Daniel Lerner, Everett Rogers were catching on.

Mediascape 2. Caribbean and Malaysia, early 1970s---Television was new to many parts of the Caribbean, to the extent that some government personnel still regarded it as primarily an educational medium; shows were mainly non-Caribbean and what local programming there was, imitated that of the United States or Europe. For example, in Barbados, *Destination USA* featured Barbadian contestants answering obscure questions about the US in competition for a trip to the US. In Malaysia, television programs (in black and white) were used by the government to promote its strict policies in the aftermath of the 1969 race riots. The government depended much on foreign programming, including American shows such as *All in the Family* and *Love American Style*. Despite its high cost (a television receiver was priced at the cost of building an *attap* house), television spread throughout the country, although the state of Sarawak was still without the medium. Malaysia and Singapore became significant training centers for radio and television broadcasting during the early 1970s; both governments also were at the forefront of using development communication to serve their pubic relations purposes.

Mediascape 3. All over India, in the summer of 1980, there were calls for delinking broadcasting from government conrol; the country had entered the satellite age with one of its own launchings; and in the Parliament, one of the debates focused on the use of television to reach people living in remote areas. The director general of Doordarshan (Indian national television), Shailendra Kumar, told a group of us that satellite television was needed for that goal and that color television would be available in time for the 1982 Asian Games to be hosted by India. The father of Indian satellite television experiments, Ramesh Chandra, explained to the same body that television news had so little impact because there were only one million sets in the country; that the government wanted to retain television as a non-commercial, non-autonomous entity; and that educational television was failing because of pressures to provide increasing levels of entertainment. In 1980, India prided itself on being self-sufficient, making its own television receivers and transmitters and producing all but five percent of its programming, granted that much of the local fare consisted of music and what Ramesh Chandra called 'third-rate Bombay films.' *I Love Lucy* was included in that five percent foreign programming.

Mediascape 4. Shanghai, 1985---As the city was making a move toward modernity, complaints surfaced about too much individualism, a lack of commitment, and the adoption of Western values inimical to Chinese lifestyles. But, Westernization was not very evident at the Shanghai television station, whose three color channels still depended on their in-house productions (the station produced 50 television films in a short span in the mid-1980s), although some from the US, Japan, and Hong Kong were used. By regulation, the television channels were permitted to air six minutes of commercials hourly, and even this time was usually not fully booked.

Mediascape 5. Caribbean, late 1980's---The satellite spill-over from the US, coupled with video and in some cases, satellite dishes, blanketed the region and changed television---and the Caribbean--- forever. Unedited US programs were available 24 hours a day, sometimes creating cultural anomalies: On Montserrat's Antilles Television, I watched CNN News, followed by *The Jeffersons, Solid Gold,* news from WGN in Chicago, along with advertisements for 'Chucks Chicken' and Chicago's windy and freezing weather forecast. By 1987, the tiny country of Belize, with its population of 166,000 had about 18 television and cable stations, at least 12 of which pirated US programming. The impact, determined by systematic research, was enormous: American products, sports, fashions, slang, and moral standards were perceived as better than, and soon replaced, those of Belize.

Other images come to mind relative to the arrival of satellite and cable television to Asia---in 1993, the ubiquitous television monitors in airport lounges of Rangoon and Bangkok, all tuned to CNN and concentrating on the floods in mid-America while large parts of neighboring Bangladesh lay under water; the same year, New Delhi newspaper photographs of individuals standing (or sitting or lying) in long queues for days waiting to obtain a precious cable franchise; and throughout the 1990s, the futile attempts of Asian film and video producers, publishers, and cartoonists to compete with STAR TV, MTV, CNN, and the many other satellite-relayed systems.

Implied in most of these observations are the issues of media imperialism and the concentration of media ownership. In recent years, the media/cultural imperialism thesis has been re-evaluated and replaced with other ideas such as globalization, cultural transcendence, geo-linguistic regionalism, and the notion of an active audience. Questioned are assumptions about: a) core and periphery countries, with arguments that media imperialism existed within and among core countries and that so-called Third World countries also committed media imperialistic acts against one another; b) the purity of native cultures, with contestations that no culture is entirely natural and that all are evolving and subject to superimposition of outside forces; c) standardized effects upon cultures, with interpretations that audiences were different and therefore, less likely to be equally affected by outside forces, that they were active, capable of deciding which messages they wanted to choose, and that too much emphasis was given to theories of maximum effects of mass media. With globalization, others explained away media imperialism by saying that with new patterns of global production, distribution and consumption, it was difficult to point to a clearly-defined local culture; that instead, the pattern is for many countries to exist in a global relationship. All of this may be partly true, but bigger truths are that globalization is still a corporate concept, beneficial to business/industrial transnationalism; that domination is still the prevailing practice in international government, trade, and communication; and that parts of national cultures are withering away under the onslaught of outside (mostly Western) cultural and media products.

Melkote, Shields, and Agrawal's book admirably discusses many aspects of cultural/media imperialism, mainly in the contexts of satellite broadcasting and India, but also relating to television flows in Asia and Europe, consumption of satellite television in East Java, corporate strategies of Asian satellite broadcasting, and pro-social entertainment television programs in developing countries. A variety of approaches---historical, political economy, audience and communicator analyses---lend credence to findings that sometimes are at odds with previous knowledge. Servaes and Malikhao look critically at research involving international flow of television programs and point out that many such studies suffer because they concentrate on the supply of television programs, not consumption or the consequences of consumption, and do not account for shifts in the dynamics of international television flows that involve a more complex pattern of distribution with satellite, cable, and privatization. Sinclair in his chapter, claims that cultural and linguistic differences prove to be substantial barriers to cultural imperialism; Singhal, Svenkerud, and Rahoi-Gilchrest propose cultural transcendence as an alternative to cultural imperialism, stating that culturally accessible programming exchanged across borders is a counterweight to cultural imperialism; and Cohen reports that television viewers of East Java have a strong satisfaction with local shows. Authors dealing with India's broadcasting situation, accuse Doordarshan of working in the interests of the state and elites, thus marginalizing rural India, and of competing so zealously with STAR and other privately-owned networks that its public service function is jettisoned.

More generally, the book brings together current topics of globalization, media imperialism, and new information technologies such as cable, satellite, and video, as they relate to India, the second most populated country. It attacks long-standing presumptions of international media influence, some of which have already been mentioned, and offers recommendations for new frameworks and concepts. Some chapters call for a move away from media-centeredness, a focus on a nations' internal dynamics, and a shift away from concentration on international media effects to national analyses.

This is an important book likely to become a model for similar treatments of satellite broadcasting systems already in place elsewhere around the globe.

Drexel Hill, PA   John A. Lent

Preface

This book explores a broad spectrum of theory, research, and policy issues arising from recent striking developments in Asian satellite broadcasting. These developments are best exemplified by the dramatic rise of international satellite networks such as the STAR-TV which currently offers an array of foreign and indigenous cultural products to millions of households across Asia. In 1991, the Hong Kong-based STAR-TV burst through the Asian skies and reached directly thousands of homes. Within a few years, the number of households reached increased from hundreds of thousands to millions. The popularity of STAR, which initially carried mostly Western programs, threatened the monopoly held largely by state controlled networks in many Asian countries. The advent of popular and intrusive 'foreign' satellite broadcasting in Asia ushered in a new phase in the history of entertainment/communications media with implications for Asia and other regions of the world.

What are the political, economic and cultural implications of these developments? More specifically, how are transnational satellite networks such as STAR-TV impacting national sovereignty, national communication systems, and 'local' cultural identity projects? Are we witnessing cultural imperialism ratcheted to a new level? Our international group of contributors take up these and related questions from a variety of perspectives. The chapters in this volume address the political, economic, social, and cultural significance and impact of transnational satellite networks, with a special emphasis on India.

The common thread that binds this collection is that most if not all of the contributions, explicitly or implicitly, intersect with and contribute to current debates concerning the continued relevance of the cultural imperialism model. As such, while the volume focuses on the south Asian context, we believe our contributors offer insights that will be useful to students of international communications around the world.

We gratefully acknowledge the editorial assistance provided by Sundeep Muppidi and Krishna Kandath. We would also like to thank Dr. Ewart Skinner for his insights and feedback on early drafts of various chapters. This project would not have materialized without the invaluable help from the contributors. Special thanks are due to all the contributors for their timely revisions and patience.

Bowling Green, Ohio   Srinivas R. Melkote
May 11, 1998   Peter Shields
                                               Binod C. Agrawal

Chapter 1

Dynamics Of Satellite Broadcasting In India And Other Areas: An Introduction

Ewart C. Skinner
Srinivas R. Melkote
Sundeep R. Muppidi

ATN, Raj TV, Sun TV, Udaya TV, Sony, ETV, ZEE, Home TV, Channel V, Star Plus, DD, ESPN, BBC, TNT, and the list goes on and on. Welcome to the world of satellite television channels in India. What makes this list interesting is that about seven years ago, Indians could access just one channel on the state-owned television network, Doordarshan. The arrival of STAR-TV, through satellite telecasting in 1992, shattered the monopoly of Doordarshan and provided four channels of English language news and entertainment. The subsequent proliferation of television channels, cable networks, and the fragmentation of television audiences has been truly remarkable. Today, major cities in India are served by at least 25 channels providing close to 24 hours of programming in several Indian languages and English. Programming content includes news, documentaries, soap operas, Indian film-based music, rock-n-roll and rap music, sports, cartoons, Hollywood and Indian films, and much much more. Today, India offers a unique opportunity to observe and document the arrival, the meteoric rise, and the impact of American, British, Australian, and Indian satellite/cable channels on the second most populous country with the second largest middle class. India provides us with a setting to test theories and notions about western cultural imperialism, globalization, regional contestations, commercialism and development communication.

The STAR TV network immediately challenged the monopoly of Doordarshan, the state-owned Indian television network, at least among the urban, middle class viewers. The immense popularity of American soap operas such as the *Bold and the Beautiful* and *Santa Barbara*, BBC news commentaries, and MTV dispelled the myth that Indians do not enjoy western television programs. The scramble for more channels, more entertainment, and more English language programming (both locally produced and foreign) soon followed and Doordarshan added several metro channels and satellite-based channels (as opposed to the largely terrestrial nature of Doordarshan's telecasting). While this may have provided some support to cultural imperialism theorists, what followed later was a more complex phenomenon. Cultural imperialism theorists have argued that transnational flow of western television programs will have a detrimental impact on national cultures usually leading to cultural erosion in the recipient (non-western) countries (Schiller, 1979,1976; Hamelink, 1983). However, this has not occurred in India. Today, most channels provide large chunks of Indian or Indian-influenced programming in Indian languages including English. STAR TV started out with an all-English menu but it is now dubbing or subtitling many of its English language programs in Indian languages and also telecasting locally produced English and Indian language programs ("Plus or Minus," 1996).

The untold story, however, is the immense popularity of privately-owned Indian language channels such as ZEE, SUN TV, Eenadu TV, Asianet, Udaya TV, etc. ("The New Buzzword," 1997). While STAR TV initially challenged Doordarshan, an interesting consequence was the creation of a space for non-Hindi Indian languages thus enabling the introduction of television program channels in Tamil, Telugu, Malayalam and Kannada languages. Until the entry of STAR TV in 1992, most of the national programming (prime time) on Doordarshan was in the Hindi language and to a limited extent in English. Acting as the cultural arm of the government in New Delhi, Doordarshan was vested with the responsibility of fostering national integration and showcasing Hindi as India's dominant language. Hindi is understood by about 40 percent of Indians and in a nation of many dominant languages, television broadcasting in only Hindi and English alienated a large section of the population (Singhal and Rogers, 1989). Other scholars have noted this pattern. Mitra (1993) pointed out in his critique of the Hindi television serial *Mahabharat,*

> By binding Hindi and north India as the central locus of practices, *Mahabharat* and other north Indian Hindi serials are able to marginalize the possibility of non-Hindi serials coming out of this center. Indeed the unity of Hindi and north Indian discourse leads to the marginalization of the discourses that are grouped around other languages......(p.130)

What these arguments bring to the fore are gaps in the cultural imperialism thesis. The cultural imperialism argument focused on the effects of western transnational programs on non-western countries and in the process presumed individual nation-states as consensual and culturally homogenous units. As such, differences within national boundaries based on culture, language, and practices and the ensuing contestations between various intra-national competing forces were ignored or not legitimated (Morley and Robbins, 1995; Samarajiva and Shields, 1990; Schlesinger, 1987; Shields and Muppidi, 1996; Tomlinson, 1991). The rise of satellite broadcasting and the unshackling of Indian television from the monopoly control of state-owned Doordarshan, has thus provided a legitimate exposure to India's other state languages that were suppressed on national television programs of Doordarshan. It also moves the discourse beyond the simplistic west to east cultural imperialism and puts the spotlight on regional contestations within the Indian state.

Another effect of the proliferation of channels is the commercialization of the Indian television scene. Almost all programs are supported by commercial sponsors and buzz words such as 'ratings' and 'market share' spell the success or doom of particular programs. Even Doordarshan is becoming increasingly dependent on advertising revenue. So, is television then a resource for the rich and those with disposable incomes? Doordarshan for decades had a public service mandate and delivered programs in support of rural development, agricultural extension, health communication, family planning and other developmental themes. The public service mandate has been looking rather weak during the last decade and, today, Doordarshan may be in the process of abandoning its historic role as a development support communication vehicle in favor of entertainment to urban and mostly middle class audiences.

In the sphere of television, the loss of one voice for all Indians (i.e. Doordarshan) and its replacement by a myriad voices raises important questions. Does this signify the end of the use of national television to create and sustain a "national culture" in a country with an amazing diversity of cultures and languages? Should and can the government play the role of the cultural guardian for its citizens in the future? What will be the effects of the emergence of strong regional and linguistic identities and the fragmentation of audiences by languages and regions on the cultural and physical unity of India?

The essays in this volume address many of the issues discussed above. Although a few chapters deal with satellite broadcasting in the pan-Asian context, the focus is on the dynamic changes occurring within India.

Review of Chapters

What type of broadcasting system to advocate has been a fundamental question for Doordarshan. Since its inception, Doordarshan has been trapped between the crush of state-controlled public service and commercial forces which have obfuscated its policy options. According to **Keval Kumar**, official accounts of Indian broadcasting do not help to clarify these options because they are over-reliant on personal accounts "presented by advocates of state bureaucracy." He argues, that the "unprecedented proliferation of transborder satellite channels" in India has raised the stakes in this exigence of options and opens the space for an appropriate critical analysis of Doordarshan's policy options.

India's "public service" media system, he writes, has "always" served the interests of both the state and the elite. Thus, while the rhetoric of a public service Doordarshan flourishes, the sub-text has been a pragmatic working out of a "special relationship" with commercial advertising agencies. Ironically, the result has been an unequal cultural exchange in which the popularity of the newer advertising-driven private channels have threatened the central government's cultural agenda, particularly its language policy.

Kumar's principal inquiry is for a democracy-inspired public service model for broadcasting. A number of guidelines for restructuring Indian broadcasting interest him: the Congress Government's Varadan Committee report to the Ministry of Information and Broadcasting (1991), the national media policy drawn up by the United Front government under Prime Minister Deve Gowda, a media report by the Forum for Independent Film and Video and the Prasar Bharati Bill.

Kumar favors "a radical restructuring of radio and television" along the lines of the Prasar Bharati Bill. A principal caveat, however, is the constraints that restructuring is likely to place on national resources. The reappropriation of the electronic media for "public welfare and service" cannot be guaranteed and, in any case, must be examined in light of the public service's historic dependence upon the public coffers. This remains a major problem for Doordarshan, insofar as the provision of basic health care, education and welfare continue to be major concerns for the Indian state.

Clear cut choices are not readily available in a media environment as dynamic and contradictory as India's. **Sandhya Rao** examines the "changing industrial dynamics" of this emerging Indian media environment and the requisite coping strategies employed by Doordarshan to withstand competition from national cable and transborder satellite networks. The sea change in the political economy of Indian electronic media comes principally from accommodations made to meet this challenge. Program sources, providers, and programming strategies have changed, and Doordarshan must adjust too.

The cable industry itself has emerged in a chaotic fashion, according to Rao, "with several thousand small budget operators competing in [a] market," crowded, and lacking in infrastructure. Nevertheless, cable now presents a major threat to the stability of Doordarshan's audience, pressing Doordarshan to introduce new international and regional Indian language channels, and to beef-up its research unit in order to compete. However, as a state-owned system, Doordarshan's fundamental prerogatives remain intact; it still brokers major cultural events and decides upon technical access issues such as uplink facilities; and, despite setbacks, it retains a much larger share of the audience because of its vast terrestrial network. Significantly, competition from cable has brought a degree of sobriety to the Doordarshan system and forced its hand as it contributes to the creation of a more plural media environment.

The preceding two chapters illustrate the current structural crisis in the Indian television system. Having to accommodate a public demand for a more diverse media and competitive pressures from STAR and other satellite channels, the commercial sector, advertisers and a gaggle of national cable operators, Doordarshan has been deflected from its erstwhile mission of national integration, consolidation and development. Presently, the dominant player in Indian media is the Indian socio-cultural environment itself. Complex, changing and demanding, it is an eager and willing host to exogenous program suppliers and investors, yet self conscious of its own remarkable potential, and unafraid of technology-bearing, capital-laden, multinational media firms.

Geetika Pathania looks closely at Doordarshan's potential and prospects regarding this new environment. Her paper "examines how the liberalization of national economic policies favorable to foreign investments in India has softened the early reception of foreign-backed media industry products, with a consequent shift in Indian cultural policy." But this shift is to be seen as a reluctant liberalization driven by the need for foreign capital. As a result, the government has lost control of its public service mandate.

With STAR's arrival Doordarshan bureaucrats were forced to respond more aggressively to the commercial challenge. They introduced some regulation of cable, privatized some of their own program content, changed content and distribution rules, restricted access to uplink facilities and to foreign exchange. STAR too had to adjust to the uncertain Indian environment. STAR introduced Hindi pop music, dabbled in cultural programming, and sought the patronage of international advertising.

In the heat of competition, it is surprising that Indian authorities did not use their power to regulate STAR out of existence. On the contrary, government found itself pandering to business groups and the "modernizing" middle classes, creating an "organic alliance between national and transnational capital on the basis of common interests." Meanwhile, STAR nudged the cumbersome Doordarshan somewhat off course and disrupted its programming agenda. One notable example is STAR's purported effect on Doordarshan's use of Hindi in national programming. Cracks in Doordarshan's monopoly allowed spaces to open for a proliferation of channels using regional Indian languages. There is much speculation about why these regional channels have emerged. It would be helpful to know whether this emergence represents the maturity of regions within the Indian union or atavistic formations seeking their own, ultimately independent identities.

Peter Shields displaces the argument from the cultural to the political and challenges two fundamental assumptions in Indian media discourse: that Indian national identity is a function of Indian media policy, and that external media are a definitive factor in the internal cultural dynamics of India. Shields contests *a priori* notions of television's influence and the idea that "national identity is portrayed as an uncontested 'natural fact'." Arguing, along with Schlesinger (1987,1991) that identity scholarship must begin with the ontological, or constitutive basis of national identity and national integration, he searches for the "key forces that have shaped the state's turbulent nation-building projects." He then presents an "examination of the changing television environment and its relations to these forces."

Shields finds that a drastic shift had taken place in India's nation-building project-- one from diversity to exclusion -- in its constitution as well as in its control of information. The "included" are represented by the Hinduized, urbanized classes and foreign economic adventurers, many from international media.

Shields concludes that there is a "crisis of representation in India" with little interaction between civil society and the state at various levels." Clearly, Shields implies, with a tone of populist democratic advocacy, that internal politics of culture (not international politics of the media) is at the core of the Indian "cultural crisis." In such a heterogeneous field as is India, cultural decision making is *ipso facto*, political decision making. As language mediates both culture and politics, language equity remains an intractable political problem begging a cultural solution.

To **Andrew Woodfield**, government policy is disappointing in its lack of explicit support for the "smaller languages or linguistic diversity." Woodfield proposes a "normative blueprint" ensuring language distributive equity in India by preserving small languages through state regulation of the broadcast media. His paradigm is based upon conditions which, if met, would suggest a *prima facie* obligation by the state to provide language service for underserved language communities. His argument is grounded in three ethical principles. The first is based on international declarations (such as the 1992 Rio Summit) and associates language scarcity to bio-diversity depletion. The next two principles are based in political philosophy: a "collective interest" approach based upon the rights of citizens to live in harmony and mutual respect; and a "language rights" approach based upon the group rights of a linguistic minority "to use its own language in the conduct of normal social and commercial life."

Woodfield argues that Indian government broadcast policy, (for example the 1996 broadcast bill) bypasses the internal language issue and instead, focuses on cultural colonialism. A corrective would be the establishment of a formal system of state supported smaller languages. Woodfield concedes, regardless of the integrity of programming schemes, that his propositions are "built on the premise that the state is a neutral arbiter in the struggle between the various language groups," a premise contested in much of the work in this book.

Binod Agrawal posits that a cursory content analysis of Indian television will reveal the influence of Indian films and film-based programs. He raises two questions in his essay: Why do Doordarshan or the satellite television channels in India rely so heavily on Indian films and film-based programs? and, is there any relationship between the content of Indian cinema and the meaning of 'recreation' as a genre of communicative arts that suits the cultural needs of the Indian viewers? He answers his questions by briefly tracing the history of Indian cinema. He points out how this medium has exploited the rich storehouse of Indian theater, song, and dance traditions and carved for itself a uniquely Indian character. Indian films are immensely popular in all regions of India. The recreation provided by the Indian film has been the impetus for the growth and support of other media such as the Indian radio and television. He concludes his essay by analyzing the cultural influence of Indian cinema and television on the viewers in India and finds the cultural imperialism argument to be problematic in the Indian context.

Shobha Das asks whether the attendant media proliferation in the Indian states says something about national unity, about impingement on the prerogatives of the nation-state, or about fragmentation into sub-national units. She explored these questions by conducting a number of ethnographic interviews with broadcasters representing the Indian Ministry of Information and Broadcasting, Doordarshan and private Indian language channels. Her aim was to explore the concept of identity itself, and come up with a sense of what national identity means to Indians. By so doing, she could "unpack" the intricacies (and contradictions) in Indians' cultural relationships. She applied a two-dimensional, (antique to modern and particular to general) framework to the text of the interviews in order to break out notions of Indian-ness represented in media producers' talk; i.e., to see whether "media producers carry with them a homogeneous articulation of national identity." Her interviews reveal that national identity ended up being a "confused and inevitably paradoxical" concept because, as regional media markets develops so too do local identities. She finds, therefore, "the idea of an over-arching national identity" a problematic one.

Srinivas Melkote, Sanjay and **Ahmed's** study is one of two chapters which looks at Indian audiences' use of television. In contrast with other studies which have focused on the source or the channel of communication, this study employed a uses and gratifications approach to conduct an audience-centered investigation of the Indian middle class. The study posited two research questions: "What are the important audience motivations for watching STAR and Doordarshan television channels?" and "what are the types of gratifications received by the viewers by watching STAR and Doordarshan television channels?" They found that compared with Doordarshan's offerings, STAR's already great impact seems to be growing, possibly because of its diversity and entertainment appeal. Melkote, Sanjay and Ahmed grant their readers a natural faith in audience autonomy and call for a revision in the way scholars view Indian audiences. Audience autonomy has much to do with the contexts in which programs are mediated, and this happens at four levels: the deeply local (or indigenous), the regional, the national and the international. Consequently, there is no simple readership of television texts.

In the urban centers of India, there is a proliferation of cable connections especially to the middle class homes. So, **Sandhya Rao** and **Srinivas Melkote** ask how Doordarshan is faring among these viewers. As the cable channels carry all Doordarshan shows (both terrestrial and satellite channels) and the privately-owned satellite channels of its competitors, this study sought to gather preliminary data on key variables such as frequency of viewing specific Doordarshan programs and satisfaction derived from viewing Doordarshan programs from cable subscribers and compare these with cable non-subscribers who can view only Doordarshan's terrestrial offerings.

A finding of this study was that cable subscribers watched Doordarshan programs for a significantly lesser amount of time per average day when compared with non-subscribers. Another finding was that cable subscribers significantly reduced their viewing time of Doordarshan programs after they subscribed to cable. Both findings imply that Doordarshan's programs have not made a positive difference in terms of the level of viewing with the urban, cabled viewers. Rao and Melkote posit that Doordarshan's efforts of adding new cable channels and programs particularly meant for urban audiences on its various cable channels have yet to make a significant positive impact on cable audiences (who have numerous private channels to choose from) at least in terms of the level of viewing. Another finding of the study that --- cable subscribers were significantly less satisfied with Doordarshan programs compared with cable non-subscribers --- may be an indication that cable subscribers derive greater satisfaction by viewing programs of the privately-owned satellite channels.

When STAR TV first entered India, there was a fear that foreign programs may have an adverse impact on Indian culture. This fear was based on the assumption that Indians would spend many hours watching American or British television shows. However, the initial popularity of American soaps such as *Bold and Beautiful* and *Santa Barbara* seems to have waned according to Rao and Melkote. In their study, it was found that western serials were least frequently watched by both cable subscribers and non-subscribers. Both categories of audiences were also least satisfied with western serials. This finding questions the cultural imperialism thesis that presumes a dominant cultural impact of western programs on non-western countries.

John Sinclair's "Culture as a 'Market Force': Corporate Strategies in Asian Skies" argues that political and cultural barriers determine how international broadcasting is disseminated and received in nations and regions. He argues for an alternative paradigm in the cultural imperialism debate in which local socio-political traditions actively work to subvert the effects of cultural imperialism. His case in point is Asia where regimes in control of leading nation states have successfully withstood the considerable forces of globalization. They have actually reinforced their power and secured their interests, both private and state, in their own communication industries, and have done so with cultural imperialism as their ideological rationale.

Again we see that cultural and linguistic differences have in themselves proved to be more substantial barriers to foreign programming than the classic theory of cultural imperialism would have predicted. It is clear that global media services have, in many cases, to accede to the cultural demands in the host nations. Political leaders end up using their cultural guests to meet their own nationalist ends. Because of its complex matrix of languages and cultures within national borders, Asia has a natural advantage in this method of resistance. The situation is different in Latin America where cultural dominance by oligopolistic groups is easier to accomplish because of the relative cultural uniformity of the region.

Naive interpretations of television texts naturally give way to significations of local languages, regional affiliations, national prescriptions, acceptability of cultural imports and a host of other cultural values. **Hart Cohen's** contribution examines this issue in the Indonesian context. He summarizes research done by himself and four colleagues in 1995 in Surabaya, East Java. The researchers developed "base-line [quantitative] data on the local consumption of global television" to investigate what cultural values are important in the mediation of foreign satellite television texts. Primary research interest was in communication processes because "these processes (which) are at the focal point where spheres of culture and commerce cross." Sharing Shields', Sinclair's, and Woodfield's concern that too little attention is paid to socio-political contexts, Cohen's summary examines "cultural values of Indonesian media," through "the larger context of political values" which constrain them. Although biased toward "highly educated and wealthy" Indonesians the chapter gives an informed view of what they watch, and how they watch satellite television. The backdrop is a sense of nation centeredness, critical viewing of news and current affairs and "strong satisfaction for local programming." The robustness of local media culture it is believed, is established through its relationship to older Indonesian cultural and political formations such as the concepts of "Guided Democracy," and *Pancasila*, which extend across the Sukarno and Suharto regimes.

As global media are consumed and disputations between the local, national and international levels of identification arise, it is the meta-narrative of the "national" which defines the limits of democracy and finds itself in conflict with the "local." In the midst of all this stands the audience member as individual arbiter. Is it possible that in this space of individual interpretativeness one finds avenues of transcendence, a common intelligence that allows the successful transference of cultural forms from one society to the next?

Arvind Singhal, Peter Svenkerud and **Rita Rahoi-Gilchrest** discuss cultural transcendence as an alternative to cultural imperialism. They look at the role of pro-social entertainment television programs in developing countries, particularly the phenomenon of globally transcendent programs which are accepted in a variety of settings over a long period of time. Their argument draws on the view of the audience as active agent comprising, in simple appreciation of the same program, a coherent crossnational viewing community based on a transcendent aesthetic of values. Such culturally accessible television programming exchanged across borders could be a counterweight to cultural imperialism because they resonate with commonly appreciated social values. The substantive evidence from programs such as *Oshin* from Japan, *Simplemente Maria* from Peru, and *Consequences* from Zimbabwe demonstrate the appeal, relevance, and hence, marketability of these programs. Principally a South-South exchange, these programs "can help developing countries pool resources, fight common development problems, reduce their dependence on imported programming, and promote regional and local independence."

The substantive argument here is not without its pitfalls and the authors offer cultural and logistical limitations which temper an overly utopian interpretation of these possibilities. Regardless of whether transcendent, prosocial, crossnational programs can be deliberately created --- or are a result of unspecifiable magic that "just works" --- developing countries ought to consider the ease with which recent advances in telecommunications could facilitate international cultural exchange.

Jan Servaes and **Patchanee Malikhao's** "critical examination of a UNESCO study of television flows in Europe and Asia," advocates a novel methodological approach to explicate heretofore under-examined assumptions of international television flow. They summarize two UNESCO reports of "television supply consumption in five European and four Asia-Pacific countries" conducted using a methodological and theoretical frame developed by Sepstrup (1990).

The rationale for the new approach is simply that the dynamics of international television flows have shifted to a more complex pattern of distribution. The bi-continental nature of the report provided the researchers a measure of critical appreciation for the difficulties of conducting genuinely crossnational research. They concluded that the climate in which television consumption takes place, and other factors such as the scheduling of programs, the culture, and socio-economic development, are stronger determinants of transnationalization of television consumption, than demographic criteria such as gender, age, education or urbanization.

En route to their conclusion the authors found that there were difficulties of 'streamlining' a comparative and international research program. They attribute this difficulty to the unevenness of levels of development and social complexity of societies in which research was to be carried out. This frustrates researchers' attempts to attain proper cross-national comparisons. They suggest a system be developed for standardized, "centrally supervised" research to be executed at the national level, and that there should be international agreement about how the variables "program categories" and "country of origin" should be defined. Finally, the authors seek theoretical clarification on the topic of international research.

Organization of the Book

The first part of the book deals with chapters that focus on India. The earlier chapters in this section examine the phenomenon of satellite broadcasting in India from historic, cultural, political, and economic contexts.   These essays which have a qualitative bent are followed by two chapters that use quantitative surveys of television audiences to examine the relative uses of and gratifications derived from watching STAR and Doordarshan networks.

The second part of this volume comprises critical essays of satellite television in the Asian and other contexts.   Sinclair examines the political and cultural implications of transnational satellite networks in the Asian context while Cohen examines similar themes within Indonesia.   Singhal, Svenkerud and Rahoi-Gilchrest look at flow of cultural transcendent pro-social television programs across developing countries while Servaes and Malikhao examine television flows in Europe and Asia from a "consumption" perspective.   **Ewart Skinner** and **Krishna Kandath** summarize the contribution of all the chapters in the book and weave them together to distill the main arguments made by the various authors.   These authors provide a critical summary of the chapters, challenging their fundamental assumptions and propositions.   They argue that the authors of the chapters have given up too much of the heuristics of the global in attempting to ascribe agency at the local level, and that media as a subject, in and of itself, should remain close to the center of the discourse.

References

Hamelink, C. (1983). *Cultural autonomy in global communications.* New York: Longman.

Mitra, A. (1993). *Television and popular culture in India: a study of the Mahabharat.* New Delhi: Sage.

Morley, D., and Robins, K. (1995). *Spaces of identity: global media, electronic landscapes and cultural boundaries.* London: Routledge.

Plus or Minus? (1996, October 21). *Business India,* pp. 172-176.

Samarajiva, R., and Shields, P. (1990). Integration, telecommunication, and development: power in the paradigms. *Journal of Communication* 40(3): 84-105.

Schiller, H.I. (1976). *Communication and cultural domination.* New York: M.E. Sharpe.

Schiller, H.I. (1979). Transnational media and national development. In K. Nordenstreng and H.I. Schiller (Eds.), *National sovereignty and international communication.* Norwood, N.J.: Ablex.

Schlesinger, P. (1987). On national Identity: some conceptions and misconceptions criticized. *Social Science Information* 26(2):219-264.

Schlesinger, P. (1991). Media, the political order and national identity. *Media, Culture and Society,* Vol. 13: 297-308.

Sepstrup, P. (1990). *Transnationalization of television in western Europe.* Acamedia Research Monograph 5, John Libbey, London.

Shields, P., and Muppidi, S. (1996). Integration, the Indian state and STAR TV: policy and theory issues. *Gazette,* 58(1): 1-24.

Singhal, A., and Rogers, E. (1989). *India's information revolution.* New Delhi: Sage.

The New Buzzword. (1997, June 22). *The Hindu,* p. III.

Tomlinson, J. (1991). *Cultural imperialism.* Baltimore, MD: Johns Hopkins University.

PART I

The Indian Context

Chapter 2

History of Television in India: A Political Economy Perspective

Keval J. Kumar

On the threshold of the 21st century, India has perhaps one of the largest radio, television, cable and satellite television networks in the world, and further expansion and commercialization is expected with the introduction of digital and direct-to- home (DTH) broadcasting in Asia. Both radio and television continue to be public service networks, though since September 1997 they are under the direct control of the recently established statutory body known as the *Prasar Bharati* (Broadcasting Corporation of India) rather than that of the federal government in New Delhi. Like private channels, however, they do carry advertising spots and sponsored programs, with many of the programs (including news and current affairs) produced by private sector production companies and advertising agencies. All India Radio (AIR) and Doordarshan (DD) have held a monopoly over the airwaves since their inception, but this is now being challenged by transborder satellite networks (such as STAR-TV, CNN, ABN, BBC,

Discovery, ESPN, HBO, TNT, Sony and NBC) as well as by several private Indian language channels (Zee-TV, Jain-TV, ATN, Sun TV, Vijay TV, Raj TV, Asianet, Eenadu TV, and Home-TV) based within the country but uplinking their channels from outside its borders. To meet the challenge, All India Radio and Doordarshan have extended and revamped their services; FM radio channels have been introduced in the metros and in the state of Goa, as well as 14 Indian language satellite television channels that cater to diverse cultural groups across the nation. With set-top converters, Indian viewers can now access, via their local cable networks, more than 50 satellite channels. The government has so far favored an 'open skies' policy (unlike Singapore and Malaysia), and it is unlikely to overturn this policy, despite protests against 'cultural invasion' and 'media imperialism'.

This chapter attempts to rewrite the history of Indian broadcasting from a political economy perspective --- a perspective that is wanting in the linear, and often personal, historical accounts of radio and television provided by former directors of All India Radio.   These include Awasthy (1965), Mullick (1974), Duggal (1980), Masani (1985), Luthra (1987) and Chatterji (1987). The focus is on Indian television though the early years of radio are addressed. In particular, it attempts to critically analyze recent developments in Indian broadcasting in the context of the unprecedented proliferation of transborder satellite channels in Asia.   The chapter argues that Doordarshan, the public service network, has been further commercialized in an effort to compete with the transnational satellite networks. To buttress this argument, the structure of programming on Doordarshan is analyzed. In conclusion, the Indian government's proposed National Media Policy as reflected in the amended Prasar Bharati Act (Govt. of India, 1990) and the Broadcasting Bill (Govt. of India, 1997) is discussed.

Early Radio in India

From Private Enterprise to Government Monopoly

Broadcasting in India began as a private enterprise by Indian businessmen who believed that it had the potential of developing into a major entertainment business. It was the early 1920's and the only model available at the time was that of the British. But large investments were required, transmitters, studio equipment and even receivers had to be imported; the financial risks were enormous indeed. The early twenties saw the rapid establishment of amateur radio clubs in Calcutta, Madras (now Chennai), Bombay (now Mumbai) and Lahore, though even before the clubs came to be established, several experimental broadcasts were carried out in Mumbai and the other cities. The *Times of India* records that a broadcast was transmitted from the roof of its building on August 20, 1921. However, the first transmitting license was granted only on February 23, 1922. The first to start functioning was perhaps the Radio Club in Calcutta, in November 1923. The Madras Presidency Radio Club was formed on May 16, 1924, and began broadcasting on July 31 of the same year. By 1927, these radio clubs came together to form the Indian Broadcasting Company (IBC), a private company, 'fired by the financial success of European broadcasting' (Fielden, 1960). IBC built 'two weak little stations at Calcutta and Mumbai with a meager capital. 'In the following three years they had gathered some 7,000 listeners and lost a great deal of money. They decided to go into liquidation' (Fielden, 1960). Poor earnings from commercial broadcasts and radio license fees forced a shut down of its business in 1930 (Rao,1986). It was then that 'vested interests of radio dealers' bullied an unwilling Government of India---which considered broadcasting a 'curse', according to Fielden (1960)---to buy up the transmitters and to continue the service. What perhaps finally influenced the government's decision was the start of the BBC's Empire program on short-wave, and the irresistible temptation of making money out of it. But the government soon put a stop to commercial broadcasts with the growth in the revenue accruing from receiver licenses collected by the post offices. A fifty per cent hike in the import duty did not affect the rising interest to acquire radio sets.

The government's radio service came to be called first the Indian State Broadcasting Service (ISBS), and later, All India Radio or AIR, under the mistaken notion of Fielden (who took all credit for hitting upon that name, and getting the then Viceroy to accept it) that 'broadcasting' was an unpronounceable word for Indians! Fielden (1960) summed up his stint at All India Radio in his autobiography thus:

In India, I had lost confidence not only in England and the West, but also, and seriously, in myself. Four years of hard labor had produced 14 transmitters and a competent staff - and in four years the 400 million people of India had bought exactly 85,000 wireless sets. It was enough to make a cat laugh. It was the biggest flop of all time (p.204).

According to estimates available at the time, there were little more than 100,000 radio receivers in 1940 for a population which was already past the 400 million mark (Mansell, 1982).

War Years and Underground Radio

During the 1930s, and until the departure of the British colonialists in 1947, radio catered to elite interests. As a government operation, its mandate was to engage in colonial propaganda and maintain the status quo, not to serve the people. The war years only reinforced this task (Eapen, 1996). During the war years AIR, like the BBC itself, was transformed into a vehicle for anti-Nazi propaganda. In 1939, the External Services Division was launched first with short-wave broadcasts in Pushtu (the language of Afghanistan) and later in other languages of Asia. At the height of the Second World War, as many as 27 news bulletins were broadcast each day. The External Services Division as also a Monitoring Service were set up as part of the Military Intelligence Wing. The Germans and the Japanese, it was feared, were succeeding in their efforts to win the war of words in the Indian sub-continent.

The Indian nationalist leaders were divided over whom they should support. While Subhas Chandra Bose and his National Army opted to align with the Axis powers, Mahatma Gandhi went to the support of the Allies in the hope that independence could be wrested from the British on this ground. However, access to radio continued to be denied to leaders of the 'Quit India' movement. Hence the emergence of underground radio which was used by Gandhians such as Usha Mehta to whip up nationalist sentiments in Mumbai and other cities; however, the extent of coverage and the actual listenership of underground radio is unknown.

AIR on the Eve of Indian Independence

On the eve of independence in 1947, AIR had no national network; it had six stations in metropolitan areas, five in the princely states, a few low power transmitters and a mere 250,000 receiver sets for a population exceeding 400 million. The Nehru government gave priority to the expansion of the radio network across the country, especially in the border states of Punjab and Jammu and Kashmir, and by the 1950's, 25 stations had been established and several pilot stations and low power transmitters installed. During the First (1951 - 56) and Second (1956-61) Five Year Plans, a total of Rs. 78.6 million was invested in radio broadcasting (Rao, 1986). Receiver sets increased from 0.2 million sets to 0.7 million in 1951 and jumped to 2.2 million in a decade. However, the cost of receivers continued to be far too high for the rural residents, despite the incentives of community listening schemes and rural broadcasts in several Indian languages.

Vividh Bharati: The Commercial Channel

Ever since India's independence, it was a matter of AIR policy not to air Indian film songs on the network. No advertising or sponsorship was permitted on the public service radio network, but on October 2, 1957 a full-fledged commercial service called the *Vividh Bharathi* was launched to counter the popularity of the Sri Lanka Commercial Broadcasting Service's Indian film-oriented music programs. By the 1990s, Vividh Bharati had 30 commercial broadcasting centers, and devoted sixty per cent of total broadcast time (around 16 hours every day) to Indian film music, ten per cent to advertisements, and the rest to devotional music, light music and spoken word programs. Now, *Vividh Bharathi* brings in an annual advertising revenue of about Rs. 370 million.

The border war with China in 1962 and the war with Pakistan in 1965 led to the expansion of broadcasting in the border regions of the country. Auxiliary relay centers were commissioned before the end of 1966 (Rao, 1986). The introduction of transistor radio led to a dramatic increase in the number of receiver sets, particularly in the urban areas. In the same year, the Chanda Committee on Broadcasting and Information Media submitted its report recommending the establishment of two autonomous corporations for radio and television. This recommendation found no favor with the central government though other recommendations related to the strengthening of the external services, reorientation of rural broadcasts and the introduction of commercial broadcasts were readily put into effect. Three super-power transmitters were installed to enhance coverage of the external service, as well as a number of high-power medium-wave transmitters for achieving wider coverage for the domestic services, so that by the early 1970's coverage was as much as 80 per cent of India's population. Political and economic reasons were crucial for this rapid expansion.

Table 2.1 Growth of Radio Network After Independence

Year	AIR Centers	Radio Receivers (in millions)
1947	10	0.2
1951	21	0.7
1961	30	2.2
1971	65	12.8
1985	86	35.0
1995	177	111.0
1996	187	115.0 (est.)

(Sources: Rao, 1986; *Doordarshan-1997*)

Television in India

Early Experiments in Television

The government of Prime Minister Nehru in New Delhi had little interest in television considering it a luxury which a developing country could ill afford to finance. However, various economic and political factors came together to bring television to India. It all began, most likely, with the offer in 1959 by Phillips (India) of a 500-watt television transmitter at a nominal cost. The multinational company had earlier demonstrated the use of television at an industrial fair in New Delhi. The government accepted the offer with the aim of employing it for a pilot project to train personnel, and partly to discover what television could achieve in community development and formal education. A UNESCO grant of $20,000 for the purchase of community receiver sets then came to the assistance of the government. 'Teleclubs' or community television centers (with 20 to 25 members each) were introduced in the capital to receive an half-hour weekly service, courtesy of UNESCO. Two years later, the government won a Ford Foundation grant to set up a small experimental in-school television (Mody, 1988). Mody (1988) comments, 'This capital-city centered deployment of television technology ensured that all these subsequent so-called public rural service applications would privilege the already privileged capital-city residents even further'. Mody (1988) further notes that 'this pattern of television introduction --- early public service rhetoric, educational experimentation, and then implementation on a large scale for elite pacification through entertainment --- has been noticed' in other parts of the developing world too. Besides, in India's case 'strategic considerations' (Luthra, 1987, p.413) such as the need to counter Pakistan's television programs was also a vital element in the pattern. From August 1965, entertainment and information programs were introduced in addition to social education programs.

By 1970, the duration of television service was increased to three hours and included news, information and entertainment programs, two weekly programs running 20 minutes each for 180 teleclubs, and another weekly program called 'Krishi Darshan' for farmers in 80 villages around New Delhi. The number of television sets in that year stood at around 22,000 excluding the community sets. During the next few years, television stations were launched in Mumbai, Calcutta, Chennai, Lucknow and the border areas of Srinagar and Amritsar. By the mid-seventies Indian-manufactured sets were in the market and in a few years, the number of television sets crossed the 100,000 mark. Manufacturers, television set owners and the advertising industry pressured the government for further expansion of urban-oriented programming. From January 1, 1976, commercials were allowed on television, and three months later, Doordarshan (DD), the television wing of AIR was established as a separate organization. But, it would take another decade before the first commercially sponsored indigenous soap-opera would be telecast. This was 'Hum Log' sponsored by Maggi Noodles, a product of a Nestle subsidiary. It was directly inspired by the Mexican tele-novella (Singhal & Rogers, 1989; Kumar, 1995), and its thumping success launched Indian television on the road to commercialization.

Table 2.2. Growth Of Indian Television Network (1976 To 1997)

Year	Number of Transmitters	No. of TV Sets (in million)	Population with Access to TV (in million)
1976	8	0.5	2.9
1978	15	0.7	4.1
1979	17	0.9	5.4
1980	17	1.2	6.9
1981	18	1.5	9.3
1982	39	2.1	12.6
1983	41	2.1	12.7
1984	166	3.6	21.8
1985	175	6.8	40.5
1986	179	11.0	52.5
1987	243	13.2	65.0*
1988	335	17.3	86.5*
1989	519	22.5	110.5*
1990	527	27.8	139.0*
1991	531	30.8	150.0*
1992	540	34.8	195.0
1993	553	40.3	218.8*
1994	564	45.7	241.8*
1995	698	52.3	246.0*
1996	792	54.0*	270.0
1997	921	55.5*	296.0

* Estimates. (Source: *Doordarshan - 1994, 1995, 1996, 1997*)

The Satellite Instructional Television Experiment (SITE) took the television medium to 2400 villages in six States (Rajasthan, Bihar, Orissa, Madhya Pradesh, Andhra Pradesh and Karnataka) for one year, from August 1, 1975 to July 31, 1976. The project was inaugurated with a telecast by Prime Minister Indira Gandhi; SITE was also utilized for nationwide telecasts of Independence Day, Republic Day and other national celebrations. Official evaluations of the project (see Agrawal, 1981) were euphoric about its success, but independent evaluations (see Gore, 1983) suggested that the results were far from dramatic. For instance, Luthra (1987) noted:

in matters like agriculture especially, it was an unrealistic presumption that one common program would meet the needs of the huge Hindi speaking area of Bihar, Rajasthan and Madhya Pradesh with the wide variety of soil, climatic conditions, incidence of rainfall and irrigation facilities available (p.418).

But the era of 'satellite television' had dawned, though it would take another decade and a half for multi-channel round-the-clock cross-border satellite television to reach Indian viewers. The defeat of prime minister Indira Gandhi at the polls and the suspension of the state of internal emergency in 1977 raised hopes for the autonomy of state-controlled radio and television networks. The new government set up the Verghese Committee to examine the procedures for the granting of autonomy to the broadcasting network. The Verghese Committee's Report (*Government of India*, 1978) and its recommendations for the establishment of *Akash Bharati* (or the National Broadcasting Trust) were accepted by the new Janata Party government, and a bill was prepared for introduction in parliament. However, the newly elected Janata government was soon replaced by Indira Gandhi's Congress Party that re-emerged victorious in the ensuing elections. The Verghese Committee's report was put in cold storage until 1990.

Television Comes of Age

Table 2.2 lists the growth in television from 1976 to 1997. The Asian Games (the Asian equivalent of the Olympics), held in New Delhi in 1982, was a major impetus for the rapid expansion of the national television network during that decade. In the mid-1980s, a second channel was introduced, first in Delhi and Mumbai, and later in the other metros; this second channel was to evolve into the popular Metro Entertainment Channel (or DD-2). With the success of *Hum Log* and other soap operas like *Buniyaad* and *Khandaan*, Doordarshan's revenue from advertising soared, and the sponsorship of indigenous soaps and other serials provided a spurt in production, sometimes taken up by the advertising agencies themselves (such as Lintas' production of a popular detective serial *Karamchand*). The climax of the Indian soap opera was the phenomenal blockbusters in the form of the religious epics, the *Mahabharat* and the *Ramayana*. The mid-eighties saw the emergence of indigenous sitcoms (*Yeh Jo Hai Zindagi* and *Nukkad*), children's stories (*Vikram Aur Betaal*), women-oriented stories (*Chehere*), political satires (*Kakaji Kahen*) and tragedies of the Partition (*Tamas*). By 1987, over 40 serials had been produced; on average two were being screened each evening. American serials such as 'I Love Lucy' 'Some Mothers do Love 'Em' were edged out gradually; so were several prime-time talk-shows, quiz programs, and film-based programs. In 1987-1988, Doordarshan's revenue shot up to Rs.136.3 million; it zoomed to Rs.256 million at the end of 1990. By the end of that decade, there were more than 28 million television sets in the country, with over a million connected to neighborhood cable networks.

Cross-Border Television: The Beginnings

In Asia, cross-border television is a post-Gulf War phenomenon. It began with five-star hotels in India and other parts of Asia hooking up to CNN to give their customers live coverage of the war. These hotels already had local cable and/or CCTV facilities. All they required to plug in to CNN was a dish antenna. By the time the Gulf War drew to a close, CNN had become a byword for 'news as it happens' in print and electronic media of Asian countries. The national television networks had used CNN footage extensively for their war coverage. And, current affairs magazine programs like 'The World This Week' used CNN's actuality footage to lend authority to their own coverage (see Kumar, 1990 for a detailed analysis). Cross-border television had arrived in Asia, and few voices of protest were heard from national governments or from the public. But it was the launch of STAR-TV by the Whampoa Hutchison group of Hong Kong using the Chinese satellite ASIASAT I that brought as many as 38 countries of Asia within the footprint of cross-border television. This occurred in April 1991, with four 24-hour channels, and later a fifth channel, the BBC World Service Television (BBC-WSTV). (Now rechristened 'BBC World', it has moved from Murdoch's Asiasat platform to that of Panamsat-4).

Asian governments were taken by surprise (since they were neither informed nor their permission sought, as per ITU and WARC regulations), but the western and Indian media hailed the event in rhetoric characteristic of media hype. TIME magazine, for instance, announced that 'A STAR is born in Asia'. Sections of the English press in India termed it 'an invasion from the skies', but welcomed it as an alternative to the state-controlled national network. Cross-border satellite television has been most successful in those countries in Asia where domestic television showed little sensitivity to audience interests, and more importantly to the diversity of languages and cultures. In India, audiences who spoke languages other than Hindi had been taken for granted. For over two decades, Doordarshan could not see beyond Delhi and Mumbai; most software was oriented to Hindi and to North Indian culture. Other regions of the country could take it or leave it.

Table 2.3. Growth of Cable TV Networks (1984 To 1997)

Year	Number
1984	100
1985	450
1988	1200
1989	2000
1990	4000
1991	6000
1992	15000
1993	125000
1997	200000 (est.)

(Estimates by Khare, 1993)

Soon, with an increase in transmission hours and in the number of STAR TV channels, the domination of American mainstream network fare became evident. The BBC dominated the news and current affairs programs, while companies from the United States, Britain and Australia dominated soap opera and other entertainment fare. A Mandarin Chinese channel as well as a Hindi channel (Zee TV) were added later. An increasing number of cable operators (no less than 6,000 at the time of STAR's launch) hooked up to the satellite channels via large dish antennae and supplied their neighborhoods with satellite programming. By 1993, there were more than 125,000 cable operators in India and around ten million cable homes (see Table 2.3)

Round-the-Clock Movie Channels

On October 1, 1994, the first encrypted 24-hour movie channel was launched in Asia. This pay or subscription satellite channel was launched on the southern beam of Asiasat-I by the STAR-TV network. The new subscription channel, STAR Movies, proposed to beam sixty to seventy Hollywood films each month via local neighborhood cable networks in fifty countries of the Asian continent. The majority of films to be screened were inevitably to be from Twentieth Century Fox which, like STAR-TV, is owned by Rupert Murdoch. The films were 'rated' 'G', 'PG', '18' '15' and '12', and parents were expected to monitor their children's viewing round the clock. The films were sub-titled in Hindi for Indian viewers, or in Arabic for West Asian viewers. The main regions targeted were the Indian sub-continent, Saudi Arabia, and the United Arab Emirates. (A similar subscription-based channel was launched a few months earlier on the northern beam of Asiasat, targeted primarily at Taiwan and the Philippines).

However, STAR-Movies is not the only player in the field. Free and subscription channels for Hindi films were also launched during the months that followed by Doordarshan, CNN, Zee TV, STAR-TV and other satellite networks. The idea of subscription services had already been tested in Europe by Murdoch's Sky Channel, for instance, but it had not proved to be a thumping success. The strategy has, however, succeeded in shaping the kind of software made available on both basic and pay television. (A good percentage of the software is imported from the United States). In the process, Asia has already become a dumping ground for American, European and Australian software (for instance, 'Small Wonder', 'The Bold and the Beautiful', 'Baywatch', 'The Simpsons', 'Adam's Family', 'Denis the Menace, 'I Dream of Jeanie' and 'Celeste').

Structure of Programming on Doordarshan

According to the annual surveys of DD's Audience Research Unit (*Doordarshan*, 1994, 1995, 1996, 1997), as well as the surveys by IMRB, MARG and ORG, feature films and film-based programs (such as film songs, interviews with film makers and film stars, etc.) clearly dominate Doordarshan's programming on the national network, the metro channel, the Indian language satellite channels, and the regional television stations. On the national network, around 25 per cent of the total number of programs telecast comprise films and film-based programs, while on the regional channels over ten per cent is given over to similar program types. Serials and plays make up another 20% on the national network, and 12.5% on the regional channels. News bulletins in English and various Indian languages form over 15% and 10% respectively of programs telecast on the national and regional channels. Current Affairs comprise about seven per cent on both the national and regional channels. Music and dance receive a little more attention with eight and eleven per cent respectively on the national and regional channels. Sports would appear to be prominent on both channels, but in reality comprise barely three to five per cent on each channel. Programs for women and children comprise around three per cent, while special programs (health, education and development) directed primarily at rural viewers comprise about ten percent on the regional channel, but hardly figure on the national network. Other program genres that find some place on both channels include educational programs (for school and college students), documentaries, interviews/discussions, parliamentary coverage, etc.

In terms of language, Hindi dominates the national network as well as the Metro Channel, while the official state languages dominate the regional stations. As much as 47% of telecast time on the national network is devoted to Hindi language programs, and as much as 45% to English language programs, with the result that other Indian languages are side-lined on the national network broadcast from New Delhi. The politics of language is thus played out on the small screen. The Central Government policy on the promotion of Hindi as the national language, and as a corollary of North-Indian culture, is thus subtly imposed through television program structure, and the various genres that make up that structure (see Mitra, 1993; Kumar, 1997, for further discussion).

The monopoly of Hindi programming is, however, threatened by the growing popularity of the private channels of Sun-TV, Asianet, Eeenadu TV, Udaya TV, Vijay TV and Raj TV, which telecast programs in south Indian languages. However, decentralization of Doordarshan whereby state governments, local governments and non-government organizations have a role to play in the development of community-specific and language-specific software, has not yet been perceived as an important issue. Neither the Prasar Bharati Act (Govt. of India, 1990) nor the Broadcasting Bill (Govt. of India, 1997) discuss the issue. This is primarily because Doordarshan's major concern these days is not so much with the development of culturally diverse software as with keeping its advertising revenues in a competitive market. Table 2.4 provides data on the growth in Doordarshan's revenue from advertising since 1990.

The time consumed by advertisers in 1996 rose by 52% over that consumed in the previous year, with Doordarshan's national network recording the highest growth in advertiser time (76%), followed by DD-Calcutta (57%), DD-Bangalore (54%), DD-Metro Channel (53%) and DD-Chennai (39%) (Patel, 1997). In 1997, the total number of advertising hours on Doordarshan rose to 1,096. Indeed, it is the advertisers who are calling the shots.

Advertising Agencies and Television Software Producers

Television software producers, advertisers and advertising agencies are playing an increasingly vital role in shaping programming on Indian television. Not only are they dictating terms to Doordarshan, but calling the shots where advertising rates and program schedules are concerned. Further, they are actively involved in the production of programs. By Doordarshan's own admission, over 40% of

Doordarshan's programs are produced by independent agencies, and 3.6% are foreign programs (*Doordarshan*, 1996). Further, on the metro channel (DD-2) up to 60% of the programs are sponsored, 17% are acquired/imported, 15% are commissioned, and barely 8% is produced in-house (*Doordarshan*, 1997). Several of the independent agencies are advertising agencies or extensions of advertising and public relations agencies. Of the top ten advertising agencies in India, more than half have strategic alliances or affiliations with multinationals. These include HTA, Lintas, Ogilvy and Mather, Tara Sinha-Mcann-Ericsson, MAA- Bozell, and Trikaya-Grey. And of the top twenty advertisers on Doordarshan, the majority are multinational companies: Procter and Gamble, Hindustan Lever, Colgate Palmolive, Nestle, Coca Cola, Pepsi, Phillips-India, Brooke Bond and Cadbury's. The Indian companies that figure in the list are: Godrej Soaps, Nirma, BPL, Dabur, Parle and Bajaj Auto. The top ten products advertised on Doordarshan are: toilet soaps, toothpastes, detergent powders, shampoos. soft drinks, facial creams/lotions, corporations, motorbikes and motor scooters, shoes and cosmetic oils (Patel, 1997).

Table 2.4. Revenue Earned From Commercials on AIR and Doordarshan (1990 To 1997)

Year	All India Radio (Million Rs.)	Doordarshan Million (Rs.)
1990-91	393.0	2538.5
1991-92	527.3	3006.1
1992-93	589.1	3602.3
1993-94	643.5	3729.5
1994-95	652.1	3980.0
1995-96	809.0	4301.3
1996-97	950.0 (est.)	4800.0

(Source: *Doordarshan - 1997*)

That Doordarshan and the top advertising agencies have a special relationship is shown in the formation in January 1987 of the *Lok Seva*

Sanchar Parishad, a non-profit voluntary body whose objective is 'to promote production of attractive packages of   public service communication' (*Doordarshan,* 1994). The members of the *Parishad* are representatives from media, advertising agencies, market research and other fields. While Doordarshan provides the funds for the 'quickies' on national integration and other social issues, it is the advertising agencies that produce the advertisements, offering their creative talents free, or so it is claimed (see Kumar, 1992; 1997). In the bargain, however, the agencies make a tidy package, all at the cost of the public exchequer. Another instance of how closely Doordarshan and advertiser-producers work together is the wide use in sponsored programs of imported visual material which is bought cheap on the international market.

Towards A National Media Policy

The Indian government's initial response to the illegal transmission and distribution of cross-border television channels was one of toleration rather than of resistance. According to the Wireless Telegraphy Act of 1885 (instituted by the British colonial administration), the Government of India held monopoly of both the transmission and reception of all forms of wireless signals over Indian territory. But in the early 1990's, the Congress party which had ushered in a new economic policy of liberalization, did not wish to give the impression that it wanted in any way to restrict or block the transnational television channels. It allowed the free growth of cable and satellite television until 1995 when the Cable Television Networks Regulation Act was promulgated to introduce some kind of control and order in the industry. The Act made it obligatory for cable operators to register their companies with the post office and to pay entertainment taxes. More significantly, the Act made the transmission of at least two Doordarshan channels obligatory, and drew up a Programming and Advertising Code, the adherence to which would be the responsibility of the operator.

The Varadan Committee

Perhaps the first step the Congress government in New Delhi took to respond to the new developments in cross-border satellite television was to set up the Varadan Committee (Ministry of Information & Broadcasting, Govt. of India, 1991) with the task of re-examining the Prasar Bharati Act (Govt. of India, 1990). The Committee's report offered a set of guidelines to deal with the emerging situation. The following four guidelines were suggested for Doordarshan as an 'autonomous' broadcaster:

1. Not more than 10% in terms of time of the programs broadcast on each channel should be imported from abroad;

2. At least 20% of total broadcasting time on each channel should be socially relevant and necessary for developmental purposes;

3. The programs broadcast should not be the means for furtherance of the interests of any political party, or any one linguistic group or community;

4. While dealing with any matter of controversy, the programs shall present all points of view in a fair and impartial manner.

Ram Vilas Paswan Committee on National Media Policy

The United Front government later sought to go beyond the question of autonomous broadcasting. It showed interest in drawing up a National Media Policy, though the earlier Congress government had laid the foundations for initiating discussions on the policy (see for instance, Gupta and Dayal, 1996). The media policy was to lay down norms for decentralization of television to the regional and local level, and for the grant of uplinking facilities to private networks. Besides, the plan was also to draw up norms for the following: regulating single media ownership, cross-media ownership, partnership and collaboration of Indian with foreign media houses, proportion of indigenous to foreign content of software, proportion of advertising to programs or editorials, role of advertisers in production of software, and restrictions on the advertising of products like tobacco, alcohol, and chewing tobacco. The Ram Vilas Paswan Committee set up in 1996 for this purpose, submitted an 104-page working paper with 46 recommendations on public and private electronic media, newspapers, news agencies and film. The Committee hammered out a consensus on the National Media Policy. Some of the recommendations were incorporated in the Broadcasting Bill introduced in parliament in May 1997.

The Broadcasting Bill (1997)

The Broadcasting Bill, once approved by parliament, was to establish the Broadcast Authority of India (BAI), an independent authority for the purposes of facilitating and regulating broadcasting services in India. However, some political parties wanted amendments to the Bill, hence a Joint Parliamentary Committee was formed to have a second look at some of the controversial clauses of the Bill. The Bill spells out details on licensing procedures for terrestrial, cable, satellite and direct-to-home channels, the extent of foreign equity, cross-media ownership, and uplinking services for private satellite channels.

The Bill makes it mandatory for all channels whether Indian or foreign to transmit their programs from Indian territory. Licenses will be granted only to Indian companies for satellite channels though these companies would be permitted to have up to 49% foreign equity. No foreign equity for terrestrial channels would be allowed. Further, the Bill bans cross-media ownership (newspaper publishing houses can have no more than 20% equity in television or cable companies), and foreign ownership (though equity up to 49% is allowed for satellite channels). Besides, no advertising agencies, religious bodies, political bodies or publicly funded bodies will be granted a license to own a television broadcasting company. Direct-to-home services would be licensed only to two companies after a bidding process. And, the Cable Television Networks (Regulation) Act would stand repealed once the Bill came into effect.

The Broadcasting Bill set off panic waves among foreign satellite television companies. The *Economic Times* ("Broadcast Bill," 1997) reported that the United States ambassador to India called on the Secretary to the Ministry of Information and Broadcasting 'to convey the anxiety of American channels about certain provisions of the proposed Broadcasting Bill'. The provisions related to the cap on foreign equity and on mandatory uplinking from India. It was also reported that the American channels (ESPN, STAR-TV, CNN,

Discovery, CNBC and NBC) had clubbed together to set up an 'informal committee' to draft an alternative Bill to be submitted to the Indian government. The American Business Council (ABC), the BBC and the British High Commission in New Delhi have also lobbied against the Bill (see "Foreign Channels," *The Economic Times*, June 5, 1997).

The Broadcasting Bill, it must be noted, was introduced in direct response to the Supreme Court of India's direction to the central government in February 1995 to take immediate steps to establish an independent autonomous public authority representative of all sections and interests in the society to control and regulate the use of the airwaves. It ruled that the broadcasting media should be under the control of the public as distinct from the government. The Court was opposed to the privatization of broadcasting, observing that 'private broadcasting, even if allowed, should not be left to market forces, in the interests of ensuring that a wide variety of voices enjoy access to it'. The Court saw 'a potential danger flowing from the concentration of the rights to broadcast/telecast in the hands of (either) a central agency or of a few private affluent broadcasters'.

Nitish Sengupta Committee

The United Front Government's Common Minimum Program made a commitment to broadcasting autonomy, though it rejected entry to the foreign press. It set up a high-powered Committee on Prasar Bharati (the Nitish Sengupta Committee) to re-examine the Prasar Bharati Act (Govt. of India, 1990), drawn up by the earlier Congress Government. The primary concern of the Committee was 'an autonomous structure for Indian broadcasting, with plurality tempered with social responsibility'. It recommended that the government should consider granting licenses to satellite channel operators, domestic and foreign, with uplinking facilities from the Indian soil. The major spin-off from such policy, it argued, would be the generation of substantial revenue, creation of employment opportunities, and regulatory control to ensure that private operators fell in line with the Prasar Bharati Act. A second major recommendation of the Committee was that the government should 'loosen its grip on Doordarshan and let it function as an autonomous

Table 2.5. Countdown To Broadcasting Autonomy

1966: The Chanda Committee Report recommends autonomous status for All India Radio.

1978: The Verghese Committee Report recommends the formation of a National Broadcasting Trust, an autonomous statutory body for Indian broadcasting. The Congress Government shelves the Report.

1989: Prasar Bharati Bill introduced in Parliament by the National Front Government.

1990: Prasar Bharati Bill approved by Parliament after several amendments; receives the President of India's assent.

1991: STAR-TV starts beaming its satellite channels to India in May.

1991: Congress government asks for review of the Prasar Bharati Act in the light of new developments in cross-border satellite broadcasting; the Varadan Inter-Departmental Committee set up to examine the implications for Indian television.

1992: Zee-TV launches its Hindi channel on the STAR-TV network.

1993: Deodhar Committee formed to examine implications of apportioning air-time.

1995: The Supreme Court pronounces landmark judgment on 'airwaves as public property' (Union of India vs. Cricket Association of Bengal).

1995: Ram Vilas Paswan Committee on National Media Policy set up; Cable (Television Networks) Regulation Act promulgated.

1996: Nitish Sengupta Committee constituted to look into the Prasar Bharati Act and to suggest amendments. Submitted report in August

1997: Broadcasting Bill introduced in Parliament on May 16. Joint Parliamentary Committee headed by Sharad Pawar set up to suggest amendments.

1997: Prasar Bharati (Broadcasting Corporation of India) established in September by a Presidential Ordinance.

1997: Prasar Bharati Board is constituted in November, and takes over charge from the Ministry of Information and Broadcasting.

corporation with a paid-up capital of Rs. 2000 crores'. The United Front government amended the Prasar Bharati Act by deleting three clauses (Nos. 13, 14 and 15) that related to the appointment of a 22-member Parliament Committee (whose task was to 'oversee' the functioning of the proposed Corporation), and the establishment of the Broadcasting Council, a forum for consumers' complaints; the Broadcasting Authority would take over the Council's function instead.

Prasar Bharati Act and the Broadcasting Bill

The Prasar Bharati (Broadcasting Corporation of India) began functioning in late November 1997, with the appointment of a Board comprising a Chairman, an Executive Member (who is the Chief Executive), six part-time members, directors of AIR and Doordarshan, and one representative of the Ministry of Information and Broadcasting, and two representatives of the Corporation's employees. The Board has independent authority, its primary duty being 'to organize and conduct public broadcasting services to inform, educate and entertain the public and to ensure a balanced development of broadcasting on radio and television'. Thus, its mandate is that of a public service broadcaster much like the BBC, funded by the federal government but autonomous in its policies and functioning. Thus broadcasting has ceased to be a unit of the Ministry of Information and Broadcasting, and instead functions as an autonomous body as recommended by the Chanda Committee (Govt. of India, 1966), the Verghese Committee (Govt. of India, 1978), and the Nitish Sengupta Committee (Govt. of India, 1997).

An Alternative Broadcasting Structure

Meanwhile, the Forum for Independent Film and Video, an association of independent film and video professionals circulated, in August 1996, a 13-page paper entitled 'A Vision for Television: An Argument for a Public Broadcasting Service'. The paper was debated in various fora, and a set of recommendations were submitted to the Ministry of Information and Broadcasting, the Parliamentary

Consultative Committee attached to the Ministry, as well as to the Speakers of both Houses of Parliament.

The paper proposed an alternative structure for Indian Radio and Television with a Broadcast Licensing Authority, an independent body (which would not be a part of the Prasar Bharati Corporation), but which would create two supervisory bodies: the Broadcasting Standards Council and the Broadcasting Redressal Council. To ensure a significant place for public service content, the Forum recommended that Prasar Bharati demarcate three parallel streams: official, commercial and public broadcasting service. The official platform would reflect the government's policies and programs and be run by government officials; the commercial platform would be geared to programs determined by the needs of advertising; and the public service platform would offer alternative programming produced by NGOS (Non-Government Organizations) or other independent groups. Funding for the public service platform would come from a percentage of advertising revenues collected by the official and the commercial platforms, license fees for uplinking facilities, and from sales of programs to other channels in India and abroad.

Conclusion

Five years after the 'satellite invasion' by foreign and Indian channels (both free-to-air and pay channels), Doordarshan continues to be the dominant player with a total of 921 transmitters, 17 transponders (on INSAT satellites), 41 production centers and a staff of 19,576. Supported by an annual budget of over Rs. 10.8 billion and an advertising revenue of Rs. 4.3 billion, Doordarshan reaches out to 448 million viewers, with a potential coverage of as much as 86% of the nation's population of 930 million (*Doordarshan*, 1996; *Doordarshan*, 1997). AIR has an even more extensive reach with over 300 transmitters, 250 stations, and a reach extending to more than 111 million sets and a coverage of almost the entire population (*Doordarshan*, 1997).

Actual access to both radio and television in India is, however, still limited. Receiver sets are priced far beyond the reach of the urban and rural poor. At the close of 1997, there were around 57.7 million television households in the country out of which barely 15 million were in rural India. Of the 30 million urban households with access to television, around 18 million were connected to cable, but a mere 10 million to the satellite channels via cable networks. Over a million of these urban homes used a remote control to surf the satellite channels, and 3.5 million homes owned more than one television set each. However, barely three million could access more than a dozen satellite channels. Over 75% of the television households were in Western and Northern India, with the South possessing only 15%, and the East and North-East together a mere 10% (*Doordarshan*, 1997).

The total reach of the metro channel which was launched in 1993 for urban areas is about 12 million households including nine million by terrestrial and three million by satellite (*Doordarshan*, 1995, 1996, 1997). All the five (now extended to eight) STAR-TV channels have a viewership of about 6.5 million in India, with ZEE TV taking more than fifty per cent of this share. Less than two million watch BBC, and fewer than three million the STAR-Plus channel. They stand no comparison with Doordarshan's national network whose viewership touches 400 million. In fact, the metro channel of Doordarshan, though restricted only to 42 major Indian cities, commands a much higher viewership (112 million, according to *Doordarshan*, 1997) than any foreign channel. Thus, the only real competitor to Doordarshan is the ZEE channel on the STAR-TV network, though in south India, the private satellite channels such as SUN TV, Eenadu TV, and Asianet are challenging Doordarshan's supremacy. According to an IMRB survey for the week ending December 1996, 18 channels vied for prime time (7.00 to 9.00 p.m.). Doordarshan's national network was way above other channels, obtaining 71.5% of the total viewership, with ZEE TV getting 18%, Sony TV 13%, and STAR Plus 8.3%. BBC, CNN, Home TV and the various music and sports channels have a very low viewership in India.

From 9.00 p.m. to midnight, cable has over fifty per cent of the audience share (*Doordarshan*, 1994). Hindi and English movies are the main software for the cable networks. In the mid-nineties, a distinct trend in urban India was the revival of interest in cable which offered local language, 'neighborhood' programming, interactive community games (such as 'housie'), and phone-in facilities. Further, the local cable operators have found that most subscribers are unwilling to fork out additional fees for the pay television channels (like ESPN, for instance). In the metros, small cable operators have united under the INCABLENET (promoted by the Hinduja Group) and SITICABLE (a subsidiary of ZEE-TV) networks.

Moreover, there is evidence that many Indian viewers of the satellite channels are turning to the newly started regional language satellite channels of Doordarshan (Channels 4 to 13), the revamped channels of DD I (the National Network) and DD II (the Metro Channel), as well as to the SUN-TV channels (Tamil), Udaya TV (Kannada), Gemini TV (Telugu), Raj TV, Vijay TV, Eenadu (Telugu), Asianet (Malayalam), and several Hindi channels such as ZEE-TV, EL-TV, JAIN TV, ATN, Sony and CVO (a joint venture of Hinduja's and CableMaster), the first Hindi movie cable channel for ten cities launched in late 1996. The growing success of the Indian language channels has forced English language transnational channels (for instance, STAR-Plus and STAR-Movies) to dub or sub-title their programs in Hindi, and to screen original Indian soaps during prime-time.

DD-India, an 18-hour international service beamed via PAS-I and PAS-4, was launched in March 1995 to reach audiences across the world. Several cable channels in Europe, the Americas and West Asia carry Doordarshan's programs on their networks. In Sri Lanka, Singapore, and Malaysia, SUN-TV's Tamil channels are easily accessed; so are Asianet's Malayalam channels and ZEE and ATN's Hindi channels in the Gulf countries. Thus Indian television companies have turned 'transnationals' and are competing for viewers (and advertising revenue) in the global market.

Issues Beyond Autonomy

More than a decade ago, the Joshi Working Group on Software for Doordarshan (Govt. of India, 1984) raised two simple questions: Television for whom and for what? The questions still remain very pertinent after the government decided to grant autonomy to the broadcasting industry in late 1997. The Working Group took note of the 'credibility gap created by the growing hiatus between profession and practice, between official policy pronouncements emphasizing the use of television for development and education, and the increasing drift and departure from them in actual programming'. It made a plea for 'education with entertainment', and for an 'Indian personality for

Indian Television'. It strongly urged that 'software planning be utilized as a means of preventing the appropriation of television by the emerging forces of commercialism and consumerism'. Ten years on, as television in Asia enters the digital and Direct-to-Home era, the Broadcasting Corporation of India continues to use the rhetoric of 'education and social development', but in actual practice draws closer to advertisers, advertising and marketing agencies, and media professionals. One hopes that the radical restructuring of radio and television envisaged by the Prasar Bharati Act and the proposed Broadcast Authority of India will lead to a 'reappropriation' of these electronic media for public welfare and service.

References

Agrawal, Binod C. (1981). *SITE Social Evaluation: Results, Experiences and Implications.* Ahmedabad: Space Applications Center.

Awasthy, G. C. (1965). *Broadcasting in India.* Mumbai: Allied Publishers.

Baruah, U. L. (1984) *This is All India Radio.* New Delhi: Publications Division.

'Broadcast Bill sets off panic waves in foreign channels.' (1997, May 12). *The Economic Times,* p.1.

Chapman, G.; K. Kumar; C. Fraser; & I. Gaber. (1997). *Environmentalism and the Mass Media: The North-South Divide.* London/New York: Routledge.

Chatterjee, P. C. (1987). *Broadcasting in India.* New Delhi: Sage Publications.

Chowdhary, N. (1996). 'STAR-TV shines in India.' *International Herald Tribune,* July 16.

Chowla, N. L. (1991) *Listening and Viewing.* New Delhi: Sage Publications.

Doordarshan - 1994. New Delhi: Audience Research Unit, Directorate General, Doordarshan.

Doordarshan - 1995. New Delhi: Audience Research Unit, Directorate General, Doordarshan.

Doordarshan - 1996. New Delhi: Audience Research Unit, Directorate General, Doordarshan.

Doordarshan - 1997. New Delhi: Audience Research Unit, Directorate General, Doordarshan.

Duggal, K. S. (1980). *What Ails Indian Broadcasting?* New Delhi: Marwah Publications.

Eapen, K. E. (1996). 'India's Radio System: The Unmet Challenges of Local Broadcasting.' Paper presented at IAMCR Conference, Sydney.

Fielden, L. (1960) *The Natural Bent.* London: Andrew Deutsch.

'Foreign Channels to link up against Bill.' (1997, June 5). *The Economic Times,* p.1.

Forum for Independent Film and Video (1996). *A Vision for Television - An Argument for a Public Service Broadcasting Service.* New Delhi.

Gore, M. S. (1983). *The SITE Experience.* Paris: UNESCO.

Government of India (1966). *The Chanda Committee Report.* New Delhi: Publications Division.

Government of India (1978). *Akash Bharati: National Broadcast Trust* (The Verghese Committee Report), Vols. I and II. New Delhi: Government of India, Ministry of Information and Broadcasting/ Publications Division.

Government of India (1984). *An Indian Personality for Television: Report of the Working Group on Software for Doordarshan,* Vols. I, II and III. New Delhi: Publications Division.

Government of India, Ministry of Law and Justice (1990). *Prasar Bharati Act.* New Delhi.

Government of India, Ministry of Information and Broadcasting (1997). *The Broadcasting Bill.* New Delhi.

Gupta V.S. & R. Dayal (1996). *National Media Policy.* New Delhi: Concept Publishing Company and AMIC.

Khare, V. C. (1993). 'Cable TV Scenario in India.' Paper presented at International Broadcasting, Cable and Satellite Conference, October.

Kumar, K. J. (1990). 'The West This Week, Every Week : A Content Analysis of The World This Week.' Paper presented at the International Television Studies Conference, London, July. Reprinted in French, David and Michael Richards (Eds.) (1996). *Contemporary Television: Eastern Perspectives,* New Delhi: Sage.

Kumar, K. J. (1992). *Advertising: A Critical View.* Pune: Nirali Prakashan.

Kumar, K. J. (1994). 'The Politics of Satellite Television in Asia: Implications for Media Education.' Paper presented at the IAMCR Conference, Seoul, Korea, July 3-7. Reprinted in Ludes, Peter (Ed.) (1996) : Informationskontexte fuer Massmedien, Westdeutscher Verlag.

Kumar, K. J. (1995). *Media Education, Communications and Public Policy: An Indian Perspective.* Mumbai: Himalaya Publishers.

Kumar, K. J. (1996). 'The Emerging Media Scenario in India: Challenges for Media Education.' Paper presented at IAMCR

Conference, Sydney, August 18-22.

Kumar, K. J. (1996). *Mass Communication in India.* Mumbai: Jaico.

Kumar, K. J. (1997). *Mass Communication: A Critical Analysis.* Mumbai: Vipul Prakashan.

Luthra, H. K. (1987). *Indian Broadcasting.* New Delhi: Publications Division.

Mansell, G. (1982). *Let Truth Be Told.* London: George Weidenfeld & Nicholson Ltd.

Masani, M. (1985). *Broadcasting and the People.* New Delhi: National Book Trust.

Ministry of Information and Broadcasting (1995). *Cable Regulation Act,* New Delhi.

Ministry of Information and Broadcasting (1991). *Varadan Committee Report.* New Delhi.

Mitra, A. (1993). *Television and Popular Culture in India: A Study of the Mahabhara.* New Delhi: Sage Publications.

Mody, B. (1988). 'The Commercialization of television in India: A Research Agenda for Cross-Country Comparisons.' Paper presented at ICA Conference, New Orleans.

Mullick, K. R. (1974). *Tangled Tapes: The Inside Story of Indian Broadcasting.* New Delhi: Sterling Publications.

Patel, M. (1997). 'The Year of Reckoning in Brand Equity.'*The Economic Times,* Mumbai, February 19-25, p. 4.

Rao, B. S. S. (1986). 'All India Radio: The New Challenges.' *Gazette* Vol. 38:101-113.

Singhal, A. & Rogers E. M. (1989*). India's Information Revolution.* New Delhi: Sage.

Tunstall, Jeremy (1977). *The Media are American.* London: Constable.

Chapter 3

The New Doordarshan: Facing The Challenges of Cable and Satellite Networks in India

Sandhya Rao

Cable television signaled the beginning of a new era in the history of Indian television. In terms of content as well as diffusion, television is now growing at an explosive pace, offering an array of viewing choices to a public that not so long ago had to be content with monotonous programming on one or two channels of the government-owned terrestrial network.

This chapter examines the changing industrial dynamics, resulting from the rise of cable connections in India. In particular, it analyzes the implications for Doordarshan in this changing television environment. How has Doordarshan coped with the challenges presented by cable and transborder satellite networks? What have been the resulting changes in the quantity and quality of programs offered to Indian audiences? Before addressing these questions, the chapter will briefly review the history of Doordarshan. This will provide a transition to the first section of the chapter.

Brief History of Doordarshan

The evolution of Doordarshan, the state-controlled television network, spans over three decades; a growth that has been sporadic rather than consistent. The first television transmitter was set up in the capital New Delhi in 1959 as part of an experimental UNESCO project to train personnel and evaluate television as a tool for education and national development. Television sets were installed in a few community centers around Delhi and hour-long programs were beamed twice a week. Encouraged by the positive impact of this experiment, educational programs for schools were added and telecast once a week for ten weeks in 1961.

The year 1965 marked the beginning of regular television broadcasts in New Delhi. The program content focused on education, development, news, and entertainment (Malhan, 1985). After a gap of seven years, a second television station was set up in Mumbai. In the year that followed, a relay station in Pune and stations in Srinagar and Amritsar were established. In 1975, Calcutta, Chennai (Madras) and Lucknow were placed on the television map of India.

Instructional and development programs formed the backbone of Indian television, at least until the mid-1980's. In August 1975, the government attempted to reach rural viewers by launching a novel one-year project -- the Satellite Instruction Television Experiment (SITE), using NASA's Applications Technology Satellite-6 (ATS-6). Instructional programs were beamed to 2,400 villages in the states of Andhra Pradesh, Karnataka, Rajasthan, Bihar, Orissa and Madhya Pradesh. One of the primary objectives of SITE was demonstrating the potential of satellite television in providing practical instruction in areas such as health, hygiene, agriculture, nutrition, national integration, and adult literacy to the villagers.

The year 1982 saw the emergence of a period of aggressive growth of Doordarshan. This was the year when Doordarshan started broadcasting in color. The ASIAD, a major Asian sports event, that India hosted in 1982 provided an impetus for the expansion of the Doordarshan network, which grew to include 40 transmitters. During 1984, which marked the silver jubilee of Doordarshan, the government commissioned one new transmitter a day for a period of more than four months, taking the total number of transmitters to 172 and covering 52 percent of the country's then 800 million population (Malhan, 1985). By December 1988, India had 274 stations. This momentum continued through the end of the 1980s. By 1990, Doordarshan had 510 transmitters (*Manorama Year Book*, 1992).

From Development to Entertainment Media

In the beginning, ambiguity prevailed regarding the nature of television programs and the diffusion of the medium. Because television was conceived as an audio-visual medium that would be used for educational and development purposes, the programs tended to be geared toward the rural audiences. However, the diffusion of television transmitters as well as the receiver sets were concentrated in the urban areas. In fact, Singhal & Rogers (1989) noted that "one of the most controversial policy issues in New Delhi in this decade (1980s) has been the proper role of television, centering on whether it should be used for entertainment or for education" (p. 61). Furthermore, Mitra (1993) contends that a "...source of tension around Indian television is the opposition between educational and entertainment programs and its relation with the rural-urban dichotomy in India" (p. 25).

The programs were far from appealing to the urban audiences, most of whom owned television sets compared to their rural counterparts who owned far fewer television sets (Singhal & Rogers, 1989). This was evident in the 1980s with the rapid increase in the number of transmitters and in the purchase of television sets. In 1988, about 75 percent of the 11 million television sets were concentrated in the four metropolitan cities of Delhi, Calcutta, Chennai and Mumbai (Singhal and Rogers, 1989). In the 1980s, there was a slight increase in the variety of entertainment programs that included Indian language soap operas, feature films, film song picturization, and quiz shows. *Chitrahaar*, a program featuring songs from Hindi films, was one of the most popular programs. English language programming was limited to national news bulletins and a few imported serials such as the American comedy, *I Love Lucy* and the British comedy, *Are You Being Served?* In most cities, Doordarshan operated just one or two channels and the time had to be divided between the national telecast in Hindi, the news in English and the regional telecast in the language spoken in the Indian states. This was frustrating for viewers especially in the non Hindi-speaking states because the regional telecast was allotted only one or two hours during non-prime time in the evenings and in many areas the transmission was interrupted by power outages. Even though there has been general criticism that Doordarshan programs carried propaganda messages for the government of the day, some of the programs have been very successful. For example, the documentary *Ramayan*, based on the well-known Hindu epic of the same name was a phenomenal success. This religion-based program was patronized alike by both urban and rural audiences across the nation and served to reinforce the message of national integration. It also served to inflate Doordarshan's coffers considerably because of the numerous commercials aired just before and after the show. *Ramayan* was followed by the documentary broadcast of *Mahabharat*, another ancient Hindu epic.

Hum Log, a soap opera that was broadcast in the mid-1980s introduced a new trend in programming by combining entertainment with pro-development messages relating to family planning, family harmony, and national integration. This combination was so successful that Singhal and Rogers (1989) noted, it "...convinced national leaders in other Third World countries to launch pro-development soap operas" (p. 89). *Hum Log* was sponsored by advertisers who paid for the production costs in return for commercial spots. There were several successful television programs that were launched at this time including *Buniyaad, Rajni*, and *Yeh Jo Hai Zindagi*.

Cable Television Emerges

Cable television entered the Indian communication scene in a significant way in the 1990s and heralded a new era in the history of Indian television. In terms of content as well as diffusion, cable television registered a tremendous growth. The number of cable operators rose from 150 in 1985 to roughly 12,000 in 1992 (Thomas, 1993) and about 30,000 by 1995 (Agarwal, 1995a). Hong Kong-based STAR TV, the first commercial pan-Asia satellite television service (Chan, 1994), entered India in 1991 with five channels (Karp, 1994). By the end of 1993 about 25 percent (7,278,000) of the total TV households were estimated to have STAR TV reception capabilities in India through cable connections (Chan, 1994). ZEE TV, a private satellite television service began in October 1992 and EL TV, a sister company of ZEE TV was launched by the end of 1994. ZEE TV's entertaining Hindi-language quiz shows, soap operas and serials posed serious challenges to Doordarshan programs (Karp, 1994). By August 1994, viewers could access a total of 25 channels including CNN, ZEE TV, Jain TV, SUN TV, ASIANET and ATN (*Manorama Year Book*, 1995). Currently, this number has grown to about 35 channels in most major Indian cities. Jain TV was the first 24-hour Hindi-language channel while SUN TV is a Chennai-based Tamil, Kannada, and Telugu language service. The number of television households was estimated to be over 42 million (Karp, 1994; *Manorama Year Book*, 1995) in the mid-1990's. By February 1998, there were 65 million television homes (*Doordarshan, 1998*). Today, India has 270 million urban, middle-class people --- an attractive audience for those who want to market products to this segment via television commercials.

The cable industry however, is beset with problems. The growth of cable networks has been chaotic (Agarwal, 1995b) with several thousand small budget operators competing in the market. Apart from lacking the necessary infrastructure to distribute the available channels, the cable operators are finding it unprofitable to provide specific channels that meet limited subscriber choices. Additionally, most of the subscriber television sets lack the capacity to receive numerous channels. Big companies such as Indusind Media Communications owned by the Hindujas and ZEE TV-owned Siti Cable now provide large-scale cable services, sending in the process, small operators out of business (Agarwal, 1995b). On the technology front, there is a likelihood of a merging of telephony and cable television which offers great hope for better services (Agarwal, 1995b).

Doordarshan Responds

Since the entry of cable in 1990, there has been much introspection, rethinking, and a reorientation by Doordarshan, according to N. G. Srinivas, station director of Doordarshan in Bangalore, India (personal communication, July 1996). Earlier, Doordarshan had complete monopoly over viewers in India but the emergence of cable/satellite services has provided a good deal of competition in attracting and retaining audiences. In an attempt to gear itself up to meet the challenges posed by cable, Doordarshan has initiated many changes, including the introduction of new---both international and regional Indian language---channels, increasing the entertainment content of existing channels, and conducting ratings research.

Doordarshan has registered a rapid growth in the 1990s in terms of adding several channels to the one or two channels that existed earlier. In 1996, there were about 15 channels including the regional Indian language channels (*Doordarshan* '96). There has also been a decided shift towards providing more entertainment. Since 1993, the content of DD-1, the primary (national) channel, has been restructured to accommodate more entertainment programs. Additionally, the four terrestrial transmitters that provided a second channel to viewers in Delhi, Mumbai, Calcutta, and Chennai were linked through satellite. This has enabled Doordarshan to provide more entertainment for urban audiences in these cities. This channel, DD-2 (the metro channel), can be accessed in 42 cities terrestrially and by using a dish antenna in other parts of the country. The metro channel fare includes entertainment programs, sitcoms, films and talk shows in both Hindi and English. DD-3, introduced in 1995, caters to an upmarket audience. Theater, arts, literature, classical music, travel, and in-depth coverage of news are featured on this channel. In addition, Doordarshan started a Movie Club channel, the only free to air channel of Indian films in India. During 1993, Doordarshan introduced regional Indian language satellite programs in ten languages many of which are spoken by more than 50 million people. Doordarshan has also entered into a mutual agreement with CNN, for news coverage (*Doordarshan* '96). While Doordarshan accommodates CNN news and current affairs programs, CNN in turn, is expected to allot a certain amount of time to news on India and project the Indian point of view on international issues to an international audience (Srinivas, N.G., personal communication, July, 1996). The DD-CNNI is a 24-hour current affairs channel with programs from both Doordarshan and CNNI. Doordarshan's plans include launching new channels such as the one similar to MTV, devoted exclusively to music, and a sports channel. Exclusive channels such as the Business channel and Money channel are in the pipeline also. These channels are expensive, complicated, and demand high-quality programs, labor and sophisticated technology (Srinivas, N.G., personal communication, July, 1996).

Table 3.1: Milestones in the Growth of Television in India

Year	Milestones
1959	First television transmitter is set up for educational broadcast on an experimental basis in New Delhi.
1965	Regular television station is set up in New Delhi.
1972	Television station is set up in Bombay.
1975	SITE is launched in 2,400 villages in six states. At this time there are television stations in eight Indian cities.
1982	Color television is introduced in part due to the ASIAD held in New Delhi. The number of transmitters rises to 40.
1989	The momentum of growth increases in the 1980s. By 1989-90, the number of transmitters rises to 510.
1990	CNN's images of the Gulf War are telecast via satellite.
1991	Hong Kong based STAR TV enters India.
1992	Number of cable operators increases from 150 in 1985 to about 12,000. 25% of the total TV households have STAR TV connections.
1993	Doordarshan restructures national programs to accommodate more entertainment. Doordarshan commences audience research TV ratings. Metro Channel, Regional Language Channels and several other channels are launched.
1995	Number of cable operators rises to about 30,000. DD-India, International Channel, Doordarshan Movie Club, DD-CNNI and DD-3 are launched. Doordarshan has 792 transmitters and reaches 86 percent of the population.
1996	Cable provides about 35 channels on average to subscribers
1998	Doordarshan operates 17 channels, has 934 transmitters, provides over 1,400 hours of programs every week and reaches 87% of the population.

Sources: Agarwal (1995a), *Doordarshan '96*, Karp (1994), Malhan (1985), *Manorama Year Book* (1992, 1995),Thomas (1993) and *Doordarshan-98*.

It can be seen from Table 3.1, that television has come a long way since the first transmitter was set up in 1959. It was in the 1980s that television began to diffuse rapidly. The spread of cable television since 1990 has led to an increase in the number of commercial satellite as well as Doordarshan channels available to the audience. Despite rapid cable penetration, Doordarshan continues to enjoy a much larger share of viewers because of its vast terrestrial network. By 1995, there were 792 television transmitters. Today, Doordarshan is accessible to 87 percent of the country's 950 million population *(Doordarshan '98)*. There are an estimated 65,000 community sets. Among the 660 million rural dwellers, 205 million have access to television on Doordarshan *(Doordarshan '96)*. Doordarshan beams programs from INSAT 1D, INSAT 2A, INSAT 2B, INSAT 2C, and PAS-4 satellites.

During the 1996 Olympics, Doordarshan had a decided edge over cable operators and won the rights to cover the games at a low rate because of its membership in the Asian Broadcasting Union. Satellite networks such as STAR TV would have incurred a higher price for the same privilege, according to B.S. Chandrasekhar, director of audience research for Doordarshan (personal communication, August, 1996).

A major advantage Doordarshan has over the cable networks is the immediacy or the currency factor. Cable has a problem of uplinking, according to Srinivas, N.G. (personal communication, July, 1996). Cable operators have to take the programs to Hong Kong or Singapore to uplink to the satellite and this process involves a time lag. Doordarshan, on the other hand, has the facility to cover news instantly. However, this national policy is being debated and deliberated and the government proposes to make a decision on the issue (see Pathania chapter in this volume for an extended discussion). Srinivas points out that the satellite channels are basically for entertainment and not for news, except for international news. STAR TV and private regional Indian language channels do have news programs but for a limited time, whereas Doordarshan covers local and national news extensively. Doordarshan is also making use of the immediacy factor to present live programs. For example, the former prime minister Deve Gowda participated in a live program on television when he was the Chief Minister of Karnataka State, prior to becoming the Prime Minister. He answered questions from people across the nation. Cable, due to limited access to technology, is not able to do this (Srinivas, N.G., personal communication, July, 1996). However, only those who have access to telephones can participate in the live programs.

The percentage of the audience watching DD-1, Doordarshan's terrestrial channel, and DD-2, Doordarshan's metro channel, together accounts for a large segment of the audience in Delhi, Chennai, and Mumbai. According to the results of a study conducted by the Indian Market Research Bureau (IMRB) in Delhi, the two channels have a combined viewership of 95.1 percent of the audience on Sunday mornings, 82.7 percent on Sunday evenings, and 84.7 percent on weekdays. In Chennai, the percentage of viewers on weekends and week days varies from 88.8 to 96.5 percent. In Mumbai, the percentages are lower, ranging from 66.6 percent to 74 percent. However, even in Mumbai, Doordarshan enjoys the majority of the audience's attention with the nearest competitors having less than ten percent of the market share.

Future Challenges for Doordarshan

Doordarshan certainly offers more channels and more variety in its programming. However, all the new channels that Doordarshan has added are on cable. The idea was to attract cable viewers surfing the channels who would then have the choice to view Doordarshan cable channels as well. Doordarshan's major objective has been to keep the cable audience within its fold. However, those who cannot afford cable continue to get only the national and regional Indian language programs. According to Srinivas (personal communication, July 1996), Doordarshan's audience is not lost but splintered. DD-2 for example, was started to counter the Hindi entertainment channel, ZEE TV. ZEE TV posed a direct threat in terms of shifting Doordarshan's audience patronage. As a media manager, the government had to think in terms of countering that in a way that would win back the audience. DD-2 is now a competitor to ZEE TV.

Though channels in several regional Indian languages are available, these only reach people with cable connections. Besides, even those with cable connections would be able to receive a particular channel only if the cable operator decided to provide the channel. Cable operators provide channels based on the demand in their geographical areas of operation. At present there is no solution, says Chandrasekhar (personal communication, August, 1996). Doordarshan does not have the resources to expand the terrestrial channels and has to use the existing one or two channels to an optimum extent. Regional-language Indian programs are also more expensive to produce. Doordarshan has social goals to fulfill on the one hand and commercial aims on the other. For instance, 6.30 p.m. may be a good time for rural programs but it is also a good time for a documentary that may fetch Doordarshan more advertising money.

With the influx of Western programs on cable, questions have been raised about their impact on the local culture. Doordarshan officials contend that Western soap operas shown on cable cannot make competitive inroads into the country due to differences in language and culture (Srinivas, N.G., personal communication, July, 1996). Doordarshan's own urban soap operas, *Swabhiman* and *Shanti* have enjoyed good ratings. Participatory, slick, imaginative programs such as *Close-up Antakshari*, a music-based program, have survived cutthroat competition. Foreign-language programs on Doordarshan constitute about 2-3 percent, according to Chandrasekhar. DD-2 has some German and British programs, but barring a few movies, hardly any American content.

Competition from cable has made Doordarshan take a serious look at its program ratings. Earlier Doordarshan used to conduct social research but has now changed its emphasis to commercial research. In 1993, for the first time Doordarshan paid serious attention to ratings research. Doordarshan found that research conducted by some private firms was biased against Doordarshan because they were based in cities where satellite/cable penetration was higher. When the country is taken as a whole, Doordarshan has a large and continuous audience (Chandrasekhar, B.S., personal communication, August, 1996). Doordarshan Audience Research Television (DART) has panels in 33 cities and covers 20 cities each week. The diary method and people meters are both used. Consolidated ratings at the national level are provided. A typical DART sample has 51 percent male and 49 percent female; four income groups ranging from less than Rs. 1000 per month to above Rs. 4000 (1 USD= Rs. 35); and ages ranging from 8 to over 45 years. Homes with cable account for 28 percent and homes without cable account for 72 percent of the sample.

Conclusion

Doordarshan has restructured itself in a number of ways in the 1990s to meet the challenges posed by cable. Currently, Doordarshan continues to attract large audiences nationwide compared to cable. A likely explanation for this is that Doordarshan has a vast terrestrial network and reaches a large percentage of the population, especially those living in the rural areas, unable to afford cable. Besides, cable is still in its infancy in India. The dilemma of reaching different types of audiences in rural and urban areas has not been solved. Srinivas and Chandrasekhar posit that Doordarshan basically caters to a general, mixed audience and is accountable for fulfilling social goals as well. While the stress is now on sponsored, entertainment-oriented programs, Doordarshan continues to broadcast programs that are development-oriented. However, people are now selective and do not watch programs that they do not like. Thus, Doordarshan's strategy to please urban and rural audiences may end up pleasing neither. According to Doordarshan authorities, this dilemma may continue until Doordarshan gets exclusive channels (for rural and urban audiences), adequate and up-to-date technology and software (Srinivas, N.G., personal communication, July, 1996).

While the officials in Doordarshan assert that programs continue to be produced for the upliftment of the masses (socio-economic development), Kumar in his chapter points out that very limited resources have been set aside for development-oriented programs relative to the production of entertainment for the urban middle class. Thus, the argument that Doordarshan does not have the resources to fulfill social goals needs to be evaluated against the time and money spent on entertainment-oriented programs and channels for the urban elites.

While the allocation of resources between rural, development-oriented and urban entertainment-oriented programs may seem inequitable, overall lack of resources and infrastructure continue to be a problem for Doordarshan. In terms of investment, the government continued to give priority to basic sectors such as health, nutrition, education, and national defense. Though Doordarshan's budget has increased from Rs. 776 million in 1982 to Rs. 10,890 million in 1996 (*Doordarshan* '96), the investment is a very small percentage of the country's total investment in all sectors. Doordarshan's commercial earnings have registered a growth from Rs. 159 million in 1982 to Rs. 4300 million in 1996 (*Doordarshan* '96). With regard to software, the actual program output from Doordarshan's 40 production centers in 1998 was 1400 hours per week (*Doordarshan*, 1998) which falls far short of the estimated total program hours of about 13,000 required by all the channels. The gaps are filled by showing repeats. In terms of talent, India has not only a vast pool of talented people but is also rich in talent such as folk artists. However, the problem is that Doordarshan is not able to tap this talent adequately due to resource constraints. Doordarshan has limited satellite news gathering vehicles with uplink facilities for adequate coverage of rural areas. Infrastructural problems including the unreliable power supply (frequent power outages), pose a hindrance to regular television viewing. Though Doordarshan has increased investment on equipment such as transmitters, new camera and studio facilities, this equipment is expensive and the investment is inadequate.

The question of autonomy for Doordarshan has been addressed again in the Indian parliament. In July 1997 the government announced that it was granting Doordarshan an autonomous status. Since then, a board has been constituted under the provisions of the Prasar Bharati Act 1990 that seeks to grant autonomy to the government-run electronic media ("Board for Media," 1997). But, already there was increasing privatization within Doordarshan in terms of program content. For example, news programs such as *Aaj Tak, News Tonight* and most of the documentaries are produced by private program producers at their own risk. So, it is not certain to what extent an autonomous status would further the objective of Doordarshan to provide meaningful programs to rural audiences. In the 1960's and the 1970's, the Chanda Committee and the Verghese Committee recommended autonomy for All India Radio (AIR) and Doordarshan. It was felt then that an autonomous status would provide freedom from intrusive government control over programming decisions and content. However, successive governments have resisted granting autonomy because they felt development-oriented programs that usually require substantial investment would be sidetracked and commercial interests would become more important in programming decisions and content (Malhan, 1985). Today, programming is dominated by the interests of advertisers, advertising agencies, and media professionals (see Kumar's chapter). Doordarshan has become increasingly dependent on advertising revenue. Moreover, problems such as lack of credibility due to political influence and corruption continue to exist. So, it remains to be seen whether an autonomous status for Doordarshan will be a boon or a bane with respect to the social goals of Doordarshan programming.

References

Agarwal, A. (1995a, January 31). The survival of the fittest. *India Today*, 228-229.

Agarwal, A. (1995b, August 15). Choking on its own growth. *India Today*, 116-117.

'Board for media autonomy is constituted.' (1997, December 5). *India Abroad*, Vol. XXVIII, No. 10, page 14.

Chan, J. M. (1994). National responses and accessibility to STAR TV in Asia. *Journal of Communication, 44* (3), 112-131.

Doordarshan '96 (1996). New Delhi: Directorate General, Doordarshan.

Doordarshan 1998. Home page of the government-run television in India at http://www.ddindia.net

Karp, J. (1994). TV times. *Far Eastern Economic Review, 157* (50).

Manorama Year Book. (1992). Kottayam, India: Malayala Manorama

Manorama Year Book. (1995). Kottayam, India: Malayala Manorama.

Malhan, P. N. (1985). *Communication media--yesterday, today and tomorrow.* Meerut, India: Link Printers.

Mitra, A. (1993). *Television and popular culture in India: A study of the Mahabharat.* New Delhi, India: Sage Publications.

Singhal, A., & Rogers, E. M. (1989). *India's information revolution.* New Delhi, India: Sage Publications.

Thomas, P. N. (1993). Broadcasting and the state in India: Towards relevant alternatives. *Gazette, 51,* 19-33.

Chapter 4

Responses to Transnational Television in a STAR-struck land: Doordarshan and STAR-TV in India[1]

Geetika Pathania

As the forces of liberalization sweep through the world, the opening of economies, and hence markets provides an increasingly receptive context within which the trade of cultural products is carried out. The success of Hong Kong-based Satellite Television Asian Region (STAR TV), which, in 1991, started direct broadcasting via satellite to Asia, has underlined the attractiveness of Asian markets to the corporations of the media saturated West. The mainly American programming which arrived without any prior consent of national governments has also demonstrated the ambivalence with which governments are viewing the manifestations of the foreign capital they so eagerly seek. This chapter examines how the Indian government's liberalization policies, which favor foreign investors, has softened the early reception of foreign-backed media industry products, with a consequent shift in Indian cultural policy.

Advertising-supported STAR TV has been owned, since August 1993, by western media mogul Rupert Murdoch, one of the "lords of the global village" (Bagdikian, 1989). The early regulatory response to STAR TV in India is notable since it occurred at a time when the process of India's slow and somewhat erratic economic liberalization was coming under increasing pressure to stay on track. As transnational interests responded to possible access to the previously closed Indian market, the government began to find itself at odds with the media agendas that were no longer under its control. This chapter discusses the context within which Doordarshan and STAR TV operate and their strategies for greatest market share and revenue. The Zee companies are treated here as part of the STAR TV umbrella.[2] Transnational links of the advertising industry in India will be discussed, and an analysis of the political economy of liberalization in India will be attempted. By way of conclusion it will be argued that the timing of STAR TV's arrival in India, when the credibility of internal reforms was vital, was key to its official reception in India.

Doordarshan

At the time of independence in 1947, the concern with developmental issues made radio, and later television a natural choice of the government for the centralizing tendency of the state (Chatterjee, 1987.)[3] When television broadcasting began in 1959, it was a modest, if controversial beginning. A single studio in Delhi transmitted an hour of programming twice a week. For several years, farm programs for rural audiences, folk dances and music, and women-oriented programs were the mainstay of Doordarshan's programming (Vasudeva & Malhotra, 1992). Indira Gandhi, India's Prime Minister for fifteen years, was a strong supporter of television, and her government made significant efforts to improve television infrastructure development. The Satellite Instructional Television Experiment (SITE) in 1976 provided an impetus for the use of television for development purposes, and state-controlled Doordarshan, has been under the purview of the Ministry of Information and Broadcasting since 1976.

Doordarshan began a slow shift away from its original mandate of social education in 1982, the year India hosted the Asian Games, yet the rhetoric remained. Vasant Sathe, then Minister of Information and Broadcasting, introduced color television ostensibly to improve the quality of educational programs. Pendakur (1991) however, suggests that "adding prestige to the ruling party" (p. 242) was a more plausible rationale for this action.

At about the same time, soap opera *Hum Log* inspired by Mexican *telenovellas*, began its 159 episode marathon run. The tremendous

audience response generated by the serial inevitably caught the attention of advertisers. Doordarshan, realizing that allowing limited commercialization of broadcasting could painlessly provide capital needed for expansion, encouraged sponsorship of the immensely popular subsequent serials such as *Buniyaad,* the *Ramayan* and *Mahabharat.*
Financial pressures encouraged this trend. Lacking a license fee, and with the government urging Doordarshan to "fend for it's own revenue and stand on it's own feet" ("DD To Cut Down," 1996) Doordarshan has become increasingly vulnerable to market pressures of audience ratings and advertising revenues. Vestigial remains of its original orientation are still to be found in its agricultural programs and folk music[4] and also in the documentaries on issues such as the environment and drugs. On the whole, however, the drift has been in the direction of what former Minister for Information and Broadcasting, Sangma, recently referred to as "unbridled commercialization" ("Teletalk," 1996a).

Indian television policy, according to Pendakur (1991), "simultaneously serves it's own propaganda needs as well as the demands of indigenous and transnational capitalists, along with the entertainment prerogatives of the middle/upper middle classes" (p. 242). Pendakur's criticism that there is "no evidence... that the state television policy is either designed for, or even accidentally related to, social improvements for the vast majority of Indian people" (p. 242) is especially sharp since it portrays Doordarshan as no better than an instrument of corporate and class interests. However, Mankekar (1993) posits that Doordarshan discourses are directed at co-opting the upwardly mobile classes into the project of constructing a national culture; these classes are, on the one hand, 'captured' simultaneously as a market for consumer goods advertised by sponsors of programming, and, on the other hand, as an audience for nationalistic serials. Thus, Doordarshan is not just acting as a mere instrument of the corporate interests but actively working on its own agenda. While Doordarshan's role as a broadcaster attempting to maintain internal social control deserves to be criticized, it is worth noting that Doordarshan was an arm of the Indian government, whose policy interventions might well constitute the only buffer between Indian citizen-consumers and "global capitalism in its drive for the deregulation and privatization of the cultural industries" (Sinclair,

1996). Smith (1980) has talked about the "restraints of both the market-place and government; both lead to distortion of information" (p. 15). Therefore, the role of an overarching state and the efficacy of unregulated market forces to achieve desirable ends must be questioned.

STAR TV represents one such market force, and it is challenging Doordarshan's political and economic agendas. For one, it is subverting government attempts at national integration which, according to Joshi (1989), is a primary objective of Indian television. Foreign news television helps citizens look behind what Meyrowitz (1985) calls "on-stage" political behavior of inaugurations and speeches, to the hitherto hidden "backstage" behavior of failing policies and their frequently violent outcomes, thus weakening the government's authority. STAR TV is also siphoning-off Doordarshan's advertising revenues. In 1995, STAR TV and Zee TV together had 25% of the total advertising pie, up from 18% in 1993 and 23% in 1994 ("Teletalk," 1996b). Doordarshan's share fell correspondingly from 82% to 75%, and then to 69% ("Doordarshan: Opening," 1994) even though it rose in absolute terms, from $145m in 1993 to $160m in 1994, and to $227m in 1995 ("Teletalk," 1996b).

Table 4.1 Advertising Revenues of Doordarshan (DD) and STAR-Zee TV

	DD Advertising Revenue	% of Total	STAR-Zee TV Advertising Revenue	% of Total
1993	$145 m	82	$32 m	18
1994	$160 m	75	$49 m	23
1995	$227 m	69	$83 m	25

The Information and Broadcasting Ministry's response to STAR TV can be roughly classified in the following way: (i) incipient cable regulation, (ii) privatization of program content, (iii) changes in content, and (iv) limiting access to uplink and foreign exchange.

Incipient Cable Regulation

The Cable Act, first promulgated as a Presidential ordinance in September 1994, and since then ratified by parliament, leaves the cable market a free-for-all, though high investment remains a formidable entry barrier for small operators. The Act stipulates that all cable equipment must meet Bureau of Indian Standards (BIS) specifications, and that cable operators must abide by government programming and advertising codes. It allows foreign companies up to 49% of equity in cable operations (Inamdar, 1995). State governments are left to decide how the cables are to be laid ("The Survival," 1995). Small cable operators, typically neighborhood entrepreneurs on a shoe-string budget who wire 8-10 adjoining buildings and provide a menu of film and satellite television programs to urban dwellers, are beginning to face fierce competition in the market, mainly from Zee's Siticable and Hinduja's Incable. New rules also call for cable operators to be officially registered and maintain a record of programs being broadcast each month. In the words of Siticable's Bombay-based General Manager, L. Sharma (personal communication, April 16, 1996):

> Government will no longer let you put cable tree to tree and pillar to pillar and it is a very expensive proposition. Ultimately what we all see is the death knell for the cable operator... he will not be able to subsist this time. He will not have the money.

This regulation, with its pro-large enterprise bias, is an attempt to bring an element of control and accountability. But, foreign program providers are afraid that it does not go far enough. STAR TV has criticized the bill for not providing adequate intellectual property rights protection, an increasingly contentious problem as new subscription-based channels go on the air (Da Cunha and Groves, 1995).

Privatization of Program Content

Doordarshan now allows private Indian companies to bid for programming slots on Doordarshan, while still running the channels. This is all the encouragement needed by independent software production companies like UTV (United Television) and Nimbus. These companies are flourishing in the virtual seller's market for programming created by the plethora of twenty-four hour channels. Yet not all programming is home-grown. For instance, Doordarshan has aired MTV fare until quite recently, it has a programming alliance with CNN, and it continues to air Disney programming. Disney's V. Puri (personal communication, April 26, 1996) explains how the process works:

> Basically, Doordarshan works in half hour slots. And they give out half hour slots to all producers. As far as they're concerned, I'm a producer. I pay them a telecast fee to run my program. In return for which they allot me a certain amount of free commercial time. I sell that free commercial time, and I generate a certain amount of advertising revenue... The difference between the two, if you add the software costs and the telecast fee, the difference between the two is the money that we make[5]

The proliferation of new Doordarshan channels probably contributes to Doordarshan's new, more circumscribed role as a broker of time slots. Between 1992 and 1995, Doordarshan added an average of 2.8 channels every year, at the end of which it was running eighteen channels[6]. Doordarshan, by itself, simply cannot provide all that programming any longer.

Changing Content

Doordarshan not only carries American serials like *The Valley of the Dolls* in their original form, but also Western fare which has been Indianized through cosmetic changes such as dubbing or local hosting, as in the case of Disney cartoons. Mankekar (1993) maintains that Doordarshan has, in this way, allowed itself to become a conduit for American programming to reach Indian audiences. The advertising code has become less stringent. It now allows the exhibition of foreign models and locales, and permits foreign banks, airlines, and other foreign firms with investments in India to advertise ("Upendra," 1994). It still bans advertisements for items of conspicuous consumption such as "jewelry or precious stones," as well as "cigarettes, alcohol, tobacco products and other intoxicants[7]." These admirable sentiments pertaining to the advertisements are somewhat belied by the nature of the programs themselves.

The issue is whether Doordarshan can avoid becoming more and more like its rivals as it attempts to regain lost market share. The example of the British Broadcasting Corporation (BBC) may be relevant in this context. In Britain, a wave of deregulation saw public broadcaster BBC, suffer "severe competitive disadvantages compared with its private sector rivals" (Curran, 1986, p. 325). As a result, the BBC had less money to spend on its programs, paid its skilled technical staff inadequately, had lost light entertainment stars to Independent Television (ITV), and was under strong pressure to shift towards major series only in collaboration with outside partners.

Limiting Access To Uplink And Foreign Exchange

Doordarshan is not pleased at the challenge to its erstwhile monopoly. Piqued at being out-bid for domestic telecast rights, Doordarshan denied STAR satellite uplink facilities for the 1993 Hero Cricket Cup ("Talking Sport," 1993). A legal wrangle ensued, with the Cricket Association of Bengal (CAB), as well as the Board of Control for Cricket in India (BCCI) filing cases against the Information and Broadcasting Ministry. The Ministry resurrected a fossilized 1885 Indian Telegraph Act to claim the exclusive right to uplink. In a January 1995 ruling of great legal importance, the Supreme Court upheld the rights of citizens to access the airwaves and subsequently weakened Doordarshan's monopolistic position. A parliamentary sub-committee, headed by Ram Vilas Paswan has recommended that private Indian broadcasters be allowed to uplink from Indian soil, but implementation is slow ("Panel Favours," 1996). Madhwani (personal communication, April 22, 1996), Managing Director of a Zee subsidiary claims that "even though the Supreme Court has cleared it, the Information and Broadcasting Ministry is dragging its feet on it, and hasn't really allowed for free uplink out of India." In the meantime, STAR and Zee continue to uplink out of Hong Kong.

Another regulatory issue is the Exchange Control Act, which limits the advertiser base of foreign broadcasters to companies that have export earnings. The regulations allow exporting companies to retain a quarter of their foreign exchange earnings abroad and then choose to spend this on expenses such as advertising. Since "everyone except Doordarshan is a foreign broadcaster because they're broadcasting from outside," as R. Nair (personal communication, April 18, 1996) of MTV India puts it, Doordarshan has a virtual monopoly on local rupee advertisements. Regulations also prohibit media companies from making payments in foreign exchange for the leasing of transponders (Inamdar, 1995). This leads to perforce convoluted arrangements. Zee Telefilms, for instance, exports software to Asia Today Ltd. (ATL) in Hong Kong, which is jointly owned by Murdoch's NewsCorp and Zee. In turn, Zee's advertising subsidiary gets a 15% commission on ATL's advertising from exporting companies in India. Having burdened its competitors with bureaucratic restrictions, it is interesting to note that Doordarshan's own bureaucracy seems to slow it down only slightly. Just days before Zee was to launch a new movie channel in April 1995, for instance, Doordarshan moved surprisingly fast and started its own, meeting the competition head-on.

One is left to wonder why Doordarshan did not make a pre-emptive strike to ban STAR TV outright when it first arrived, as it happened in China, Singapore, Bangladesh, and Malaysia ("Chinese Law," 1993). Why did the Information and Broadcasting Ministry not put pressure to ban downlinking, and not just uplinking? Even if it could overcome the enforcement difficulties brought on by technological advancements of small satellite size, and not alienate the middle class urbanites who continue to watch STAR TV, the mild reaction was surprising. With Doordarshan's incredible terrestrial reach, and its ability to leverage the regulatory playing field in its own favor, Doordarshan yields considerable clout in the Indian media environment. It certainly appears that the commitment to liberalization is one of the important reasons for the government's decision to tolerate the presence of what must surely be an irritant.

STAR TV

Television's main impulse, according to Smythe (1981), is not to deliver messages to the audience, but to effectively deliver the audience to the advertiser. According to A. Carnegie (personal communication, April 25, 1996), General Manager of STAR, India, a third of STAR's advertising revenue comes from advertisers interested in Indian audiences. STAR's global apparatus is primed to capture this local audience. Under Rupert Murdoch, STAR TV has altered it's original pan-Asian strategy, and split its beams to offer far more customized and country-specific programming to consumers. STAR channels have significantly increased their share of Hindi language programming on the Southern beam.

STAR's Channel [V], has provided a tremendous boost to the popularity of Hindi pop music. Channel [V] uses Indian videos in it's programs, its local hosts speak 'Hinglish', a mix of Hindi and English, and Indian staff are given significant creative autonomy. The Channel [V] formula seems depressingly simple: "You make nice, cool packaging, you put a sexy girl in there, speaking, you know, 'Hinglish', and you make it a fast-paced program," says Ed Sharples (personal communication, July 19, 1996), the man responsible for Channel [V] first in India and Dubai, and now in Thailand. As on Doordarshan, imported product is frequently localized on STAR channels, though ratings are low for such programming. Hindi subtitling is quite common on STAR Plus, and Zee carries *Celeste*, a dubbed Mexican soap opera.

An increase in Hindi programming may be a politically savvy way for Murdoch to allay fears of Western images inundating Indian skies. In Europe, for instance, Murdoch's satellite channels met with political resistance to the overwhelmingly American and British content. What remains unsaid is how much of this programming is a reproduction of Western formats with a local twist, as Ed Sharples' comment suggests. The growing competition for the Hindi audiovisual space, however, is accompanied by the increasing success of niche private regional Indian language satellite operations such as SUN TV, Eenadu TV, Udaya TV, Asianet, etc., which are especially popular in south Indian states. By following a strategy of differentiation, these south Indian language channels command a smaller but intensely loyal audience following.

Local partners and employees frequently assist in the process of localization. McAnany and Wilkinson (1996) suggest that these are partnerships to produce, distribute and disseminate programs entered with local partners who understand the market and share the risks. In India, Newscorp has partnered two local players, Zee, and software company UTV, respectively. "One was broadcasting, one was a production deal," says Carnegie (personal communication, April 25, 1996). He believes that "it does help a lot when you've got relationships." Channel [V]'s part ownership by BMG Records, Warner Records, EMI Records, and SONY pictures has benefits in music programming, just as Newscorp's relationship with Prime Sports and ESPN has benefits in sports programming.

Being part of a global media empire confers significant advantages on STAR. Global media companies like STAR are able to move resources like money, programming and managerial talent around the globe as needed. "The real advantage is money," says Carnegie (personal communication, April 25, 1996). "You've got to have a lot of money to survive; deep pockets to take the losses."

But losses are not what STAR's managers are thinking of. In India, where the cable environment is limited by the number of channels that a television set can receive, the STAR platform channels have begun to 'bundle' their offerings, as well as engage in sophisticated market segmentation in order to retain viewers within a bouquet of channels called the 'prime band'. Cross-channel advertising within STAR is common, and cross-media spinoffs, such as a 'Channel [V] Hits' CD, and 'Quick Gun Murugun the Movie' demonstrate that global managers are applying valuable lessons learnt on other multi-channel environments and satellite systems to India. Sophisticated forms of windowing[8] encourages multiple exploitation of media assets:

Over Territory. STAR Plus in Asia airs Fox's *The Simpsons* after it has been aired in North America

Over Time. For the next ten years, Zee Telefilms Ltd. (ZTL) will supply channel runner Asia Today Ltd. (ATL) software for a one-time telecast only ("Zee Telefilms," 1996). Programs like *Antakshri, Khubsoorat, Khaana Khazaana* are subsequently sent to other Zee subsidiaries in the United Kingdom and Mauritius for additional telecasts.

Over Technology. Zee Telefilms Ltd. programming, after a satellite run, is shown again on Siticable through cable.

More broadly, STAR TV has made concerted efforts to be culturally inoffensive to the host countries in its footprint. Still, cultural sensitivity is a relative term, and in some eyes, STAR TV cannot try hard enough. It's very presence on Asian air-waves is an irritant for some. Former Indian Information and Broadcasting Minister Singh Deo, in 1993, denounced the "cultural invasion by foreign television networks" and even blamed foreign saboteurs for the rocky start of the five new Doordarshan channels. Yet, despite these early indictments, Murdoch has had several cordial meetings with Indian Prime Ministers Rao and Gowda ("Much Ado," 1996). STAR has frequently flattered Doordarshan, for instance, by telecasting India's Republic Day celebrations and Zee TV has telecast the budget proceedings of parliament on its channel ("Murdoch in New Delhi to Woo TV Viewers," 1994).

Transnational Advertising

By far the greatest advantage to STAR TV is the patronage of multinational firms who can advertise to multiple countries within the STAR footprint. These companies benefit from using global campaigns and consolidating all their advertising with one agency. Companies like Proctor and Gamble find that applying an existing advertising campaign to a new market can decrease costs and help the company move faster ("Make It Simple," 1996). Global alignments are reflected in the Indian context. Euro RSCG, for instance, handles the Philips account world-wide. In India, the lion's share of the Philips brands converge at the Indian Euro subsidiary. The entry of satellite media closes the circle for these globally affiliated advertising agencies purveying global brands ("The Brand," 1996). Advertisements on the *Philips Top Ten*, one of the most popular programs on Zee, for instance, has a global advertising tagline "Let's Make Things Better," but is localized inasmuch as it carries testimonials by Indian cricket star Sachin Tendulkar. Such attempts at localization, Maxwell (1996) points out is for the "benefit of a transnational firm hawking a local sale... so that a foreign clients' products appear as local goods."

Schiller (1991) has noted that the impact of the global arena of cultural domination has not decreased in the 1990's. Reinforced by new delivery vehicles such as the communication satellites and cable outlets, the image flow is now heavier than ever. Schiller claims that the media, public relations, advertising, polling, cultural sponsorship, and consultants the industrial giants use and support are hardly distinguishable from the same services at the disposal of American-owned corporations. Thus, economic liberalization makes India an especially attractive market. As Carnegie (personal communication, April 25, 1996) of STAR TV puts it, "there are international brands being launched almost every day, so if you're a seller of advertising space, you should be able to make some money." This prognosis is borne out by companies like Zee, which became a profit-making channel from its very first year of operation.

The Political Economy of Liberalization

India's development strategy, when it became independent from British colonial rule in 1947, was based on the Nehru/Mahalanobis model and favored import substitution, a large public sector that took on heavy industrialization as well as other "commanding heights" of the economy, and a highly regulated private sector. The sheer unwieldiness of India, with its ethnic and linguistic complexity, contributed to a centralizing force within the government and the constitution. On the international front, in a world increasingly divided by Cold War tensions, India decided on a policy of non-alignment.

Almost five decades later, according to Kohli (1989), there is a sense of 'failure of socialism' and with the erstwhile Soviet Union and China embracing the free market, there seem to be few exemplars left in the world that could help sustain anti-market arguments. Competing explanations for industrial stagnation in India center around three alternative hypotheses: the inefficiencies of the state as a productive enterprise, low aggregate demand, and "bottlenecks" in infrastructure caused by declining public investment (Ahluwalia, 1985). The models of state-induced, free market-like competitiveness that spur economic growth, as seen in the East Asian NIC's and also in Latin America, appears to appeal to government advisors (Kohli, 1989). However stripping away public functions may not necessarily lead to a more efficient and productive private sector. Thus, the quality of intervention rather than its elimination may be an important factor.

Under pressure from both an adverse balance of payment situation and institutional foreign lenders, India intensified the process of liberalization in almost all sectors of the economy in July 1991. The reforms undertaken under former Finance Minister Manmohan Singh, were primarily aimed at reducing fiscal as well as external deficits and comprised expenditure cuts, devaluation, and measures to encourage foreign capital inflows. India's "cooperation" on this front was rewarded by a $2.2 billion standby loan to India to replenish its foreign exchange reserves which had dwindled to dangerously low levels. Some important highlights of the Narasimha Rao-Manmohan Singh 1991 reforms included devaluation and convertibility of the rupee, the abolition of import licensing and almost all industrial licensing, reduction in tariffs and excise duty, and a commitment to formulate "exit policies" to downsize the public sector ("Market Reports," 1993). By 1992, foreigners could control 51% of joint ventures and buy and sell on the Indian stock exchange. Overseas investors took note of this development.

When STAR programming first reached the Indian air-waves, there was still some skepticism about India's genuine commitment to the reforms (Kohli, 1993). Until 1993, India had not attracted as much investment as had been hoped subsequent to the opening of the economy. Of the projects worth $3 billion cleared by the Foreign Investment Promotion Board between 1991 and 1993 (involving companies such as Kellogg's, General Motors, International Business Machines, Coca-Cola and Dupont-Nylon) only about $500 million had been invested (Jain & Sanotra, 1993). The government was, therefore, probably loathe to send out signals that were indicative of less than full commitment to a reduced role for the state in the economy. Further, concerted attempts to encourage domestic manufacturing to make the satellite and cable industry in India more competitive were underway.

India's strong ideological stand on the international regulation of direct broadcasting satellite and its strong support for a New World Information and Communication Order in the 1970's makes it evident that a very different political climate had settled in New Delhi starting with former Prime Ministers Rajiv Gandhi and Narasimha Rao and former Finance Minister Manmohan Singh. Its effects are still continuing under the new administration, as the liberalization of the economy continues to be given top priority in the pro-business political climate.

Early attempts to liberalize the domestic economy, according to Kohli (1989), had already begun under Prime Minister Indira Gandhi. Electoral expediency led Gandhi, who had earlier taken visibly socialist actions such as the nationalization of banks, to adopt a more pro-business stance. Yet it was her son Rajiv Gandhi who is most closely associated with India's first attempts to liberalize. The reforms he announced in the 1985 budget, included tax concessions to business, import liberalization in priority sectors, and the relaxation of licensing regulations. These reforms provided a boost for consumer electronics. Production of television receivers registered an impressive 44 percent compound annual growth during the period between 1980 and 1988, mainly due to the boom in kit assembly brought on by the introduction of color television (Guhathakurta, 1992).

Not surprisingly, business groups and the middle class favored the reforms. Yet the opposition to the reforms by rural groups, the moderate left as well as the rank and file of the Congress Party ultimately slowed down the reforms. Rajiv Gandhi acquired the most damaging of labels for a leader of a poor country: "pro-rich," and the pace of reforms decelerated. The 1991 Rao-Singh reforms, which were precipitated by a foreign exchange crisis, received a somewhat skeptical reception as a result of this earlier back-tracking. The foreign exchange situation itself has improved considerably in recent years. Foreign investment in 1995 was $5.3 billion, up from $132 million in 1991 ("Conflict Of Interest," 1996), and foreign reserves were a comfortable $20.2 billion ("Emerging Market Indicators," 1996). Dogged opposition, however, continues to greet the entry of multinationals such as Enron and Kentucky Fried Chicken.

Conclusion

Contradictions abound in STAR TV's early Indian reception. The Information and Broadcasting Ministry unhesitatingly unleashed rhetoric decrying foreign cultural imperialism, yet did not attempt to regulate its competition out of existence. Was it because technological advances in the form of diminishing satellite dish size made attempts at regulation hopelessly unenforceable? Or was it because the business groups and the middle class, the same segment of the population that favor economic liberalization, were watching STAR TV and liking it? In this context, Mattelart (1984) discusses society as the site of confrontation and negotiation between social groups that serve to mediate national communication policies. The organic alliances between national and transnational capital on the basis of common interests that Mattelart points to, finds a ready example in the Zee-STAR link-up, with STAR literally launching Zee's success.

To add another dimension, the International Monetary Fund (IMF)-World Bank structural adjustment programs for debtor countries have been criticized for serving the interests of transnational corporations that have followed close behind. The movement towards economic liberalization in India may have occurred due to the pressure from lending institutions. The middle class, whose savings finance domestic capital through the stock market in India constitute the last link of this national/transnational alignment in a world where "international relations are increasingly internalized into the global operations of transnational businesses" (Maxwell, 1996). It is only through an understanding of the larger context of these many layers--- which includes the World Bank, transnational corporations, domestic business groups, the state, the middle class, all influencing and being influenced by each other---that we can begin to comprehend STAR TV's continued and unhindered presence in India.

The Indian government seems to be collaborating with transnational capital, motivated no doubt by a desire to invigorate the domestic cultural industries and improve its own competitive and export position. Doordarshan's terrestrial reach and ability to tap into the strong Indian film industry appear to be advantages that presage the beginning of a viable domestic television industry. Given the taste preferences of Indian viewers for local programming, somewhat more culturally proximate offerings for Indian audiences are likely. As greater competition stimulates the rapidly changing Indian television industry, Doordarshan will most probably benefit from a larger advertising pie. Yet, surely memories of its younger, more idealistic years serve to remind Doordarshan of how it stumbled off its chosen path of social welfare for the less privileged and reached where it is today, peddling soap and capitalist dreams to Indian audiences.

Notes

[1] This chapter is a revised version of an earlier article that appeared in the *South Asia Graduate Research Journal, 1*(1) (May 1994): 60 - 78. The author thanks the following individuals for their interviews: Andrew Carnegie, General Manager, India; Leena Sharma, General Manager-West, Siticable; Vineet Puri, Senior Business Manager, Buena Vista T.V.; P. Govindrajan, Finance Manager, MTV; Rajmohan Nair, Account Manager, Network Development, MTV; and especially Ed Sharples, General Manager, Thailand, who despite being the man responsible for encouraging the 'bimbo phenomenon' on Channel [V], was a font of useful information.

[2] Zee uses the STAR TV uplink and satellite facilities, and is 49.5% owned by Murdoch. The rest is owned by Zee promoters Subash Chandra and other Non-Resident Indians.

[3] Newspapers and film escaped this centralizing tendency, probably because they had already evolved into mature industries at the time of independence.

[4] For instance, on a typical day (March 4, 1996) DD's schedule included an agricultural program, a development program, classical music, and a program on consumer awareness. Private channels showed light entertainment almost exclusively ("TV Schedule," *Indian Express,* March 4, 1996)

[5] Disney revenue = advertising revenue - (telecast fee + software cost)

[6] DD added two new channels in 1990 and three in 1991.

[7] "General Rules of Conduct for Television and Radio Advertising." Information and Broadcasting Ministry, Government of India.

[8] Turow (1992:686) defines windowing as the "ability of news and entertainment materials to pay for themselves when moved through different channels, or windows of distribution

References

Ahluwalia, I. J. (1985). *Industrial growth in India: Stagnation since the mid-sixties*. New Delhi: Oxford University Press.

Bagdikian, B. H. (1989, June 12). The lords of the global village. *The Nation*, 805-820.

Chatterjee, P. C. (1987). *Broadcasting in India*. New Delhi: Sage.

Chinese law on satellite dishes blocks access to foreign stations. (1993, October 9). *The Guardian*, 14.

Conflict of interest. (1996, April 12). *Asiaweek*.

Curran, J. (1986). The impact of advertising on the British mass media. In R. Collins, J. Curran, N. Graham, P. Scannell, P. Schlesinger, & C. Sparks (Eds.), *Media, culture and society: A critical reader*. pp. 309-35, London: Sage.

Da Cunha, Uma and D. Groves. (1995). Tapping a Vast Market. *Variety*, June 12-18.

DD to cut down on ads during Hindi films. (1996, March 26). *Bombay Times*.

Doordarshan: Opening up at last. (1994, April 15). *India Today*, 53.

Emerging market indicators. (1996, September 28). *The Economist*, p.172.

General rules of conduct for television and radio advertising. Information and Broadcasting Ministry, Government of India. [Jayaram, C. Market Reports. National Trade Data Base, Lexis Nexis, 17 August, 1993].

Guhathakurta, S. (1992, April). *Electronic policy and the television manufacturing industry: Lessons from India's liberalization efforts*. Berkeley, CA: University of California, Berkeley, Institute of Urban and Regional Development.

Inamdar, T. (1995, November). The great Indian media race. *Jardine Fleming Industry Review*. JF Publications.

Jain, S., & Sanotra, H. (1993, November 15). Economic reforms: Questioning the pace. *India Today*.

Joshi, P. C. (1989). *Culture, communication and social change*. New York: Vikas.

Kohli, A. (1989). Politics of economic liberalization in India, *World Development, 17* (3), 305-328.

Kohli, I. (1993, April 16-18). *Symposium rapportage: Economic liberalization in South Asia.* Berkeley, CA: University of California, Berkeley, Center for South Asia Studies.

Make it simple: How Proctor & Gamble is paring down. (1996, September 9). *BusinessWeek,* 56-61.

Mankekar, P. (1993, August). National texts and gendered lives: An ethnography of television viewers in a North Indian city, *American Ethnologist, 20* (3): 543-63.

Market Reports: India Country Marketing Plan 1993: National Trade Base. [Lexis Nexis, August 1993]

Mattelart, A., Mattelart, M., & Delcourt, X. (1984). *International image markets: In search of an alternative perspective.* London: Comedia Publishing Group.

Maxwell, R. (1996). Out of kindness and into difference: The value of global market research. *Media, Culture and Society, 10* (1), 105-123.

McAnany, E., and K. Wilkinson. (1996). Introduction. In E. McAnany & K. Wilkinson (Eds.), *Mass Media and Free Trade: NAFTA and the Cultural Industries.* pp. 3-29. Austin, Texas: University of Texas Press.

Meyrowitz, J. (1985). *No Sense of Place.* New York: Oxford University Press.

Much ado about a meeting. (1996, July 15). *India Today,*

Murdoch in New Delhi to woo TV Viewers. (1994, February 10). *Inter Press Service.*

Panel favours legalizing private broadcasting. (1996, March 30). *The Times of India.*

Pendakur, M. (1991). A political economy of television: State, class and corporatenfluence in India. In G. Sussman, & J. Lent (Eds.), *Transnational Communication: Wiring the Third World.* Newbury Park: Sage, pp. 234-62.

Schiller, H. I. (1991). Not yet the post-imperialistic era. *Critical Studies in Mass Communication, 8,* 13-28.

Sinclair, J. 1996. Culture and trade: Some theoretical and practical considerations. In E. McAnany & K. Wilkinson (Eds.), *Mass Media and Free Trade: NAFTA and the Cultural Industries.* pp. 30-62. Austin, Texas: University of Texas Press.

Smith, A. (1980). *The geopolitics of information: How western culture dominates the world*. New York: Oxford University Press.

Smythe, D. W. (1981). *Dependency road: Communication, capitalism, consciousness and Canada*. Norwood, NJ: Ablex Publishing Corp.

Talking sport: Pulling the plug may short-circuit India's World Cup plans. (1993, November 16). *The Daily Telegraph*, 35.

Teletalk. (1994, March 20). *India Today*.

Teletalk. (1996a, March 15). *India Today*.

Teletalk. (1996b, April 20). *India Today*.

The Brand has but one face. (1996, March 27- April 2). *The Economic Times*.

The survival of the fittest. (1995, January 31). *India Today*.

Turow, J. (1992). The Organizational Underpinnings of Contemporary Media Conglomerates. *Communication Research*, Vol. 19, No. 6.

TV schedule. (1996, March 4). *Indian Express*.

Upendra for limited media autonomy. (1994, February 22). *Hindustan Times*.

Vasudeva, A., & Malhotra, L. K. (1992, October). India: T.V. at the crossroads. Indian Television Programs Fiction, *UNESCO Carrier*, 37.

Zee Telefilms - Ready for competition? (1996, February 5-11). *Express Investment Week*.

Chapter 5

Putting Media Policy in its Place: The Example of STAR TV and the Indian State

Peter Shields

Media corporations are struggling for profit on a global scale. A relatively small number of transnational giants (e.g., Time Warner, Rupert Murdoch's News Corporation, the Walt Disney Company, and Sony) maneuver to deliver a plurality of audio-visual products across new swaths of geographic and social space. This has largely been made possible by the development of new forms of space-binding delivery systems such as the communication satellite and by a global policy shift to reduce the role of the state and hand things over to private enterprise. Both have rendered the boundaries of the nation-state increasingly porous.

Some believe we are witnessing cultural imperialism ratcheted to a new level. At the left end of the political spectrum, Herbert Schiller (1991) argues that these media conglomerates are combining to produce "a total cultural environment" in which "US cultural styles and techniques...have...become transnationalized" (pp. 12-13). Similarly, Richard Peet (1986) warns of "the tendency towards the production of one world mind, one world culture, and the consequent disappearance of regional consciousness..." (p. 169). In this scenario, the logic of global consumerism will eviscerate national identity and culture and thereby undercut national integration projects. The policy implications seem clear: local policy-makers must restrict the "excessive" consumption of "Western" or "Western-like" media artifacts and encourage the indigenous production of more "appropriate" fare. Here, media policy is assigned a decisive role in the struggle against domination.

A more conservative variant of this kind of thinking was evident in the 1993/4 round of the General Agreement on Tarrifs and Trade (GATT) negotiations. While the US called for the removal of quota restrictions on audiovisual products in the name of free trade and the free circulation of ideas, European interests argued for their retention in order to defend the integrity of European cultures---and to enhance the competitive position of domestic producers.

Yet there are good reasons for questioning the assumptive base of cultural imperialism arguments. An *a priori* assumption is made that large-scale ingestion of media artifacts is a central force in the life and death of national identity and national integration projects. The problem here is that "[t]elevision's power is so strongly assumed that, rather than being the object of analysis, it tends to prescribe research practices and theoretical reasoning" (Lodziak, 1986, p. 2; see also Collins, 1990; Ferguson, 1992; Schlesinger, 1991). This media-centrism has the potential to greatly exaggerate television's social significance.

The problem is compounded by the fact that the various advocates of the cultural imperialism thesis do not examine the social forces and contexts that shape the elaboration of a national identity as an important plank of the national integration enterprise (Morley & Robins, 1995; Schlesinger, 1987; Thompson, 1995; Tomlinson, 1991). Thus, national identity is portrayed as an uncontested "natural fact" rather than as something that is continually contested. As Philip Schlesinger (1991) points out:

> such identities are emergent properties of collective action...and [are] sustained by a dual process: one of inclusion that provides a boundary around 'us', and one of exclusion that distinguishes 'us' from 'them'.... [W]e should see such identities as constituted in action and as continually reconstituted in line with both internal dynamic and external balance of force. (p. 300)

Because sources of differentiation exist within nation-states (e.g., religion, language, ethnicity), multiple collective identities or even

other national identities will co-exist, often in a subordinate and antagonistic way, with the "official" state-sponsored national identity. Indeed, we may find that the real threat to "national identity" is often at this level (the strident challenge to "Canadianism" by Quebec nationalists, for example).

What is needed is a perspective that permits open-ended study of the role media play in relation to other factors in the large-scale drama of national identity construction and national integration. Schlesinger (1987) suggests the following approach:

> The problem as conventionally understood needs to be stood on its head. So far, work on and argument about communicative and cultural processes make gratuitous assumptions about the nation-state, national culture and national identity. All are taken to be unproblematic, and as communication is the central concern, they are handled as residual categories. I propose we reverse the terms of the argument: let us begin with the problem of how national identity is constituted and locate communication and culture within *that* problematic. (p. 259)

Instead of placing media (and by extension, media policy) at the center of analysis and treating national identity (and by implication national integration) as residual, we must begin with the problem of *how* national identity and national integration are constituted. It is *within* this broader inquiry that questions can be asked about the power of media (Morley & Robins, 1995, p. 72). Within this kind of inquiry, we should also be able to determine what priority should be given to media policy when pursuing democratic outcomes. What would such an analysis look like? In what follows, an answer is sketched by examining the case of India's fast-changing television environment.

The Changing Television Environment

The Indian government is involved in two related integration projects. On the one hand, the government's economic "liberalization" policies have increasingly enmeshed various sectors of Indian society in global networks of production and consumption. On the other, government agencies are involved in the perennial task of maintaining political and social order in a tension-riven society. Historically, a key element of this second integration process has been the government's

elaboration of an Indian "national identity" (Joshi, 1989; Varshney, 1993).

The government's accommodating response to the pan-Asian STAR TV initiative can be understood as an aspect of its involvement in the first integration project. Beginning in 1991, STAR TV's offerings consisted of "Western" channels such as MTV, Prime Sports, and the BBC World Service. Zee TV, which broadcasts in Hindi, was added in 1992. Constrained by its commitment to an "open-door" policy, the Indian government did not seriously attempt the difficult task of limiting the reception of these channels. To have done so, would have meant curbing the ability of transnational advertisers and program providers reaching a potentially significant audience. It would also have run afoul of the middle classes and elites who were tuning into STAR TV (Pathania, 1994).

Responding to the competition, state-owned Doordarshan augmented its regional Indian language channels and national network with new satellite channels (Entertainment, Music, Business and Current Affairs, Enrichment) which provide similar programming to STAR TV. Doordarshan also extended the metro entertainment channel to the country's four metropolitan cities (Doordarshan, 1994). Among other things, this channel carries MTV (no longer with STAR). Privately-owned Indian language satellite channels such as ATN, Jain TV (Hindi) and Sun TV (Tamil) also compete for audiences. Transnational program providers such as ESPN and CNN have recently joined the fray with their own satellite channels while others such as HBO and Disney position themselves to do so (*India Today*, November 15, 1995).

For those who can afford it, a staid state-controlled menu has given way to an abundance of domestic and foreign programming. What are the implications of the new programming environment for Indian national identity and national integration? Applying Schlesinger's approach, the analysis begins by identifying key forces that have shaped the state's turbulent nation-building project which includes the changing nature of attempts at crafting a national identity. This is followed by an examination of the changing television environment and its relation to these forces.[1]

Nation-Building

Since India's independence in 1947, the nature of the nation-building project has changed drastically. There has been a shift from a conception of national unity based on accepting myriad diversities and interests to a conception of national unity that is based on excluding large segments of the population (Kothari, 1988a, p. 2223). This shift is very much connected to the deterioration of the institutional framework erected by the Congress Party in the 1940s and 1950s (e.g., Das Gupta, 1995; Kohli, 1987; Kothari, 1989a, 1989b).

One element of this framework was the newly developed constitution which introduced protections for the people against the encroachment of state authority. It also reserved places in representative institutions and government agencies for disadvantaged classes and cultural groups (Brass, 1990, pp. 3-4). The constitution also introduced universal suffrage and adopted the parliamentary party system. A second element was the Congress Party's vast multi-tiered organizational structure that penetrated deep into the social hinterland allowing the party to appeal to and draw together a wide-ranging diversity. The Congress System was pivotal to the crafting of an inclusive notion of Indian national identity.

[I]t provided the *modus vivendi* of the Indian enterprise in nation-building, the 'net-work' through which the Indian nation reverberated.... Without the Congress System both the colonial state and the Westminster model would have left out a large part of the Indian social mosaic. *With it*, the Indian state struck deep roots and acquired a national character and a unifying credo precisely because it struck roots.... It produced and permeated a tempo and temper of nationalism and national identity that, without steamrollering any significant constituency, provided a new framework of discourse and deliberation... (Kothari, 1988a, p. 2225)

Yet it is important not to romanticize the Congress System. While Congress opened up to middle and lower middle caste and class-based interests, it still left the poor and underprivileged out of its scope. The Congress also discredited or suppressed those who threatened the integration project---for example, the secessionists (e.g., Tamil nationalists) who advanced competing national identities and the communists who advocated revolution (Brass, 1990, pp. 7-8).

Cracks began to appear in the Congress System in the 1950s and 1960s. The government's discourse of equality, justice and socialism increasingly contradicted the reality of economic policies that did not meet the growing demands of the newly "included." The socialist-inspired development model, which stressed self-reliance, state ownership and intervention and urban-based industrialization, delivered some economic growth but there was little effort to ensure the masses benefited (Kothari, 1988a, p. 2225). The limits of political accommodation---the hallmark of the Congress System---had been reached within the existing configuration of economic structures (Frankel, 1978, pp. 201-202). For example, it seemed impossible to reconcile Congress' claim to represent the interests of all groups, including the propertied classes, with acquiescence to pressures from below for land reform. There were signs that party elites (e.g., members of dominant landed castes who had "captured" local-level party organizations) opposed prioritization of such reform (Frankel, 1978, p. 200).

Erosion of the Congress Party's hegemony was manifested in widespread social unrest, the contraction of the party's popular support base, and the emergence of Indira Gandhi as leader of a bitterly divided party. Gandhi and her allies argued that political conciliation must be subordinated to the alleviation of the economic plight of the masses. The distributive issue was addressed, in part, by borrowing funds from the IMF and the World Bank. In return, the government opened up parts of the economy to private domestic and foreign investment. At the same time as the central government increased its dependence on international institutions, it asserted its independence from the lower-level tiers of the Congress System. In effect, as power centralized in Delhi, the various intermediate structures which had addressed local problems and conflicts were gutted. Without these structures, the state was unable to diffuse crises that were emerging in different parts of the country (e.g., Narang, 1986, pp. 99-100). Against this backdrop, Gandhi declared the 1975 State of Emergency. Opposition leaders were arrested, a news black-out was imposed, organizations were banned, and people were imprisoned without trial. Ousted in 1977, Indira Gandhi returned to office in 1980 with the backing of industrialists and the urban middle classes. A renewed emphasis on the liberalization of the economy followed. In the face of increasing social unrest, the state relied heavily on force to maintain social order. Rhetorically, government sources equated the fate of Indira Gandhi with the fate of India (if you oppose her the country will disintegrate). To garner electoral support, Gandhi, her allies, and many in the opposition, increasingly reverted to the strategy of manipulating Hindu-Muslim tensions (Brass, 1990, p. 202).

In the past decade, some of the trends delineated above have continued. On the economic front, the Rajiv Gandhi government and the recent Narasimha Rao government conceded more areas of the economy to private domestic and foreign investors. The process was accelerated in 1991 when the government, influenced by the IMF and the World Bank, proceeded to dismantle much of the apparatus of economic regulation.[2] For example, restrictions were removed in order to allow 51 per cent foreign equity in all industries involved in advanced technology. Restrictions on capital-goods imports were eased and private investment has been allowed in the power sector (*India Today*, October, 15, 1995). Further, the government has permitted private domestic and foreign investors to compete with the government in such sectors as broadcast and telecommunications (Mody, 1995). These measures and others have increased substantially the role of national and transnational corporations in shaping the political economy of India.

The emphasis on privatization has been intertwined with a commitment to "high-tech leap-frogging" as a route to economic development. The Rajiv Gandhi government prioritized such sectors as telecommunications and computer software development (McDowell, 1995). This policy thrust benefited certain segments of the business community and the middle classes. Thus, almost all of the government's massive allocation of resources for the expansion of telecommunication network flowed to urban areas where only one quarter of the population lives. The primary beneficiaries were the businesses, particularly those in the export-oriented sectors of the economy (e.g., software development), that demanded enhanced telecommunications services (Fernandes, 1989; Thomas, 1993).

On the political front, the state continued to employ coercion as the primary means of dealing with social unrest. For example, in 1987 the central government responded to continued separatist agitation by Sikhs in the Punjab by imposing a state of emergency. Civil liberties were dissolved and the state was placed under military control.

The perennial tensions in Hindu-Muslim relations also escalated at this time. In the Shah Bano case, Rajiv Gandhi, under great pressure from Muslim leaders, supported the decision that made Islamic personal law superior to civil law in matters concerning the "maintenance" of divorced women. Responding to Hindu outrage at this decision, the government opened a religious site at Ayodhya to Hindu pilgrimage---a site that was claimed by both Hindus and Muslims (Varshney, 1993, p. 249). Muslim demonstrations ensued and a bloody backlash from Hindu groups followed.

Particularly in the north and west of the country, this series of events fueled support for fast-growing Hindu nationalist groups like the BJP (Bharatiya Janata Party). These groups claim that since independence, the state has pampered the "minorities" at the expense of the Hindu majority. This has transpired, the argument runs, because Hindus have failed to unite. Hinduism is advocated as the source of India's identity and as the only real hope for national cohesiveness. The implication, according to Varshney (1993), is that non-Hindu groups can be a part of India by assimilation only.

The calculations of the various political parties have been affected by the increase in Hindu nationalism. In the 1989 election, the sizable support for the BJP among Hindus led Congress to compete for the communal vote, thus abandoning its traditional appeal to the Muslim minority. Rao's government continued to court the Hindu majority. In the wake of the destruction of the Babri Mosque in 1992, the country was swept by violence against Muslims. In many quarters, the government was viewed as being complicit in these events because it abdicated its responsibility to ensure the safety of a minority group (Bonner et al., 1994). The Rao government was also criticized for its violent suppression of ongoing separatist activity in Muslim-dominated Kashmir (*Economic and Political Weekly,* October 23, 1993).

The preceding paragraphs have traced the ways in which the state's inclusive national integration project has been replaced by one which is exclusive. This transpired because the political and economic framework, within which the earlier secular notion of Indian identity was embedded, failed to redistribute wealth. Against the backdrop of growing unrest, a broad-based hegemonic political process was replaced by a form of machiavellian politics that relied heavily on centralized decision-making, the exercise of coercion, the fomenting of communal tensions for political gain, and a more restricted hegemonic project aimed at the predominantly Hindu urban middle and upper classes. A new model of integration has emerged in which exclusion is understood as "a necessary correlate of preserving unity and building a strong and powerful nation that is seen to be besieged by hostile forces out to destabilize and undermine the nation..." (Kothari, 1988a, p. 2227). This model is giving rise to the phenomenon of "Two Indias." The first consists of the largely Hindu middle and upper classes who "have access to modern technology, access to sources of privilege...access to the knowledge systems that are very much tied to the structure of privilege, who are getting into the world economic market" (Kothari, 1988b, p. 2591). The second consists of the tens of millions who

are not able to have access to these advantages and privileges, the laboring classes, the unemployed...the large masses of untouchables and bonded laborers, large sections of women and children, the tribals...the various nationalities that were beginning to assert themselves for political rights but are being increasingly visited by state repression and terror. (p. 2591)

It is this India which is excluded. Here is found mass illiteracy, poor health care, and high infant morality rates. State actors have paid little attention to building bridges of mediation between the two Indias.

It is during the ascendancy of the exclusionary model of integration that television emerges as a potentially significant social force. The ways in which television has influenced and been influenced by this exclusionary model is explored below.

The "Old" Programming Environment and Integration

The forces responsible for the massive expansion of state-controlled television in the 1980s have been well-documented. Analysts place particular emphasis on the political motivations behind this substantial redirection of resources. Satellite Instructional Television Experiment (SITE), the launching of India's first generation national satellite (INSAT), Indira Gandhi's Special Expansion Plan, and the government's support for television serials such as *Mahabharatha* and *Ramayana*, have all been viewed as attempts by governing elites to extend their political and ideological control (e.g., Ghorpade, 1986; Mitra, 1993; Mody, 1988; Pendakur, 1991; Thomas, 1988; Rajagopal, 1993). The SITE was launched in August 1975. The experiment, which utilized a NASA satellite for a year, was ostensibly aimed at gaining experience in development, testing and management of a satellite-based instructional system, particularly in rural areas. Yet little energy was devoted to the design of educational programming. Also, long before the results of the educational impacts were available, the cabinet decided in favor of acquiring a satellite-based communication system. From this, Rajagopal (1993) deduces:

> [i]t could not have been a failure or oversight in policy to make so little room for effective education in SITE. Rather, the exercise was seen as an opportunity to gain expertise...concerning satellite hardware and management, as the government attempted to extend control over the information people received... (p. 96).

This interpretation is given further credence when one considers the political context in which SITE was implemented. Indira Gandhi declared a State of Emergency weeks before the commencement of the experiment. With all other media suspended during the Emergency, Doordarshan used the satellite capability to broadcast news that provided the governing elites' interpretation of events. Mody (1988, p. 5) argues that this demonstration of the utility of satellites in delivering propaganda to a significant population played a key role in the decision to invest in the first generation of INSAT satellites that were launched in 1982-3. The government's subsequent use of the expanded television infrastructure supports Mody's claim (Thomas, 1988).

The medium very much suited the form of top-down authoritarian politics that predominated in this period. As discussed earlier, successive governments led by Indira Gandhi demolished most of the institutions that provided points of contact between the state and the various groups that populate civil society. This institutional vacuum was filled, in part, by television. The expansion of television enabled Indira Gandhi and her supporters to make direct demagogic appeals to at least some segments of civil society. She attempted to use television to cultivate her image as "deliverer," and to engineer majority support for her government's policies. Her successor, Rajiv Gandhi, used television in a similar way, particularly in the lead up to the 1989 national elections. The effectiveness of these strategies are, however, open to question. In both cases, Doordarshan was widely and derisively criticized for its blatant bias (Pendakur, 1991; Rudolph, 1992). To conclude that this cynicism indicates the inherent powerlessness of mass media would be a mistake. It can be conjectured that this mistrust can be explained largely by political context. In a period when state control is marked primarily by coercion, manipulation, and insensitivity to demands, it is not too surprising that sections of the citizenry would be very wary of the state's political programming.

Who were the primary beneficiaries of the rapid expansion of television? At the beginning of the 1980s, Doordarshan's clutch of transmitters (19 in 1981) provided access to services in and around the major metropolitan areas. Doordarshan's coverage increased dramatically with the advent of satellite and the large-scale installation of transmitters. By the end of 1985, the television network covered 53 per cent of the population, and 62 percent in 1988 (Singhal & Rogers, 1989, p. 66). By 1993, Doordarshan's 553 transmitters enveloped about 84 per cent of the population (about 856 million). Doordarshan estimates that the number of television households increased from 6.8 million in 1985 to 22.5 million in 1989, to an estimated 40.4 million in 1993 (Doordarshan, 1994).

The distribution of television sets is highly uneven. For the year 1993, Doordarshan estimates that 30 per cent (12 million) of the 40.4 million television households were in rural areas. Assuming five members per household, Doordarshan concludes that there were 60 million rural family viewers. By adding to this the 50 million viewers that are believed to watch community television, Doordarshan estimates that 110 million (about 20 per cent) of India's rural population of 610 million accessed television (Doordarshan, 1994). From Doordarshan's figures, it can be estimated that in 1993 there were approximately 140 million urban family viewers (about 60 percent of the urban population). Furthermore, given the cost of receivers, only the affluent think about owning a television (e.g., Fernandes, 1989; Singhal & Rogers, 1989, p. 67; Rajagopal, 1993).

Initially, the rapid deployment of distribution hardware was not matched by new programming within Doordarshan. Rajagopal (1993) points to the contradictory source of this state of affairs:

> While on the one hand television serves as a technology of expanding state power over society, on the other hand...given the security of tenure government employees enjoy regardless of performance, and the virtual absences of incentives for merit, there is a powerful tendency toward institutional inertia (p. 93).

Yet a consequence of growing middle class access to television was the recognition by industry that television was potentially a very fruitful advertising medium. This realization, coupled with the fact Doordarshan was always in need of money for its expansion, led to television increasingly carrying commercially sponsored programs.[3] This programming, often privately produced, was primarily entertainment-oriented and aimed at the middle and upper classes-- particularly the wave of popular soap operas such as *Hum Log, Buniyaad*, and *Rajani*. Though importation of foreign entertainment programs increased, their share of overall transmission time remained low (Mody, 1988, p. 9).

Perhaps Doordarshan's biggest success, in terms of audience reach, was its serializations in the late 1980s of the Hindu epics, *Ramayana* and the *Mahabharata*. These programs, and a variety of others, have been perceived by a number of analysts as blatant attempts by governing elites to circulate a set of glorified Hindu-centered images of what constitutes Indian national identity (e.g., Mitra, 1993; Rajagopal, 1993, p. 108; Rudolph, 1992). Mitra (1993) suggests that Doordarshan has played a highly significant role in elaborating a Hindu-centric national identity:

> The image of India that is produced and reproduced by Doordarshan, and circulated as the dominant and preferred one is clearly a Hindu image... In all these serials, a certain set of similar signs have been used to signify the Hindu religion... [Thus] Doordarshan plays a crucial role in circulating an ideologically correct national Hindu image and, consequently, generating an ideological struggle to question and challenge those images and practices that marginalize large parts of the social arena... (pp. 40-42).

Mitra's textual analysis raises interesting and important connections, but the problem is that his analysis tends to assume rather than demonstrate the centrality and power of the media. The position taken here is that it is not possible to fully assess the power of the media without contextualizing its operation and reception. For example, Mitra takes little note of the fact that tens of millions of people, particularly in rural areas, had little or no access to television to begin with. They were simply not available to be "positioned" by Doordarshan's texts. Further, questions need to be asked about what kind of television viewers were more likely to watch Doordarshan's Hindu-centric offerings. Recent evidence suggests that Hindi serials are particularly popular in the north and west of India, but quite moderate in the east and south (Doordarshan, 1993). Only by taking these factors into account, can we begin to get a sense of who was actually exposed to Doordarshan's ideological images.

Finally, the influence of Doordarshan's texts on those who do view is very much dependent on the ways in which audience members are positioned by various discourses, practices, and contexts (e.g., religious, regional, class). These may offer constructions that reinforce or contradict those in the Doordarshan texts. Rudolph (1992) gives a sense of this:

> Some have argued that the emergence of a national Hindu identity [on television] automatically enhances...the stereotyping and defaming of community differences that fuel polarization, mobilization and confrontation. I am not so sure. The "Hindu" content of the mega-serials has not been explicitly communal....[B]ut the mega-serials in conjunction with the outlook and practice of the Vishva Hindu Parishad and other 'national' Hindu organizations, opens the way contextually to communalize the series. The programs may be making it possible for Hindu mobilization and cultural transformation to occur.... For example, the celebration of Ram in *Ramayana* seems likely to have helped fuel the agitation to build a temple near...the Babri mosque at Ayodhya... The intersecting of the mega-serials with the revivalism and fundamentalism of national Hindu movements and politics is not only undermining and displacing the localism and diversity of religious diversity. It has the potential for weakening the pluralist toleration and inclusiveness of pre-TV religious identity and esteem. (p. 1495)

As Rudolph suggests, in the wider socio-political context which was marked by growing Hindu fundamentalism and communal tensions, Doordarshan's subsequent Hindu-centric texts may very well have reinforced the beliefs of those viewers (e.g., BJP supporters) who were predisposed to the fundamentalist case.

The evidence and arguments presented in this section indicate that those who dwell in Kothari's "dynamic first world" were the beneficiaries of the massive investment in the state-owned television network that took place in the 1980s. These included: the ruling party elites who used the new infrastructure to appease and cultivate the support of the growing urban middle classes; the middle and upper classes; the government agencies that reaped the benefits of Doordarshan's rapidly expanding revenue base; the industrialist and advertising agencies that were provided an important means of targeting the middle classes; the national and transnational hardware manufacturers that benefited from the state's outlay on distribution technology and from the outlay by individuals on receivers; the purveyors and users of Hindu fundamentalism who may have benefited somewhat from Doordarshan's attempts at promoting a Hindu national identity. The inhabitants of the "second world"---the rural and urban poor, the laboring classes, the tribals, the unemployed---were the losers; losing out on resources that could have been used to alleviate their problems.

Yet it is important not to overestimate the centrality of the contribution of the old programming environment to the state's exclusionary integration project. Earlier analysis indicated that a number of more profound (and historically prior) forces operated to maintain and reproduce this project: a centralized power structure that was insensitive to the interests and demands of those in the "second world"; a powerful police and military apparatus that was used to quell unrest in the "second world" while providing security to the first; economic policies that increasingly integrated elements of the first world into global circuits of production and distribution; and the rise of a virulent form of Hindu fundamentalism that sought to homogenize and marginalize.

The "New" Programming Environment and Integration

With the emergence of STAR TV, the pattern of supplying television programming has been transformed. Is this new programming environment contributing to the state's integration project in the same way as the old one? Because the new environment is still in flux, the answers offered are necessarily tentative.

Of India's 40.4 million television households, Doordarshan estimates that by the end of 1993, 6.2 million (15.4 per cent) had satellite dishes (Doordarshan, 1994). But STAR TV and other foreign satellite systems have also taken advantage of the existing cable networks to reach audiences. According to a recent *India Today* (1995) report, the number of homes that have access to satellite and cable channels increased from 7.3 million in 1993 to 12 million in 1994. Most of these households are located in urban areas. If particular obstacles are removed---the growing cable bottleneck, for example--- the reach of STAR TV and other foreign satellite channel entrants is likely to increase rapidly.

For those who can afford to access Doordarshan and the foreign satellite channels, there is now a relative abundance of domestic and foreign programming to choose from. The high ratings for Hindi serials on Doordarshan and the popularity of Zee TV, which broadcasts in Hindi and provides programs that focus on Indian themes and characters, suggests a preference for domestic over foreign programming. Yet, as the Doordarshan (1993) study cited earlier indicates, most of the popularity for Hindi programming is accounted for by high ratings in the north and west of the country. Hindi programming (carried by Doordarshan or Zee TV) has fewer viewers in the south. For those in the south with access, a number of regional (South Indian) language satellite services provide more relevant programming. SUN TV, Vijay TV, and Raj TV broadcast in Tamil; Udaya TV broadcasts in Kannada; Asianet in Malayalam; and Gemini TV and Eenadu TV in Telegu. To maximize audience size, there are indications that STAR TV and other foreign satellite channels (e.g., the new Sony Entertainment Channel) will increasingly move toward provision of local language fare, particularly Hindi programming. This strategy may also aid in appeasing groups such as the BJP who warn of a "cultural invasion" (Pathania, 1994; Pendakur & Kapur, 1997).

In one sense, the emergence of the new programming environment can be understood as reinforcing the state's exclusionary integration project. A key element of this project is the placation of the burgeoning middle-classes. The new programming environment aids in this process by satisfying the middle class demand for increased program choice. Because of its competitive nature, the environment also appears more sensitive to their tastes. This "placation effect" will increase in significance as more of the middle classes join the ranks of those who can access the various satellite channels. Further, the south Indian language satellite services such as Sun TV, Eenadu TV, Udaya TV, and Asianet are beginning to meet the hitherto neglected demand of these linguistic regions to have entertainment and other fare in their own vernacular.

Yet this same dynamic may also operate to undermine television as an apparatus of state control. In the old environment, the government had more or less total control over what was televised. This made it an attractive political management tool---both in terms of elaborating a national identity by way of Doordarshan's entertainment programs, for example, and by controlling news. In the new programming environment these strategies may be undercut. Foreign satellites are offering a changed (and varying) menu of images and prescriptions from which middle class viewers may draw on in constructing their identity. These images and prescriptions, whether carried by English or Hindi channels, may sit uncomfortably with Hindu fundamentalist notions, for example. The old program environment was not devoid of this kind of tension, but it is likely to be much more prevalent in the new. Further, the proliferation of satellite channels, particularly regional Indian language channels, may lead to different notions of "nation" and "national identity" circulating through segments of the viewers.

The new programming environment may also pose a threat to state control because it has ended the state's monopoly control over televised news programming. Governing elites have already expressed concern that coverage of "sensitive" Indian issues by foreign news networks may trigger political instability. The BBC and CNN were accused of sparking a Hindu backlash against Indian Muslims after they showed Muslims in Bangladesh and Pakistan destroying Hindu temples

(Kishore, 1994, p. 100). According to Kishore, these global news sources threaten Doordarshan's policy of not naming which communities were killing each other. The government has also been critical of the BBC's coverage of the ongoing struggle in Kashmir (*India Today*, July 15, 1995, p. 99). Of course, the interpretive framework offered by these new sources may also contradict the official line on a whole range of issues. From the government's perspective, this problem is exacerbated by the long-standing and widespread distrust of Doordarshan's political programming which makes alternative news sources attractive.

Growth of the new programming environment along existing lines is likely to enhance state control by keeping the middle and upper classes content. Yet the state's ability to control politically important news programming is being undercut. The plurality of representations that may increasingly circulate in the new environment, would render ineffective any attempts at propagating a highly selective version of national identity and culture.

Conclusion

There is a crisis of representation in India. Excluded groups have little opportunity to voice their aspirations as there is little interaction between civil society and the state at various levels. Given this state of affairs, what role might media policy play in facilitating democratic outcomes?

The new programming environment may pose problems for the government but it will do little to address the crisis. This environment may promote a greater plurality of representations but it will be consumed almost entirely by the middle and upper classes. It has been argued that the problem of representation could be addressed by developing an autonomous public service broadcasting corporation, which could ensure widespread participation for the multiplicity of interests that compromise Indian society. Thus Thomas (1993) argues:

> [A] decentralized PSB system in India, within a partially de-regulated framework may be the only way to allow for the democratization of broadcasting in India, ensure access, participation and the respect for

the 'many worlds and many voices that make up Indian society'. (p. 20)

Critically, for Thomas, the ethic of public service and responsibility must suffuse the operation of this system: "[I]f such imperatives are treated as peripheral concerns to the debate on the future of broadcasting in India, the further marginalization of the poor in India will become inevitable" (p. 31).

While having much sympathy with this attempt at imagining television as a vibrant public sphere, it does seem unjustifiably media-centric. The assumption appears to be that a public service model is key to the rejuvenation of democratic processes. Given this assumption, the policy implication seems to be to deploy the model as quickly as possible in order to empower a plurality of citizens. Yet, writing in the European context, Keane (1991) suggests that the effective operation of the public service model presupposes an open government, the re-definition of sovereignty, and the establishment of a strong democratically-elected parliament able to support media "freedoms," for example. The analysis presented in this chapter suggests that these institutional preconditions do not exist and that there is in fact a more fundamental agenda than media reform. This is not to argue that mass media has no role in democratic projects. Rather the concern here is with ascertaining the weight "media" and "media policy" should be accorded in such projects.

Democracy in India can be promoted by challenging the modes of inclusion/exclusion discussed earlier. Since the early 1990s, there have been signs that these modes are being resisted by myriad movements and groups: a variety of regional upsurges and movements for cultural autonomy, a range of ecological movements, a women's movement, anti-communal movements, and a movement for homelands for tribals and hill people (Das Gupta, 1995; Kothari, 1989c, 1995; Routledge, 1993). These struggles, Kothari (1995) points out:

> [consist] of a stream of initiatives and responses, still highly scattered, often at cross purposes, involving quite a lot of fragmentation and tension...yet in many ways [they are] the only real source of hope in an otherwise dismal scenario. (p. 166)

Growing unrest within civil society poses the real danger to the state's integration project---not transborder satellite channels. The fundamental task that looms is to weld together, where possible, many of the disparate groups in civil society into a counter-hegemonic bloc that can force concessions from governing elites. This requires the development of new spaces in civil society where groups can organize and communicate in order to more effectively fend-off threats or assert rights and claims. Of course, some of the claims for recognition and equality may prove to be mutually exclusive. Situated outside of the parliamentary and party framework, a key task for this new form of organization is to develop credibility as somehow representing voices of those in the "second world" and perhaps beyond---in Kothari's terms it should project itself as the "conscience-keepers of the country." Media policy scholars can perhaps suggest media configurations and institutions that can help promote these objectives.

Notes

[1] A lengthier version of this analysis can be found in Shields and Muppidi (1996).

[2] These organizations had assisted the Indian government with a balance-of-payments crisis that ensued after the Gulf War.

[3] Mody (1988, p. 9) points out that the decision by the Information and Broadcasting Ministry (which housed Doordarshan) to accept advertising income was conditioned by the desire to gain financial autonomy from the Planning Commission and the Ministry of Finance. She notes that Doordarshan's revenues from advertising spots increased from US $0.64 million in 1976 to US $80 million in 1986.

References

Bonner, A., Ilaiah, I., Saha, S.K., Engineer, A.A., & Héuze, G. (1994). *Democracy in India: A hollow shell.* Washington DC: The American University Press.

Brass, P.R. (1990). *The new Cambridge history of India: The politics of India since independence.* New York: Cambridge University Press.

Collins, R. (1990). *Culture, communication and national identity: The case of Canadian television.* Toronto: Toronto University Press.

Das Gupta, J. (1995). India: Democratic becoming and developmental transition. In L. Diamond, J.J. Linz and S.M. Lipset (Eds.), *Politics in developing countries: Comparing experiences with democracy,* pp.263-321. Boulder, CO: Lynne Rienner.

Doordarshan, Audience Research Unit. (1993). *Doordarshan viewing pattern, January-February 1993: Results of a survey conducted in twelve cities.* New Delhi: Author.

Doordarshan, Audience Research Unit. (1994). *Doordarshan-199 4.* New Delhi: Author.

Economic and Political Weekly, Oct. 23, 1993, "Editorial," p. 2348.

Ferguson, M. (1992). The mythology about globalization. *European Journal of Communication* 7(1): 69-93.

Fernandes, C.P. (1989). Communication technologies and economic development in India. *Media Development,* 36(1): 29-32.

Frankel, F.R. (1978). *India's political economy, 1947-1977: The gradual revolution.* Princeton: Princeton University Press.

Ghorpade, S. (1986). Retrospect and prospect: The information environment and policy in India. *Gazette,* 38(4): 5-28.

India Today, March 31, 1995, "Battling for the Big Bucks," p. 120-22.

India Today, July 15, 1995, "When Beeb Blunders," p. 99.

India Today, October 15, 1995, "Economic Reform: Down to a Trickle," pp. 26-29.

India Today, November 15, 1995, "More Manna from the Sky," pp. 112-113.

Joshi, P.C. (1989). *Culture, communication and social change.* New York: Advent Books.

Keane, J. (1991). *The media and democracy.* Oxford: Polity Press.

Kishore, K. (1994). The advent of STAR TV in India: Emerging policy issues. *Media Asia*, 21(2): 96-103.

Kohli, A. (1987). *The state and poverty in India: The politics of reform.* Cambridge: Cambridge University Press.

Kothari, R. (1988a). Integration and exclusion in Indian politics. *Economic and Political Weekly, Vol. 23, No. 43,* October 22: 2223-27.

Kothari, R. (1988b). Class and communalism in India. *Economic and Political Weekly,* Vol. 23, No. 49, December 3: 2589-2592

Kothari, R. (1989a). *State against democracy: In search of humane governance.* New York: New Horizons.

Kothari, R. (1989b). *Politics and the people: In search of a humane India, Vol. 1.* New York: New Horizons.

Kothari, R. (1989c). The Indian enterprise today. *Daedalus* 118(4): 50-67.

Kothari, R. (1995). Interpreting Indian politics: A personal view. In U. Baxi and B. Parekh (Eds.), *Crisis and change in contemporary India.* New Delhi: Sage, pp. 150-168..

Lodziak, C. (1986). *The power of television: A critical appraisal.* London: Frances Pinter.

McDowell, S.D. (1995). The decline of the license Raj: Indian software export policies. *Journal of Communication,* 45(4), 25-50.

Mitra, A. (1993). Television and the nation: Doordarshan's India. *Media Asia* 20(1): 39-44.

Mody, B. (1988). The commercialization of TV in India: A research agenda for cross-country comparisons. Paper presented at International Communication Association, Intercultural and Development Communication Division, New Orleans, May.

Mody, B. (1995). State consolidation through liberalization of telecommunication services in India. *Journal of Communication,* 45(4), 107-124.

Morley, D., & Robins, K. (1995). *Spaces of identity: Global media, electronic landscapes and cultural boundaries.* London: Routledge.

Narang, A.S. (1986). *Democracy development and distortion.* New Delhi: Gitanjali Publishing House.

Pathania, G. (1994). Ambivalence in a STAR-ry eyed land: Doordarshan and the satellite TV challenge. *South Asia Graduate Research Journal,* 1(1), 60-78.

Peet, R. (1986). The destruction of regional cultures. In R.J. Johnston and P.J. Taylor (Eds.), *A world in crisis? Geographical perspectives.* pp. 150-172. Oxford: Basil Blackwell,

Pendakur, M. (1991). A political economy of television: State, class, and corporate influence in India. In G. Sussman & J.A. Lent (Eds.), *Transnational communications: Wiring the Third World.* pp. 234-262. Newbury Park: Sage,

Pendakur, M., & Kapur, J. (1997). Think globally, program locally: Privatization of Indian national television. In M. Bailie and D. Winseck (Eds.), *Democratic communication? Comparative perspectives on information and power.* pp. 195-218. Cresskill, NJ: Hampton Press.

Rajagopal, A. (1993). The rise of national programming: The case of Indian television. *Media, Culture and Society* 15(1): 91-111.

Routledge, P. (1993). *Terrains of resistance: Nonviolent social movements and the contestation of place in India.* Westport: Praeger.

Rudolph, L.I. (1992). The media and cultural politics. *Economic and Political Weekly,* Vol. 27, No. 28, July 11: 1489-1496.

Schiller, H.I. (1991). Not yet the post-imperial era. *Critical Studies in Mass Communication,* 8, 13-28.

Schlesinger, P. (1987). On national identity: Some conceptions and misconceptions criticized. *Social Science Information* 26(2): 219-264.

Schlesinger, P. (1991). Media, the political order and national identity. *Media, Culture and Society* 13: 297-308.

Shields, P., & Muppidi, S. (1996). Integration, the Indian state and STAR TV: Policy and theory issues. *Gazette,* 58(1): 1-24.

Singhal, A., & Rogers, E.M. (1989). *India's information revolution.* New Delhi: Sage.

Thomas, P.N. (1988). State monopoly capitalism and the media in India. *ICCTR Journal* 1(1): 22-37.

Thomas, P.N. (1993). Broadcasting and the state in India: Toward relevant alternatives. *Gazette* 51(1): 19-33.

Thompson, J.B. (1995). *The media and modernity: A social theory of the media.* Stanford, CA: Stanford University Press.

Tomlinson, J. (1991). *Cultural imperialism.* Baltimore, MD: Johns Hopkins University.

Varshney, A. (1993). Contested meanings: India's national identity, Hindu nationalism, and the politics of anxiety. *Daedalus* 122(3): 227-261.

Chapter 6

The Obligation to Provide a Voice for Small Languages: Implications for the Broadcast Media in India[1]

Andrew Woodfield

A Normative Issue

In recent years, linguists have begun to sound warning bells about the rapid decline in the number of languages that are spoken around the world. At the annual meeting of the American Advancement of Science held in Atlanta, Georgia in February 1995, Professor Michael Krauss claimed that up to 95 percent of the 6,000 or so languages will be either extinct or moribund by the end of the next century, if present trends continue.[2]

The loss of linguistic diversity is worrying from both the scientific and the ethical point of view. The world's languages constitute a precious cultural and cognitive resource for humanity. Linguistic diversity, like biodiversity, represents a vast storehouse of information. It is not just linguists who have an interest in this information. Language systems provide a direct or indirect source of data for many other branches of science. The irretrievable loss of data will render a whole range of inquiries difficult or impossible.

Humanity ought also to be ethically concerned about the plight of the speakers of endangered languages. These individuals are liable to be disadvantaged or harmed by the loss of their native language. It hardly needs emphasising that such loss will often carry with it the loss of an ancestral culture, a set of traditions, and a way of life. Indigenous groups are particularly vulnerable. It is for this reason that the United Nations Commission on Human Rights builds the protection of cultural and linguistic rights into its draft declaration on Discrimination Against Indigenous Peoples[3] Article 14 states:

> Indigenous peoples have the right to revitalise, use, develop, and transmit to future generations their histories, languages, oral traditions, philosophies, writing systems and literatures, and to designate and retain their own names for communities, places and persons. States shall take effective measures, whenever any right of indigenous peoples may be threatened, to ensure that this right is protected and also to ensure that they can understand and be understood in political, legal and administrative proceedings, where necessary through the provision of interpretation or by other appropriate means. (p.2)

Currently, many factors can be considered to be threatening the survival and sustainability of languages. The growth of electronic communications is one of the primary factors contributing to language loss where big languages (Big-L)[4] dominate the air waves. The dangers of linguistic and cultural imperialism have been exacerbated by the advent of satellite television broadcasting. Largely under the control of multinational companies, this technology spans most of the Third World and beams programmes which may be mostly foreign to the majority of people who live their lives under the satellites' footprints. The companies are more interested in returning a profit to their shareholders than in issues such as development or the social good of the community.

In this chapter, it is taken for granted that it is a *good thing* for small languages (Small-L)[5] to be represented in radio and television broadcasting. It is desirable in general, for scientific, cultural and ethical reasons. However, it is not easy to move from this abstract desideratum to more specific recommendations about what ought to be done. Supposing that there is a general ethical obligation to provide programming in small languages, upon whom does this obligation fall? Under what circumstances? And how might specific recommendations be implemented?

Undoubtedly, many reflective observers feel that the global communications industry could, and should, try harder to promote cultural diversity. It currently enjoys enormous power without much responsibility. It seeks to excuse its penetration of the Third World by saying: 'We increase people's range of choice of programmes. We provide the consumers with what they want.' But the business is driven fundamentally by the profit-motive. Satellite television networks will not voluntarily provide time for minority communities or languages, unless and until it becomes financially advantageous to do so.

To improve the situation, constraints must be imposed upon the industry from without. A higher authority needs to step in, *pro bono publico*. Just as polluters should be accountable for damage they cause to the natural environment, so broadcasting companies should be accountable for the effects of their activities upon the cultural environment. This means that the obligation to protect small languages from the threat of usurpation by big ones falls primarily upon national and regional governments, because governments have the power and authority to introduce language-conservationist policies on an appropriate demographic scale. However, this is based on the premise that the State is a neutral arbiter in the struggle between the various language groups. This premise is questionable and merits further exploration, something that is not attempted in this essay.

A Normative Framework

Local citizens have a *right* to receive radio and/or television in their own language. It brings a variety of social benefits. It can motivate people to become literate in their mother tongue, can help conserve oral and written literature, and eradicate illiteracy.

In this chapter, the following framework is provided for appropriate action: *in paradigm situations where a certain set of conditions obtain, the appropriate government authority ought to require that broadcasters who transmit to the population living within its jurisdiction shall provide a measure of programming in smaller local languages.*

Such a normative recommendation may fall on deaf government ears in some parts of the world. But in a democracy such as India, where the government purports to act for the benefit of its citizens, the authorities may be swayed by ethical considerations. This essay will first discuss the main elements of the normative framework before attempting to apply it to the Indian situation.

The Paradigm

The paradigm presented here is characterised by four conditions. If all four are satisfied, the situation is one in which the relevant authority has a *prima facie* obligation to act. If a situation resembles the paradigm even though not all four conditions are fully met, the ethical considerations urged in the next section may create a *prima facie* obligation there as well, but the case will not be so clear-cut. The argument here does not, of course, preclude there being other ethical considerations as well, which might imply the same obligation by a different route.

Demographic Condition

In the paradigm situation there is a country or state having a dominant language (Big-L), within whose boundaries there exists at least one sub-community speaking a different language, small-L. Small-L is a minority language within the country or state in question.

In India, the demographic condition allows the following regional languages to count as small-L's within its national boundary: Tamil, Kannada, Malayalam, and Telugu---indeed all the official state languages. But Tamil is not a minority language within the state of Tamil Nadu in India. Whether a given language counts as a minority language is relative to the boundaries of the selected state.

Socio-historical Condition

The group that speaks small-L as its first language is either indigenous to or long established within a particular geographical region and has developed its own traditions and culture in that region. This condition lets in practically all of the tribal peoples of not just

India but the entire world. In Europe, it also includes the Welsh, the Basques, the Catalans and many others.

This condition would not be satisfied by a community of recent immigrants to a country, such as the twentieth century Europeans who migrated to the United States. It is not ruled out that in some situations immigrant groups ought to have media representation in their own languages. However, such situations would not exemplify the paradigm. There is obviously a continuum of intermediate demographic possibilities where the issues become blurred. It might be relevant to consider factors such as whether the host country has appealed for immigrants in order to build a nation, and whether the immigrants entered the country with a wish to be assimilated. In the paradigm, such factors do not arise; the small-L community is living in its ancestral homeland. The rights-based arguments for small-L media representation will then apply more clearly.

Viability Condition

Small-L must be healthy enough to stand a good chance of surviving into the future. This condition is inevitably vague; viability is not a property that can be defined with absolute precision. One major index of a language's viability is the number of current speakers. But other factors enter the equation too, such as the age-profile of the speakers, their reproduction rate, and the strength of their desire to bring up their children as speakers.

Group-morale is a hard thing to measure, but its significance is undeniable. For instance, compare Scottish Gaelic with Hebrew. Scottish Gaelic is known by approximately 79,000 inhabitants of the highlands and islands of Scotland. Because jobs have been scarce, the population has dwindled over the past century. Young adults tend to move elsewhere to find work. Many Gaelic-speaking parents feel that it is not in their children's interests to speak Gaelic. The long-term future of this language is in doubt (Dorian, 1981). This fact does not disqualify Scottish Gaelic from meriting a media-presence. What is argued here is that a language which is dying does not provide the best case. Fortunately, Scottish Gaelic is in fact catered for on radio and television.

The community of Hebrew speakers, on the other hand, is small but buoyant. In the early twentieth century, Eliezer Ben Yehuda, a Russian immigrant to Palestine, took it upon himself to set up Hebrew schools. Prior to this, Hebrew was not in use as a spoken language in Palestine or anywhere else. But its use spread. Hebrew, a symbol of Jewish identity, was regarded as an appropriate *lingua franca* for a new Jewish homeland. Now, one century later, it is the official language of the state of Israel, and many young Israelis speak it as their first language (though for many older Israelis it is a second, third, or fourth language).

It is unrealistic to try to separate languages into just two groups: those that are healthy and those that are moribund. There is a large class of *languishing* languages. Also there is movement from one class to another. Which category a given language belongs to may be indeterminate. The fitness of a language can be dramatically improved if suitable policies are adopted. The argument here is directed mainly toward small languages that belong to the intermediate class.

Unfortunately, this condition has the effect of excluding a large proportion of the world's 6,500 languages from the scope of the present argument. Most of these languages are not just small but tiny, and the minorities that speak them have little chance of keeping their cultures intact in the modern world. In many cases the speakers are not consumers of electronic media at all, so it cannot easily be shown that the use of alien languages in such media has caused them any direct harm.

In India, 50 million tribal people (*adivasis*) have inherited languages that are accorded no official status. Generally these languages have no written script, and no state education is provided in them. In the state of Tamil Nadu, there are 36 such tribes (Singh, 1994). Consider the Todas of the Nilgiri hills. The Todas have been extensively studied by anthropologists and have become famous in the west through television documentaries. The speakers of Toda---a Dravidian language---numbered 825 in the 1981 census, and the present population may be double that number. But the long-term prospects for their language and culture are, regrettably, not very bright---for all sorts of reasons that have little to do with the electronic media.

In contrast with Toda, the viability condition is satisfied by many of the larger minority languages of India. For example, Konkani (spoken in Goa and along the west coast) has 4 million speakers, and moves have been made to get the language officially recognised. The will to keep the language afloat appears to be strong. Another example is Khasi, spoken by a million and a half in the north-eastern state of Meghalaya. In fact, Doordarshan already caters for these languages on its local channels. From Goa it puts out two hours of daily news and current affairs in Konkani; in the Shillong area it provides programming for an hour each evening in Khasi. But the size and importance of these languages surely warrants more hours and a wider choice. And, many other minority languages which are clearly viable do not yet have a place in electronic media.

Effectiveness condition

The circumstances and context need to be such that, if small-L were used on radio and television---in local or national news, current affairs, drama, or entertainment---this fact would significantly strengthen its viability. This condition, that use must lead to strengthening, may seem too obvious to mention. It is hard to envisage circumstances in which increasing the public use of a small language would actually harm it. Yet such circumstances are conceivable. Suppose it were the case that all the broadcasting in small-L got highjacked by a fanatical separatist party which used the media exclusively to foment hatred against the big-L community. Further, suppose that the prevailing regime were a military dictatorship that spoke big-L. Then imagine this scenario: the small-L becomes tainted, in the government's mind, by its association with the subversive messages that it is being used to carry. The government sends in the army to quell the separatist movement, giving secret instructions to liquidate the small-L community. The ensuing genocide eliminates the speakers of the language, and hence extinguishes small-L itself. The effectiveness condition, therefore, is not redundant. The likely effects of introducing small-L broadcasting must be roughly predictable, and they must be favourable to small-L. It is important to stress here that the effects could easily be decisive in saving a language that would otherwise have died.

The Proposition

It is proposed that when a small language meets the four conditions outlined earlier, the appropriate authority has a *prima facie* obligation to ensure that the language is provided with adequate representation on radio or television. This will include satellite networks owned by multinational corporations whose headquarters may be located in a different country. The compelling reason for this obligation is based on ethical considerations. The forthcoming defence of the proposition will appeal to three arguments, each one grounded in an ethical principle that commands wide acceptance. The first argument adopts a global perspective. The nations of the world, recognising the value to humanity of linguistic diversity, have a general responsibility to promote it. Linguistic and cultural diversity is linked to biodiversity. Local knowledge---of flora and fauna, culturally specific techniques for extracting valuable products from nature, sustainable methods of cultivation, etc.---need to be understood, retained and transmitted by the inhabitants of a region if their environment is to stay in balance. The signatories of the 1992 Declaration at the Rio de Janeiro Summit committed themselves to conserving languages and cultures as well as biological species. Every government that signed it thereby acknowledged that it has some responsibility to implement the measures. Such a government is bound in consistency to acknowledge that it has a responsibility to ensure a media presence for small languages within its own jurisdiction. If the four conditions are met by a given small language L, it follows that the existence of broadcasting in small-L will enhance the value and prestige of that language and will contribute in some degree to the conservation of global linguistic diversity.

The European Community (EC) provides a model of an authority that maintains an enlightened concern for linguistic minorities. Its legislative body, the European Parliament, has power to bind member states on certain matters and to make recommendations to states on other matters. The Kuijpers Resolution passed on October 30, 1987 ('European Bureau,' 1994) states (in section 9, pp. 10-11):

> The European Parliament recommends to the Member States that they take social and economic measures including:
> providing for the use of the regional and minority languages in public concerns (postal services etc.),
> recognition of the use of the regional and minority languages in the payments sector (giro cheques and banking),
> providing for consumer information and product labelling in regional and minority languages...

The Killilea Resolution of February 9, 1994 ('European Bureau,' 1994) went further, and made explicit mention of the broadcasting media:

> The European Parliament...
> Points out again the need for Member States to recognise their linguistic minorities and to make the necessary legal and administrative provisions for them to create the basic conditions for the preservation and development of these languages;
> Believes, furthermore, that all minority languages and cultures should also be protected by appropriate legal statute in the Member States;
> Considers that this legal statute should at least cover the use and encouragement of such languages and cultures in the spheres of education, justice and public administration, *the media*, toponymics and other sectors of public and cultural life...'
> (emphasis added; p. 13)

The elected members of the European Parliament voted in favour of these resolutions. Each member had his or her personal mixture of reasons. But the avowed aim of the resolutions is to safeguard and foster a certain kind of wealth that Europe is fortunate to enjoy, namely, its immensely rich cultural and linguistic heritage. This aim is built into the ideals of the European Community.

The second reason why the government of a reasonably enlightened and democratic state like India should try to provide a media voice for small languages is that it is in the collective interest of its citizens that the component linguistic groups should live in harmony and mutual respect. There must be space for public dialogue on political and cultural matters. Proposals should be debated in a way that allows all voices to be heard. The speakers of any small-L that satisfies the viability condition will, *ex hypothesi*, form a sizeable and vigorous community. Its members may share views on certain issues. If the state is a democracy, each speaker of small-L has a vote. The aggregate of small-L speakers may constitute a significant political force.[6] If such a force has no opportunity to express itself spontaneously and naturally in public in its own language, this is likely to cause tension, frustration, and dissatisfaction.

The case of Catalonia illustrates this point. In the 1960's, at the end of the Franco regime in Spain, the Catalan language had been suppressed for many years. It was not taught in schools, nor was it ever visible in public. There was no broadcasting in Catalan. Catalan-speakers continued to use the language clandestinely amongst themselves. Now, in the 1990's, Catalonia has been granted semi-autonomy. The sound and sight of Catalan are manifest throughout the region. What would have happened if this energetic and prosperous region had continued to be gagged by Madrid? Another Spanish civil war? Civil unrest?

The third argument appeals to the principle that a linguistic minority in the paradigm situation has certain group-rights, among which is the right to use its own language in the conduct of normal social and commercial life.

It is a controversial matter whether natural social groups (such as linguistic communities) have rights *over and above* the rights possessed by their individual members. Some political philosophers hold that the doctrine of group-rights implies communitarianism, and that communitarianism is incompatible with classical liberalism. Others, such as Will Kymlicka (1995) argue that there is no logical incompatibility. It's just that classical liberal thinkers did not think of addressing the issue. For example, the question of group language rights was never raised because theorists simply took it for granted that the model society was linguistically homogeneous.

In a multicultural society, the question of language rights cannot be ignored. Kymlicka (1995) writes:

> Liberal theorists debate the role of public education in promoting individual freedom, but in what language should public education be provided? What language should be used in the courts, or when public services are provided? The extent to which these rights and opportunities promote someone's freedom depends, at least in part, on whether they are available in her own language. (p. 2)

The idea of a linguistic right possessed by the group of small-L speakers can be justified or grounded in the idea that each individual speaker of small-L has the same right to equal access to information as any other citizen. This generates a supervenient right, which belongs to the individual *qua* speaker of small-L, to have access to media made available in the language of small-L. We need not worry here whether the right of the group reduces to the sum of the rights of the individual members. It is sufficient for our purposes to argue that in the paradigm case small-L citizens need to be served information spoken in small-L, if they are to get as much access to information as their fellow-citizens who speak big-L. These individuals have a right *qua* speakers of small-L. Being a speaker of small-L means communicating in small-L, and communication is an essential social activity. If only one person knows small-L, he or she will never speak it, because there is no one else to receive it. The language is already effectively dead. In such a scenario, it can hardly be argued that the lone individual has a right to be provided with access to information in small-L. Only when a community exists does it make sense to say that the individuals in it have a linguistic right.

If the argument is accepted thus far, it takes but a small step to reach the conclusion that in the paradigm case the implementation of small-L speakers' linguistic rights involves the provision of small-L broadcasting. This does not necessarily mean there has to be a channel devoted exclusively to small-L. It means there should be an appropriate number of hours of broadcasting in small-L on some channel or other, or distributed across several channels. It is the duty of the appropriate controlling authority to regulate the media industry so that the small-L speakers do get this.

In the UK, where the BBC is financed by revenue raised through receivers' licenses, this duty becomes assimilable under a more general duty to provide education and public services equally for all taxpayers. Consequently, the BBC provides regional radio and television services in Welsh and Scottish Gaelic. The European Community view is that: "Those who speak lesser used languages pay taxes and duties like all other citizens. Why deny them the right to make optimal use of public services?" ('European Bureau,' 1994, p. 6).

Small Language Broadcasting in India

The complexity of the Indian situation provides a context for an interesting and critical case study. The vast Indian sub-continent and its diverse peoples comprise nearly one billion inhabitants, ranging from indigenous groups (for instance, the constitutionally recognised scheduled tribes) to a highly educated western-oriented elite. India is a democracy and has eighteen official state languages and several hundred smaller unofficial languages. Although Hindi has been encouraged and given prominence by the central government, broadcasts in the other official Indian state languages co-exist with Hindi broadcasts. English, one of the official languages, is also prominent on Indian television channels. India is also a prime target of foreign satellite broadcasters based outside the country. Their channels mainly use English, but some channels (e.g. STAR TV) include a certain amount of Hindi programming and Western material dubbed in Hindi (including advertisements). Zee TV, the first Indian-language satellite channel, was launched in 1992. It made use of a spare transponder on Asiasat 1, leased from the then-owners of STAR TV. In 1993, Rupert Murdoch's News Corporation took over the STAR network, and shortly afterwards acquired a stake in Asia Today Limited, the holding company for Zee (Bhandare, 1996). There are commercial links between the companies based in India and the foreign companies. The recent past has witnessed much transferring of management personnel and some partial mergers. Foreign channels such as STAR and privately-owned Indian language channels transmit via satellite, using foreign bases to uplink.[7] For instance, Sun TV based in Chennai beams to India in mostly Tamil, a language spoken by 65 million. Its signals are routed---for a considerable fee---via an uplink in Singapore.

The Indian government has allowed national and international broadcasters to operate without regulation. In late 1996, former minister for Information and Broadcasting, C.M. Ibrahim sought to introduce a broadcasting bill that included the following provisions (among others) (Agarwal, 1996b):

(i) Only Indian companies will be allowed to broadcast to India. There will be a limit on the amount of foreign equity in such companies.

(ii) An independent broadcasting authority will be set up to grant licenses to satellite operators. Licenses will also be required for local, regional and national radio and TV stations. Operating without a license may be punishable.

(iii) In the case of DTH (direct-to-home) broadcasting - the new small dish technology - a minimum of two players will be given a license to operate on a national basis, and two in each language region. This measure is designed to prevent any company acquiring a monopoly.

(iv) A license holder will not be allowed to hold more than 20% stake in any other broadcasting company individually and 15% in aggregate.
(v) Newspaper owners having over 20% shareholding will not be granted any TV or radio licenses. (p. 116-117)

The general thrust of this bill seems clear. There are some Indian policy makers who perceive satellite broadcasting as a new form of cultural colonialism. In the view of some Indians, Western entertainment supplied by the foreign channels is a threat to India's cultural heritage. Minister Ibrahim tapped into this sentiment when he stated that the prime purpose of the new bill was to protect Indian culture from foreign programming. These sentiments are understandable. The unhindered penetration of India by media moguls such as Rupert Murdoch bears some comparisons with the British exploitation during the colonial era. However, the provisions of the bill oversimplify the situation. First, Indian-owned channels themselves feature Western entertainment in order to satisfy the strong viewer demand. Unless some form of censorship is incorporated in the bill, the Indian middle-classes will be able to view *Baywatch* and *Santa Barbara* even after the foreign owners' wings are clipped.

Second, there are numerous boardroom links between Indian national companies and the multinational corporations. Murdoch already owns the most successful Hindi channel, Zee TV. He has made overtures to Sun TV, a popular south Indian network. Astute tycoons whose tentacles stretch deep inside Indian firms will carry on with business as usual.

Third, there is a steady movement of top Indian television executives out of Indian companies, lured into the multinational broadcasting corporations by fat salary offers. In September 1996, former head of Doordarshan, Rathikant Basu, was appointed Chief Executive Officer of STAR TV. In an interview with the leading news magazine, *India Today,* Basu stated that one reason to head STAR was to work with the best people and 'his favourite TV producers' (Agarwal, 1996a) all of whom were going to be with STAR Plus. Top-level managers belong to the same élite, whichever company they happen to be employed by; the largest companies attract the best people, who in turn boost ratings and audience-figures, which in turn brings in more advertising.

Fourth, foreign players like Murdoch profess to supply Indian viewers with the programmes that Indians themselves want. STAR does not particularly wish to force American, British, or Australian programming into people's homes. It realised early on that English-only programmes would not attract the masses. Zee TV, the Hindi channel on STAR network, captured one quarter of all advertising soon after its launch. Further, STAR Plus Indianized its own programming with Hindi serials and news bulletins.

In a lecture delivered at the University of Melbourne in 1994, Murdoch said:

> Indian leaders have long been desperately worried about disunity in their vast, teeming, multilingual country. There has been an effort ever since independence to promote Hindi as the *lingua franca*... But the effort has failed for a number of reasons. Until now. With the coming of the electronic mass media, Hindi is finally spreading because everyone wants to watch the best television programming.

His wish to provide the best programmes was not his only reason for incorporating Hindi into Star Plus. He also wished to increase STAR's advertising share. Advertising has been STAR's only source of revenue in India (though this will no longer be true when STAR introduces Direct-to-Home services). The same motive explains Murdoch's interest in private regional Indian language channels such as Sun TV.

In light of these considerations, how effective will the new broadcasting bill be? Will it deter foreign entrepreneurs? And how far will it Indianize the content of television programmes?

In so far as the bill relates to the theme of this chapter, it represents a step in the right direction. Because licenses will be required, media companies will need to satisfy the government's conditions. But the bill is disappointing, because it does not pledge explicit support for smaller languages or for linguistic diversity. The main provisions of the bill reported in the press do not include any hint that the Information and Broadcasting Ministry wishes actively to promote the linguistic and cultural wealth of the country. Perhaps the criteria to be used in the granting of licenses to local and regional operators will include some assessment of the needs and rights of linguistic minorities within the relevant catchment areas. From an ethical perspective, such considerations ought to carry weight. However, at present the situation is not bright for smaller languages. Almost all of the languages used in All India Radio (AIR) and Doordarshan are the official state languages and the newer satellite channels are further exacerbating this trend. This does not bode well for the smaller languages.

People's desire to use their native language is strongly influenced by the image it has for them. If they perceive it as a vibrant, prestigious, message-carrying vehicle of which the wider world takes notice, they will be proud to speak it. When the media use small-L, this confers prestige. But if the speakers perceive their language to be backward or "fuddy-duddy" then they will cease speaking in it and thus hasten its demise as in the case of many native American youth. In north and west India, such a trend may be occurring. Some speakers of Punjabi and Marathi are starting to regard Hindi as having a higher status than their native languages.

If implemented, what would be the impact of the normative framework on broadcasting in India? Although it is impossible to say exactly how many languages of India would meet the four conditions, it seems reasonable to assume that the number would be well over 50. At least 20 of these are relatively big languages, major forces within their respective regions. Each of these is surely heard on television (regularly or occasionally) and on radio already. So will 30 more, if the normative framework is adopted. The most likely scenario is that these languages will be used, regularly or for a certain number of hours per week, on regional terrestrial stations run by AIR or Doordarshan or even by Indian commercial stations. The potential for local language commercial television should not be underestimated. In Wales, the exclusively Welsh-language channel S4C has benefited not only the Welsh language but also the Welsh economy, by creating *ex nihilo* a host of successful small production companies. Many S4C programmes have received international awards and won substantial export earnings. It is quite on the cards that high-quality Indian-made programmes, in small languages and with distinctive regional flavours, will prove attractive to viewers.

Notes

[1] The author wishes to thank Krishna Kandath for providing bibliographic and editorial assistance. An earlier version of this essay was delivered at the 4th International Conference on Ethics and Development in Chennai (Madras), India, sponsored by the International Development Ethics Association (IDEA) and the Centre for Research on New International Economic Order (CReNIEO). The author wishes to thank the British Academy for an overseas conference grant that paid for the travel to India and facilitated participation at the conference.

[2] Krauss's conference warning appeared in many newspapers and magazines. *The Independent on Sunday* (London) of 19th February 95 (p.11) quoted him as saying 'Languages are being lost at an unbelievable and unprecedented rate which is almost the inverse of the population curve, which we know is going straight up. The loss-of-languages curve is going straight down'.

[3] United Nations Commission on Human Rights, Sub-Commission on Prevention of Discrimination and Protection of Minorities, 45th Session, 23rd August 1993. Source: Fourth World Documentation Centre Project, http://www.halcyon.com/pub/FWDP/

[4] Big-L means a big or dominant language. Such languages have a large speaking population and/or receive continuing state support.

[5] Small-L means a small language that may or may not have a large speaking population but does not receive active state support.

[6] This argument will not carry much weight if the state is oligarchic,   because the oligarchy might perceive its own interest to lie in not maximising the collective interest of its citizens.

[7] India forbids all channels except Doordarshan to transmit signals from the Indian soil/ For additional information on Indian electronic media see chapters in this volume by P. Shields; K. Kumar; or G. Pathania

References

Agarwal, A. (1996a, October 31). A bold gamble. *India Today 21* (20), 121-122.

Agarwal, A. (1996b, December 31). Broadcast blues. *India Today 21* (24), 116-117.

Bhandare, N. (1996). Star vs Zee. *Sunday,* 29 Dec 1996 - 4 Jan 1997, pp. 12-19

Dorian, N. (1981). *Language death: The life cycle of a Scottish Gaelic dialect.* Philadelphia: University of Pennsylvania Press.

European Bureau of Lesser Used Languages. (1994). *Language rights --Individual and collective.* Brussels and Dublin: EC Publication

Kymlicka, W. (Ed.). (1995). *The rights of minority cultures.* Oxford: Oxford University Press.

Singh, K. S. (1994). *People of India: The scheduled tribes* (Vol. 3). Cambridge: Cambridge University Press.

Chapter 7

Cultural Influence of Indian Cinema on Indian Television

Binod C. Agrawal

There is very limited literature on the structure and content of programs on Doordarshan or satellite television in India. A cursory examination of the content of the most popular shows on Indian television will reveal the preponderance of Indian films and film-based programs. For example, Doordarshan includes a wide range of programming from Indian feature films and documentaries to feature film-based music programs. Mitra (1988) posits that most programs on Indian television take on a cinematic color, and the codes of television and films start to synthesize and form a unique code. This is most apparent in the serials and entertainment programs, where the visual signifiers are borrowed from cinema and do not always develop a specific television code. Even popular television serials such as the *Ramayan* and *Mahabharat* followed a tradition that was first set by the Indian feature films. This essay raises two important questions: 1. Why do Doordarshan or the satellite television channels in India rely so heavily on Indian feature films and film-based programs? 2. Is there any relationship between the content of Indian feature films and the meaning of 'recreation' as a genre of communicative arts that suits the cultural needs of the Indian viewers?

Indian Film-Based Programs on Television

The Indian film industry churns out more feature films than any other country in the world in as many as 15 languages. The majority of the films are produced in Tamil, Hindi, Telugu, Kannada, Malayalam and Bengali languages. The major centers of film production include the cities of Mumbai, Chennai, Hyderabad, Bangalore, and Calcutta.

The first full-length film was screened around 1913 in India (Barnouw and Krishnaswamy, 1980). Since then, this industry has produced thousands of films, all of high technical quality and immense audience appeal. So, in the 1970s when the fledgling Indian television setup started to establish itself, it was dwarfed by the giant film industry. Consequently, full-length feature films and film-song sequences were used to attract viewers to the television set.

Full Length Feature Films

The prime time hours on weekends have been reserved for the telecasting of a popular Indian feature film. In most states, Doordarshan telecasts a popular local language film on Saturdays and a Hindi feature film is shown on Sundays. In addition, full length Indian feature films are shown on most other days of the week. Indian language satellite television channels such as Zee TV, Eenadu TV, Sun TV have also followed a similar programming pattern. The viewership of Indian films has gone as high as 70 to 80 percent on Doordarshan (see *Doordarshan*, 1996). While Doordarshan has been dependent on film-based programs for its popularity, the satellite television channels have helped multiply the viewing of Indian cinema and emulated a programming model that was originally propagated by Doordarshan.

Film Songs

Next to full-length feature films, the film song genre is a popular item on Indian television channels. The film song is a unique staple of the Indian feature film and has been around since the first sound films arrived in India in the 1930s. In the 1970s, when television became popular in India, one of the most popular programs was the *Chaaya*

Geet, a collection of film song clips from popular Hindi films. Later, programs were added that included songs from other Indian language feature films. Today, Doordarshan, Zee TV, STAR TV, MTV-Asia, Eenadu TV and other channels carry many such commercially sponsored programs. The following list on the different channels gives the reader a flavor for the ubiquity of these film-song programs: *Chaaya Geet, Chitrahar, Rangoli* (On Doordarshan); *Cibaca Geet Mala, Lux Hit Parade, Super Hit Muqabala*(Metro Channel); *Philips Top Ten, Gaane Anjane, McDowells' Farmaish* (Zee TV); *BPL Oye* (V Channel); *Videocon Top Parade, Colgate Top Takkar* (Jain TV); and *Rin Priya Raagalu* (Eenadu TV).

Game Shows

Many game shows on television owe their popularity to films. A popular game show on Zee television is *Closeup Antakshari;* on Eenadu TV it is *Padutha Theeyaga.* These game shows involve a competition between two or more teams; the first team will sing a short snippet from an Indian film, the next team has to quickly think up a new film song that starts with the same word as the ending of the previous song. The group that outlasts all the other groups is declared victorious.

Recreational Value of Indian Films

A holistic, cultural analysis of the Indian cinema may provide a different answer to the question of dependency of Indian television on the Indian film. Indian cinema emerged in a context already rich in the ancient traditions of dance, drama, music and theatre apart from the folk art forms. The Indian cinema, from its earliest years, borrowed from the various Indian classical and folk art forms. *The Natyashastra* (ancient Indian science of drama), and other folk and local drama traditions, found a new means of exposure on the celluloid (Agrawal, 1982). Thus, the arrival of cinema as a medium of popular expression helped bring many of the folk and theatre traditions closer to the Indian masses. While the cinema borrowed from the literary tradition or the classic drama (Ghosh, 1967), it was essentially a medium of the masses. Thus, the cinema bridged the gap between "high art" and the "folk art" and took away the classical art forms from the feudal elites who held them as their exclusive preserve. The Indian cinema is uniquely Indian. This medium has exploited the rich storehouse of Indian theatre, song, and dance traditions and crafted a formula from these sources to entertain millions of Indians over the last eighty years. Indian mythology and history have contributed significantly to the plots or story lines in Indian films. The first Indian feature films were mythological epics and were inextricably linked with religion (Rangoonwalla, 1979). These epic mythological tales are popular even today. In fact, Doordarshan serials *Ramayan* and *Mahabharat* are excellent examples of films of this genre. The craving for epic mythological tales among the cinema audience has not waned in spite of the changing sociopolitical scene in India. Historical films or the lives of Indian kings and queens, brave warriors, or Indian freedom fighters is another genre of films that has continued to be popular with the Indian cinema audience. Both, the mythological and the historical cinema have also had the added advantage of cutting across regional, class, and language barriers in India. Of late, Indian films have incorporated contemporary concerns. These would include social themes such as family-related issues, political or socioeconomic themes, love stories, action films and social drama.

Whether the Indian film is a mythological tale, a historical story, or a contemporary concern, there is one ingredient that glues all the Indian films together: song and dance (Ray, 1976). An Indian movie is incomplete without classical or folk dances, playback songs and their pictorial depiction in grand and exotic locales with the actors and actresses wearing brilliantly colored costumes. The Indian cinema thus is a uniquely Indian cultural product. It has not only integrated folk and classical theater, music and dance but also invigorated these dramatic traditions by giving them a popular appeal through wide exposure. Thus, catching a movie has been an inexpensive and a wholly satisfying recreational experience to Indian film goers.

The recreation provided by the Indian film has been the impetus for the growth and/or the sustenance of other media. Indian radio programs such as *Vividh Bharati, Jay Mala* have benefited for decades from the influence and popularity of cinema songs. The Indian film was also responsible for the popularity of video cassettes in the 1980s, and today, it continues to popularize Indian television with its wide variety of offerings. Full- length feature films and song picturisations from Indian films are some of the most popular television programs today on Doordarshan, Zee TV, Jain TV, Eenadu TV, Udaya TV, Sun TV, Asianet, and many other channels.

Are there any relationships between Indian feature films and the meaning of 'recreation' as a genre of communicative arts that suits the cultural needs of the Indian radio listeners, video or television viewers? First, the difference between the meaning of 'recreation' and 'entertainment' is important and needs to be explicated. Recreation involves an onlooker's/viewer's/listener's intimate involvement in the enactment of 'extreme' situations of real or imagined lives to evoke pleasure, pain or pathos leading to some kind of catharses. *Natya Shastra*, the ancient Indian treatise on drama and a source of influence for both Indian cinema and television, describes how this type of enactment could be depicted in various art forms, drama being one such means of expression (Ghosh, 1967). Entertainment, on the other hand, is an act or instance of entertaining, a diversion or amusement. Indian film makers have followed the original dictum of the *Natya Shastra* and thus tried to provide recreation for pleasure and inspiration. In this respect, the story lines in the Indian cinema are repetitive, and its main characters are stereotypes to the extent that every move of the characters is fairly predictable. It is, therefore, the repertoire and the personal characterization of the role by the actor that is most enjoyed by the audience prompting repeat viewing of the same film.

Depiction of mythology in drama form continues to draw the largest audience when presented in an open theater, is staged, shown on the silver screen or viewed on television. In each case, it provides pleasure, pain and pathos to the audience. It is not accidental then that many popular television programs in India are mythological epics in a highly dramatized form such as the *Ram Leela* (Story of Lord Rama) which attracts the entire family, kin group and even neighbors. The same holds true for several other similar epics like *Mahabharat* (The Great War) and *Sri Krishna* (Story of Lord Krishna). Viewers are never tired of viewing these programs and probably will not in years to come.

Conclusion

The most consistent critique of globalization of the Indian cultures has to do with the homogenization of culture and issues of cultural impact. A theme running through many chapters in this book deals with the impact of the transnational satellite television channels on Indians and the Indian culture. However, any analysis of the cultural impact in India has to be examined across two dimensions: the class structure and the rural-urban divide. This may indicate that the newly developed urbanized middle class has been the most significant fallout of the phenomenon of satellite television in India. This divide is clearly apparent when one looks at India's television viewing patterns.

Television viewers in India today can be broadly classified into two major categories: Doordarshan-only viewers, and Doordarshan and satellite/cable viewers. The largest numbers of viewers fall in the first category whose number is estimated to be over 200 million. In the second category, the estimates vary from 45 million to 90 million (see *Doordarshan,* 1996). Typically, the satellite cable viewers are university-educated, white collared professionals, or businessmen/women. They tend to have small families with incomes much above the national average. They are multi-lingual (they have fluency in English and at least two Indian languages) and live in an urban and culturally pluralistic environment (see *Doordarshan,* 1996).

The present satellite/cable channels such as CNN, TNT, Discovery, NBC, ESPN, STAR Plus, Fox, Cartoon Network, etc., provide entertainment and news to this class of Indians. In that process, they are exposed to the value systems embedded in Western culture such as: individualism, freedom, and the Protestant Ethic. Whether it is a popular American serial such as *The Bold and the Beautiful, Santa Barbara,* or *Bay Watch,* they are reminded of how individuals go to any extent to protecting and maintaining their individualism and freedom of expression. The belief that hard work alone will help achieve a goal is reinforced. However, these viewers are also exposed to Doordarshan programs and Indian language satellite channels such as Zee, Eenadu, Sun, Asianet, Udaya, etc. that telecast Indian feature films, soap operas, film songs and dances. Thus, the satellite television viewers are constantly exposed to the value systems of the West and their own culture. On the surface, they adhere to consumerist and materialistic life styles, but they also reflect the deep-rooted religious and spiritual values in other matters (Agrawal, 1996). It is, therefore, argued that many of the cultural influences may be cyclical and reversible rather than being unidirectional and irreversible.

The large majority of Indians, however, live mostly in non-urban areas and can access only Doordarshan or view Indian cinema films. Many of these people may not even have a television or a cinema theater to access Doordarshan or watch films. These people are still rooted in their local and regional cultural moorings. Their television, cinema, or folk theatre viewing project and reinforce Indian themes, values, and culture. It is hard to imagine how a few transnational satellite channels can single-handedly endanger the cultural future of these millions of Indians.

References

Agrawal, B.C. (1996). Transnational television expansion and cultural domination of Euro-American life styles in Asia. Paper presented to PTC'96 at Honolulu, Hawaii, January 14-18.

Agrawal, B.C. (1982). How Indian is the Indian cinema? (Mimeographed). Ahmedabad, India: Space Applications Centre.

Barnouw, E., and S. Krishnaswamy. (1980). *Indian Film*. (2nd Edition). New York: Oxford University Press.

Doordarshan. (1996). New Delhi: Directorate General of Doordarshan.

Ghosh, M. (1967). *The Natyashastra*. Calcutta, India: Manisha Granthalaya.

Mitra, A. (1988). Significance of genres on Indian television. Paper presented at the international television studies conference, London.

Rangoonwalla, F. (1979). *A pictorial history of Indian cinema*. London: Hamlyn Publishing Group.

Ray, S. (1976). *Our films, their films*. Bombay: Orient Longman Limited.

Chapter 8

Pictures of a Native Land: Television Producers and Notions of Indianness

Shobha Das

Television in India is 37 years old. Until as late as 1991, the only television broadcaster in the country was the Indian state with its nationwide network, Doordarshan. The advent of the Gulf War provided fertile ground for the entry of Cable News Network (CNN) into Indian homes, and since then, the number of satellite channels entering the country have spiraled upwards. The STAR TV network, now majority-owned by Rupert Murdoch, started broadcasting into India in May 1991, carrying Music Television (MTV), the British Broadcasting Corporation (BBC) news, American, British and Australian serials, Mandarin and other English-language programming. Zee TV, a private Hindi channel, began broadcasting on the STAR TV network in October 1992. This was followed by a proliferation of regional, national and foreign channels, and parts of India now have access to as many as 25 channels[1] (Mathew, 1995, p. 603). Doordarshan has 12 channels, 9 of which are in regional Indian languages while the others are primarily in Hindi and English. Audiences in some cities, Chennai[2] for instance, have access to 38 channels---9 in Tamil (the regional language), 10 in English, 4 in Hindi, and 7 in other regional south Indian languages, and 8 broadcast in two or more languages ("Television Listings," 1996, p. 5).

In spite of the nationwide availability of satellite channels, only 10 million[3] of the 40.3 million television-owning households are connected to cable networks.[4] The remaining 30.3 million households continue to receive only terrestrial Doordarshan (Mathew, 1995, p. 603). Also of interest is the increasing popularity of Indian language channels as against those that broadcast in English; by 1994, Doordarshan and Zee TV had the highest ratings figures[5] in the country ("Market Diary," 1994, p. 7). But more interestingly, the popularity of regional language channels (which broadcast in Indian languages other than Hindi) is growing rapidly. For instance, viewership of Sun TV, a Tamil channel, increased from 43,000 households in July 1993 to 147,000 households in December the same year (Sun TV, 1993, p. 1). Asianet, a south Indian communications company which offers a channel in Malayalam, has an estimated 1,977,000 viewers in India. Other popular south Indian language channels include Udaya TV and Eenadu TV in Kannada and Telugu languages, respectively.

The viewership of these regional language channels provides a rich location at which to frame questions of television and national identity. Is the popularity of the regional Indian language channels a statement about the condition of national unity in India? Is this a trend that impinges in any political way on the nation-state? Does it signal a fragmentation, away from the Indian state to sub-national units, particularly linguistic-political units, as a primary location of 'national' identity? In order to explore this question, it is essential to first clarify what is meant by 'national identity'.

National Identity

National and other collective identities have little existence outside of the meanings they are given by those who experience and articulate them. Hobsbawm and Ranger's (1983) idea of 'invented traditions' and Anderson's (1983) idea of the 'imagined community' perhaps epitomize this argument. Hobsbawm and Ranger (1983, p. 13) suggest that the lines delineating the 'us' of one nation from the 'them' of another are artificially drawn, by "what has been selected, written, pictured, popularized and institutionalized by those whose function it is to do so." In Gellner's (1964) oft-quoted remark on nationalist movements, "Nationalism is not the awakening of nations to self-consciousness: it invents nations where they do not exist" (p. 169). What all these authors are hinting at is the artificial or constructed nature of national identity. In doing so, they call into question the presumed 'naturalness' of this form of collective affiliation.

This is not to suggest an absence of any 'real' content to national identity. Without doubt, national identity is experienced by national subjects as 'real', but this experience is based on a *fictive* kinship. A nation is experienced as a fully extended family, with members seeing their nation as made up of interrelated families, forming one large "super-family" (Horowitz cited in Smith, 1991, p. 22) linked by mythical ties of filiation and ancestry. The centrality of the "family" metaphor to nationhood is epitomized by terms such as "motherland," "fatherland," and "father of the nation." In India, millions of children pledge solemnly each morning in school assemblies: "India is my country, and all Indians are my brothers and sisters." This is not a rational statement intended to represent a fact; no one is expected to believe that all Indians are brothers and sisters in a genetic sense. But, it is this *myth* of kinship---referred to as ethnicity---which characterizes national identity. As Connor (1993) suggests, it is not *what is* but *what people perceive as is* which determines the extent of national feeling (p. 377).

Connor (1993) thus suggests that the nation-as-family metaphor is not a rational feeling but an emotive one; it is a bond beyond reason appealing "not to the brain but to the blood" (p. 384). The myth of common ancestry is such an integral part of national psychology that it seeps even into the self-perception of nations constituted by ethnically diverse immigrant populations, such as the US. Thus, national identity is conceptualized as a perceived politico-cultural affiliation which is strongly rooted in a sense of territory, birth and belonging (Smith, 1991; Anderson, 1983; Connor, 1993).

The importance of national identity and nation-state to media studies is manifested in the debate around the role of communication technologies in identity formation and maintenance.[6] The mass media are seen as a powerful force for integration, though there is disagreement as to whether this is negative or positive (see Schudson, 1994, p. 76; Garnham, 1993). In the negative sense, the mass media are seen as destroyers of 'original', 'pure' cultures, and harbingers of homogeneity, both common themes in cultural imperialism and globalisation debates (Schiller, 1984; Webster and Robins, 1986). In the positive sense, the mass media are portrayed as nation-builders, as a benevolent force "assimilating different peoples to a common, civil culture" (Schudson, 1994, p. 76). Prime proponents of this view are modernization theorists such as Lerner (1958), Schramm (1964), and Pool (1983).

Juxtaposing these ideas with "active" audience theory brings further conflicts to the surface. The active audience theory reasserts the capacity, and indeed the inclination of audiences to use and interpret cultural materials in diverse ways (Radway, 1984; Ang, 1985; Liebes & Katz, 1990; Dowmunt, 1993). The power of this argument compels one to rethink the notion of media influence in a profound way: if audiences read media texts in divergent ways, then how is it possible to talk of undifferentiated, uniform effects over entire national cultures? Indeed, what is a national culture? And, if the notion of a national culture is problematic, is it not important also to see how producers of media texts imagine their own nationhood? Surely, a diversity of imagination exists there too rather than only at the audience end of the continuum.

Imaginings of Professional Broadcasters

Martin-Barbero (1993) suggests that before we start theorizing the relationship between media and national identity, it is important to first problematize the idea of collectivities as monolithic entities and to acknowledge their predilection for internal differentiation. Only with this nuanced understanding of collectivities can one begin to ask questions of how the media may impinge on processes of identity-formation. There are many avenues through which we can usefully implement this mandate. Most obviously, empirical evidence may be collected to indicate the range of experiences which constitute 'Indianness' to media audiences. Or we may conduct a semiotic analysis of media texts which carry embedded messages about what it means to be 'Indian'. Here, a third strategy is proposed: an examination of producers' imaginings of nationhood.

Hartley (1992) argues that, "the way in which professional producers imagine audiences is particularly important, as it determines to some extent what goes on the air, and it may help to explain why the industry acts as it does" (p. 103). If this is true, then it seems even more important to understand how professional producers imagine *themselves* and how they articulate their own feelings of nationhood; this would indicate how the industry *thinks*, not only how it acts. The literature on this is relatively scarce compared to the extensive literature on audience readings of texts, audience reception, and audience uses of and gratifications derived from media content (Jensen, 1990; Allen, 1987; Hall, 1994; White, 1987; Morley, 1980; Philo, 1990; Rubin, 1994; Katz, Blumler & Gurevitch, 1974).

The study of producers has a number of advantages. First, it enables us to probe Anderson's (1983) suggestion that "... in the 'nation-building' policies of the new states one sees both a genuine, even Machiavellian, instilling of nationalist ideology through the mass media..." (p. 104). Anderson is implying here that media producers carry with them a homogeneous articulation of national identity---the experience of Indianness would then be uniformly the same to all producers, and this uniformity would be 'transmitted' to media consumers through media products. Earlier, Hobsbawm and Ranger (1983) made a similar suggestion; they see national identity as based on markers that have "been selected, written, pictured, popularized and institutionalized by those whose function it is to do so" (p. 13). This assumption will be questioned by observing the range of positions occupied by producers with regard to national identity.

Studying producers' imaginings of nationhood has another advantage. As they are at the same time producers and consumers of media products, they articulate nationhood in two possibly distinct registers. One, (government-employed) producers may speak for the state. In this role, they are fulfilling the 'nation-building' activity that Anderson (1983) refers to. However, they are simultaneously speaking from particular, local discursive positions. That is, they speak from their Hindi-ness, their Hindu-ness, their Delhi-ness, their Tamil-ness, etc. By analyzing their talk, therefore, we can gain access to the dynamics between these different positions, and through this, we are able to question and problematize the deeply differentiated, non-monolithic nature of national identity. What we come up with, then, is an ambivalent, diversely inflected theme of the Indian nation as united in diversity.

The broadcasters represented below were drawn from: (a) the Indian Ministry of Information and Broadcasting; (b) Doordarshan; and (c) privately-owned Indian language channels. The Ministry of Information and Broadcasting is headed by a minister and a secretary who are the key persons responsible for the generation and implementation of broadcasting policy in India. The secretary of the Information and Broadcasting Ministry was interviewed as part of this research. Doordarshan representatives were drawn from both the central office in New Delhi as well as the regional offices called *Kendras*. The interviewees in New Delhi were officials holding key positions in the central headquarters. Station directors, who are responsible for Doordarshan broadcasts within their state, were also interviewed. Representatives from the privately-owned Indian language channels were drawn from the regional stations in south and north India.

The data were collected through personal interviews with the individual broadcasters. The aims of the interviews were: 1) to clarify the meanings of common concepts and opinions, 2) to distinguish the decisive elements of an expressed opinion, 3) to determine what influenced a person to form an opinion or to act in a certain way, 4) to classify complex attitude patterns, and 5) to understand the interpretations that people attribute to their motivations to act (Lazarsfeld's description of the aims of interviews as paraphrased by Lindlof, 1995). Among the examples that follow are a few extracts from audience interviews. I present these to indicate that the frames of Indianness below are not exclusive to producers, but are shared by audiences as well.

Notions of Indianness

India, a country of sub-continental proportions is 3214 kilometers long and 2933 kilometers wide. It is home to more than 900 million people of at least six racial strains[7] and six major religious groups[8] (Mathew, 1995). It has 18 officially recognized languages[9] (Mathew, 1995), and an estimated 1652 'mother tongues'[10] (Srivastava, 1990 p. 37). Many of these are mutually unintelligible, belonging as they do to 6 distinct language groups[11] (Mathew, 1995).

India is thus a nation-state, heterogeneous in terms of race, language, and religion. Notions of collective social identity in India center around all these nodes, and this bewildering diversity of affiliative threads that criss-crosses the nation results in a national identity fraught with contradictions, dilemmas and disputes (though these problems are not unique to the Indian case). Indian nationalists believe that to emphasize the differences is to restrict one's vision to the superficial. Beneath the diversity, they argue, India is a land of one people---the 'Indians' (see for instance Vijay, 1983).

As discussed earlier, definitions of nationhood are almost always sites of contestation. As Smith (1991) points out, "some of the most bitter and protracted 'inter-national' conflicts derive from competing claims and conceptions of national identity" (p. viii). Conflicts have been initiated in the name of territory, race, language, religion, historical bonds, reflecting the diverse ways in which the same nation can be imagined by fellow nationals. In this chapter, the focus is on two recurring backdrops against which differing conceptions of national identity have been set: First, the antique-modern continuum, and second, the particular-general continuum, both of which are especially relevant to the Indian case. The first is relevant because nationalists often base their claim to India's legitimacy on the claim to a long shared history, and the second because the nation-state is at the same time so fraught with internal diversity.

This is not in any way an exhaustive typology of definitions of Indianness[12]. These divisions are suggested only as indicative of complex and possibly limitless ways of experiencing nationhood.

Continuum 1: Antique-Modern

The antique-modern continuum can perhaps be best understood by referring to two oppositional notions that emerged in the Indian independence movement and continue to be contested to the present day. One of them conceptualizes Indian history as stretching back a very long, inevitably inestimable, time (more than nine hundred thousand years by some accounts[13]), and sees the modern Indian nation-state as deriving legitimacy primarily from this claim to antiquity; "Legitimacy is a function," as Wallerstein (1991) suggests "among other things, of duration" (p. 132). This antiquity is often seen as constituted by India's Hindu[14] past.

The other strand sees India as a modern construct, emphasizing India's constructedness as the 'us' against the British 'them', and in more extreme form, advocating the replacement of all that was old and therefore 'backward' with all that was new, 'western', and therefore progressive (see Oommen, 1990). It is sometimes argued that the dominant political imagination at the time of independence was in favor of seeing India as a modern construct (see Kaviraj, 1994), but the truce within the antique/ modern dialectic has been more uneasy than this suggests. The current rise in Hindu nationalist feeling is a vociferous and increasingly popular manifestation of the 'antiquity' school.

Antique

The Hindu nationalist movement (the most public face of which is the Bharatiya Janata Party, a political party) seeks to define India in an essentialist way, by what its proponents see as the nation's Hindu roots. While it is true that the Indian nation-state was established along secular-pluralist lines, it is also true, as Smith (1991) notes that:

> The modern bureaucratic state... was captured by northern... Hindu elites, and they have been trying to weld together the many Indian regions and ethnic communities into a single secular, territorial nation by means of a series of interlocking institutions and cross-cutting ties and through Hindu myths,

symbols and customs. (p.113; Also see Das and Harindranath, 1995)

Look for instance at the following comments from a media consumer (initials of all respondents have been changed; SD is the researcher).

SD: Is India united?

NMT: We are united. Ask a Muslim, don't ask this question from a Hindu. We will say we are united, because we are Indians, born in India, we are 100% Indians. Ask those who themselves think that they are pro-Pakistan. Their leanings are towards Pakistan not towards India. Ask this question from the Muslims.

And later, reinforcing the fundamental nature of the religious divide,

NMT: They [the Muslims] don't like you [the Hindus]. When a cricket match is going on and Pakistan loses, they will hoot (i.e. heckle) like anything. These are actual facts, and everybody knows.

The generalized 'you' in NMT's statement refers (through the researcher) to the Hindu community. (S)he supports the Hindu fundamentalist discourse which is emerging as an essentialist and exclusivist means of defining national identity in India. This discourse of Hindu supremacy is an attempt to turn the clock back. It is the "regressive, the anachronistic, element in the national cultural story," concealing (not well in NMT's case) "a struggle to mobilize 'the people' to purify their ranks, to expel the 'others' who threaten their identity, and to gird their loins for a new march forwards" (Hall, 1992, p. 295). It is an attempt to return to a mythical time when the nation was 'great', and relies on a presumed sense of purity in the national people. But of course, this is an impossible aspiration---most modern nations were unified through processes of violent conquest. Even 'the British people', as Hall (1992) shows, "are the product of a series of such conquests---Celtic, Roman, Saxon, Viking and Norman. Throughout Europe, the story is repeated *ad nauseum*" (p.295). The same is certainly true in the case of India, where wave upon wave of cultural and military settlements and conquests have resulted in the multi-layered texture of the Indian nation-state. Following is another instance of a similar articulation of Indianness from an interview with a Doordarshan official, in which the 'ancient' and 'Hindu' themes are clearly forefronted:

> SLT: You're talking of historicity over three thousand years or two thousand years. ...even in the earliest literatures in scriptures or otherwise..., India is referred to as one land. [...] Let's take the folklore of Ramayan for example. A north Indian king goes all the way down to south India. ...

Here, the example chosen to strengthen the point about India's claim to antiquity is that of the *Ramayana*. The *Ramayana* is a Hindu religious text but SLT makes it stand as a cultural artifact of 'Indianness', not just of Hinduism. At another level, the *Ramayana* is a religious text spawned of Aryan Hinduism; Dravidian religious practice which pre-dates Aryan Hinduism in India, is marginalized by this equation of *'Ramayana'* and 'Hindu'.

This pattern is repeated by another Doordarshan official; modern India is again seen as being constituted in ancient history, and this ancient history is linked intimately with religious structures:

> CH: Historically, India has been an entity. ... you will see the identity emerge in terms of religious structures more than anything else. The fact that the Shankaracharya (a Hindu thinker who lived in 8th c. A.D.) could in fact move around India, what was India then? There was no India. But he moved across this land mass. ... The invaders who came in underscore this point. Every time they'd come, whether it was the Afghans or whether it was the Turks, all of them came because they saw 'Hindustan'.

Note again the conflation of India and Hindu, evident in the equation of 'invaders', and 'Muslim'. Again, this example picks up the question raised earlier in the section---is it possible to define with any conviction an 'original' national population? By naming the Muslims as 'the invaders', CH names, by implication, the pre-Muslim inhabitants, i.e. the Aryans, as the 'true' owners of the national space. This argument is premised on an Indian history that starts after Aryan conquest and settlement (for the debates around the veracity of the Aryan invasion, see Deshpande, 1994, p. 1865), and thus marginalises an entire history of the subjugation of the original tribes of India, now called *vanavasis* or forest-dwellers[15] (see Oommen, 1990; 1994). It is believed that the area now covered by India was once home to Dravidian people, who were gradually pushed south by Aryans coming in from the North. This theory is based largely on speculation, of course, as is much ancient history, but seals and inscriptions recovered from the Mohenjodaro and Harrappa civilizations (in present-day Punjab and Baluchistan) of 2500 BC seem to belong to the Dravidian language group, rather than the Indo-Aryan one which now predominates in northern India. Also, there still remains a pocket of Dravidian speech on the Pakistan-Afghanistan border---the language Brahui which is spoken by about 250,000 people in the highlands of Baluchistan (Marr, 1975, p. 31).

As Oommen (1990) indicates:

> There are several routes through which a people come to identify themselves with a territory: birth, immigration, colonization and conquest. The first is the most natural in that the legitimacy of such identification is not contested. The last is the most problematic in that one has to gradually convert a claim based on physical force into a moral claim.
> (p. 11)

It is for this reason that narratives of power within what is now known as the 'Indian' population are hidden away or collectively 'forgotten' by large sections of the population. As Renan remarks, "these violent beginnings which stand at the origins of modern nations have first to be 'forgotten' before allegiance to a more unified, homogeneous national identity could begin to be forged" (cited in Hall, 1992, p. 297).

Modern

In this formulation, it is primarily the fact of being a nation-state as part of the modern world-system which gives rise to national identity. National identity here becomes more a political than a cultural construct. Oommen (1990) suggests that as

'Indian consciousness' emerged during the movement for liberation from the British, 'national' becomes more a political than a cultural referent in India (p. 39). Such a framework demands that aspects of culture which highlight internal differentiation, signaling them as locations of contestation, are made secondary and unimportant. Two examples of this come from officials in the Indian Ministry of Information and Broadcasting.

> CH: If you go to Tamil Nad, if you go to Kerala, the same institutions, the same structures, exist there and work perfectly in harmony with the people of that place. The same structures exist in the northeast. Same structures exist in the east and the west and the north. So it's really this which, .. whatever you want to call it ... you want to call it a network of television stations, or a network of post offices, or a network of railways, they're great unifying things.

And similarly,

> SLT: There is a very, very remote connection (between Indianness and language), nothing beyond that. Depends on what hat you want to wear. Do you want to be a chauvinist ... while you're just speaking a language ...? Or do you want to be wearing the hat of an Indian, who as a free citizen of this country, is free to adopt any religion, free to speak anything he wants, in any manner that he wants.

Note how, in the second excerpt, the connection between language and nationhood is made insignificant in an exaggerated ("very, very remote connection") manner. What is noteworthy in this example is not the idea of linguistic or cultural chauvinism he refers to, but the vehemence with which the uneasy connection between Indianness and language is denied.

Here is an example where the respondent not only highlights points of internal difference in the Indian polity, but celebrates this diversity, thus turning it from a potential threat into an asset:

> UDS: Because there are many languages, ...many languages; thousands of castes (*jaati*). There are no other places which, there are no other countries which have so much diversity,

are there?

SD: Is that good, or is that a problem?

UDS: It's good, isn't it? When people from outside see us, even if there are questions, the unity is still there, with many languages. There is so much difference but even then we are one.

SD: Are we one?

UDS: Even if there are small questions on the surface, we are still adjusting and carrying on, aren't we? Which is not true of any other country.

The above example from an audience member epitomizes the predominant 'nation-building' strategy adopted by the Indian state. In this strategy, India is presented as united in the face of all 'superficial' appearances of diversity. We return to this theme in the discussion on the 'general' mode of imagining India.

Continuum 2: Particular-General

The second continuum emerges from India's essentially pluralistic nature. The numerous axes along which the Indian state and society are divided---politically, linguistically, by religion, by caste---mean that an Indian is, along with being an Indian, always also something else. The author, for instance, apart from being an Indian, is also a Keralite,[16] a Malayalee,[17] a Hindu,[18] a Nair,[19] a middle-class urban-dwelling woman, etc. One's position on this axis is determined by which of these levels of identification is perceived as primary: the particular (regional, linguistic etc.) or the general (Indian).

The inevitability of flux on this continuum highlights the notion that every person possesses multiple identities, which can be seen as "a series of concentric points of reference whereby individuals participate in many different intersecting circles, none of which can command their individual allegiance" (Drummond, 1993, p. 3). This model points to differing strata of identification, each with its own level of (variable) potency. An intense loyalty felt by a large collectivity towards a nation may, at one moment, result in nationalistic struggles for statehood, as it did in the Indian case in the 1930s and 40s. However, the potency of this level of affiliation may wane once the immediate goal of statehood has been achieved, with a new circle of affiliation, for instance affiliation with the linguistic group, taking primary political place. It is important to note that such fluctuation need not result in an eventual resolution in the sense of 'true' and ultimate identification. Rather, identities are stories that are continually unfolding, that are always formed in the past and are always to be formed in the future (see Hall, 1995).

Particular

The 'particular' refers to that mode of imagining India in which the existence of strong affiliative ties to collectivities smaller than the Indian state is acknowledged, legitimized, and considered more 'authentic' than ties to the larger nation-state. This sentiment, when very intense, may contribute to separatist movements. Notice the tendency in the following respondent to forefront the differences between the various geographical regions of India, and his/her professed affiliation with a linguistic region as the 'national' group.

SD: If I asked you which country do you really belong to, would you be able to answer?

ULK: Most likely I have to say that I am a Keralite.

SD: Can you identify with something called India?

ULK: See, normally we say integration. Many people defer to that. Mainly because we are not having a common culture, no common values, no common psyche. So what commonality is there?

ULK (an audience member) argues that if there was true unity among the people of India---i.e. unity in cultures, values, or psyche---then there would be no need for national integration projects (such as the television short films discussed during the interview). Another audience member makes a similar point:

QLT: I'm really surprised that after forty-eight years of independence we have got to really remind ourselves that we are Indians. I'm ashamed of it, aren't you? I wouldn't like a foreigner to see that film at all. It's not a new country where you've got to have this kind of film to show you that these are Indians .... No! We should have known this much earlier!

Note this respondent's ambivalent use of 'we'. 'We' are the Indians, and in that sense he is part of this collectivity, but 'we' are also an object of shame for not being fully constituted as a collectivity ---"It's not a new country where you've got to have this kind of film to show you that these are Indians ... No! We should have known this much earlier!" (The films QLT refers to are short television films on national integration). But the 'them', the foreigners, are decidedly those who do not belong to Indian territory, and further, according to QLT, they seem to come from countries with a well-developed sense of national identity. Thus the feeling of shame for India in comparison to them.

Here is another example of the particularistic mode of identification, this time from a senior producer of a regional language channel in south India.

TL:...all along, we've emphasized national integration in some kind of perverse sense, as some kind of foisted national identity, which comes from Delhi. But the Delhi-centric view of national integration obviously isn't serving the purpose. (But) ...you're a Malayalee first, you're a Tamilian first, a Telugu first, an Oriya first, a Bengali first and there's a sense of fulsomeness in that identity. ... Indianness comes from that. ... I can't say I'm an Indian first and a Malayalee next you know, because that's like not being rooted. ... It doesn't work that way, you go from the particular to the general and that's the right way to go.

A similar particularistic mode of identification is evident in the response of a senior producer of a Tamil language channel.

LN: (If Tamil television cuts off people's exposure to Hindi), it's not the television. The reason why I'm

> watching Tamil programs is because I don't know Hindi.
> I can't follow Hindi. That's the case with everybody. ...
> In fact, if you take the statistics of Tamil Nadu, 98%
> don't know Hindi. People don't know Hindi. That being
> the scenario, what can I do about it?

Note how the discourse of difference is cloaked in the language of pragmatism. The tension surrounding the Hindi language in Tamil-speaking territory is taken as a starting point, rather than as something demanding exploration and deliberation. By using the market as the apparent prime definer of what is broadcast, this person is in effect legitimizing Tamil Indian identity as separate from the Hindi Indian identity.

This point is underlined by the first respondent in his delineation of the phases of nationhood. In this formulation, he creates space for particularistic modes of identification as a valid and indeed natural way of experiencing nationhood.

> TL: I think in the history of a nation, there will be a phase ...
> of consensual identity. Because you're fighting the British,
> because you're talking about national independence and
> national liberation, there was a need for that kind of phase.
> After that, you evolve into a different phase ... you evolve
> into a phase of truly identifying yourself as *part* of a nation,
> and it is the process of identifying yourself as *part* of a nation
> that sometimes tends to be called separatist.

Particularistic identification becomes, in this formulation, a natural phase of the evolution of the nation-state. This view is more commonly articulated in the south of India, where Hindi is and has been uneasily received as the official language. The presence of particularistic identification as a common mode of identification seems indicative of resistance to two ideas---first, mainstream India as Hindi-speaking, and second, the centralization of political power in northern, Hindi-speaking India.

General

By 'general' mode of identification, is meant the idea of India as defined by a sense of unity rather than diversity. This mode does not rely on the denial of diversity, but only on placing it as secondary to the larger unified India.

The following response is from an owner/Chief Executive Officer (CEO) of a Tamil television channel who tries to define the mainstream by reference to external comparisons, rather than internal divisions. That is, India is defined by its difference from what is territorially not India, rather than what is within Indian territory. The only legitimate mark of Indianness becomes loyalty to the nation, as defined by lack of loyalty to the 'other'.

> LN: ... me watching a Tamil language program doesn't mean I'm out of the mainstream. Right? Me supporting Pakistan is out of the mainstream. Or me supporting Sri Lanka is out of the mainstream. ... Me going to church doesn't mean I'm out of the mainstream. Mainstream is patriotism and loyalty to the nation. And mainstream has nothing to do with your religion or your language or your cultural background .... What about Indians who are sitting there in America for years, who are citizens there? (I don't) mean they're not patriotic to the US government; they are. But their roots are still in India, right?

Of interest here is the conflation of patriotism and mainstream, and the vociferous denial of any link between mainstream and language or religion. For LN, 'mainstream' seems to be a purely spatial construct, and is not seen as being impinged upon by any cultural factors.

And finally, the words of a private television producer, who has produced advertisements on national integration for Doordarshan. Even through his inability to articulate what his sense of Indianness is, he emphasizes the idea that there is an underlying cultural similarity that overrides external differences:

> QQ: Value systems (among Indians) don't differ. It's an expression which may be the result of the way that society evolved. The systems and the values, they have some common threads. ... I don't think it's easy to define.

What is remarkable in this example is that even a person charged with designing a media message to engender national identity remains unable to articulate in specific terms what constitutes this identity.

However, other examples suggest quite the opposite. They suggest the idea that resistance to the notion of nationhood can also arise only from knowledge of the latter, and that the existence of political unity need not involve cultural unity. This is exemplified by an audience member.

SD: Do you think there's something unifying the country?

> QLT: What unifies? Your dress itself is different. You're wearing *churidar* which is a north Indian dress, right? Every state has a different way of dressing, where is the unification? Can you symbolize the Indian woman in one particular dress? Can you imagine? Yes, you look at a foreigner, you say a British woman would be this. Right? American is like this or a (Chinese) is like this, or a Taiwanese will be like this. You can straight-away say that.

An interesting illustration of internal contradiction emerges from the above excerpt. QLT considers British/ American/ Chinese/ Taiwanese as 'them', signaled clearly in using the term 'foreigner'. While QLT is articulating doubt about the existence of cultural similarity within India, QLT nevertheless uses 'us' to relate to this very same India.

Conclusion

It is a fitting comment that while many of the above examples were obviously taken from statements of different respondents, many of the contradictory statements were often made by the same person. This emphasizes the confused and inevitably paradoxical nature of national identity, and such evidence is crucial to the globalisation debate---it suggests that we must weave in an understanding of the manner in which new communication technologies are facilitating not only new *global* identities, but also new *local* identities. With the trend towards more global interdependence, Hall (1992) notes:

> national identities remain strong ... especially with respect to such things as legal and citizenship rights, but local, regional and community identities have become more significant. Above the level of national culture, 'global' identifications

begin to displace, and sometimes override, national ones. (p. 302)

In the Indian case, the emergence and initial popularity of STAR TV and its primarily Western programming suggested that the 'cultural supermarket' had arrived in the country. It seemed that Indian identities would be disembedded from their 'local' moorings and tied into supra-national levels of affiliation. It seemed that the consumerisation which would inevitably result from this 'cultural supermarket' would erode the sovereignty of the nation-state to control and define its own cultural destiny, and that the West was winning its post-colonial cultural battles through the airwaves.

In this chapter, the possible problems with such hypotheses have been illustrated. While it may still be true that 'globalisation' is not quite as 'historical' and 'transnational' as some of its proponents make it out to be, at the same time, local identities are on offer. I have tried to show how these local identities, as obtained from producers' imaginings, are articulating themselves in India through, *inter alia*, the fragmenting, regionalised media market. These new localized media (relying paradoxically on global technologies) may not only fulfill the needs of emerging local identities, they are at the same time fueled by them.

As illustrated in this chapter, the idea of an overarching national identity is a problematic one; studies attempting to define the role of the media in the process of national identity formation must be informed by this realization. I do not hesitate to accept the central role the media play in developing national identity in the modern state. As Anderson (1983) points out, these are imagined communities heavily reliant on representations for their persistence through time. Mass communications are central to the production and distribution of such representations. However, one must be wary not to draw hasty conclusions about the relationship between the two. As Schlesinger (1991) says:

> ... we now need to turn around the terms of the conventional argument: not to start with communication and its supposed effects on collective identity and culture, but rather to begin by posing the problem of collective identity itself, to ask how

it might be analyzed and what importance communicative practices might play in its constitution. (p. 307)

The examples and discussion in this chapter are intended to throw a few incipient ideas into the ring to set off an empirical examination of the diversity inherent in national identities. This chapter, then, is a limited exercise in that sense; presuming only to start-off the process of questioning. It is also limited in the sense that it asks the reader to take broadcasters' assumptions at face value. Needless to say, broadcasters' public statements are made within constraints imposed by their public position. However, I have desisted from merely quoting them unproblematically, choosing instead to ferret-out underlying assumptions and contradictions in these statements in order to illustrate some of the discursive positions they adopt in articulating Indianness. A possible bias in this methodology is that it is assumed (as opposed to demonstrated) that officials' notions of Indianness will be a factor in deciding what kind of programming is broadcast.

Notes

[1] This is a conservative estimate. It has proved difficult to find official statistics for the number of channels broadcasting into India.

[2] Chennai is the new name for Madras. Also, Bombay is now renamed as Mumbai.

[3] 7.2 million by Chan's (1994) estimate.

[4] A few households have privately-owned satellite dishes. For the most part, however, reception equipment is owned by small entrepreneurs who re-transmit satellite signals via local-area cable to surrounding households for a small monthly or annual fee.

[5] This includes their film-based programs.

[6] For an exhaustive overview of the debates in the area, see Tomlinson (1991).

[7] Proto-Australoids, Mongoloids, Mediterranean or Dravidian, Western Brachycephalis, and Nordic Aryans.

[8] Hindus, Muslims, Christians, Sikhs, Buddhists, Jains, and other religions.

[9] The Constitution originally recognized 15 languages in its 8th Schedule - Assamese, Bengali, Gujarati, Hindi, Kannada, Kashmiri, Malayalam, Marathi, Oriya, Punjabi, Sanskrit, Tamil, Telugu, Urdu, Sindhi. But, three more---Konkani, Manipuri, Nepali---were added in 1992.

[10] This figure is from the 1961 census. It represents the number of respondent-reported mother tongues. For a discussion of problems with such estimates, see Oommen (1992).

[11] Negroid, Austric, Sino-Tibetan, Dravidian, Indo-Aryan, and others.

[12] For an elaboration of the debate on what constitutes Indian culture, see Deshpande, G.P. (1994) "'The Kingdome of Darknesse' or the Problem of Culture" in *Economic and Political Weekly*, July 16th 1994.

[13] See G Pandey (1994a) "Modes of History Writing: New Hindu history of Ayodhya" *Economic and Political Weekly* June 18th 1994, pp.1523-1528 for a fascinating account of recent Hindu revisionist history. See also G. Pandey (1994b) "The new Hindu history" in *South Asia*, Vol. XVII, Special Issue, pp. 97-112.

[14] I use the term 'Hindu' here to refer to the people who profess to, or are categorized as belonging to, the Hindu religion. The term is sometimes understood as a collective for the inhabitants of *Hindustan*, the territory. For a discussion, see Oommen, T.K. (1994) "Religious nationalism and democratic polity: The Indian case" in *Sociology of Religion* 55:4, pp.455-472.

[15] The 400-odd tribal communities of India claim to be the original inhabitants of the land, or 'first people' in Bennett and Blundell's (1995), "First peoples" in *Cultural Studies*, 9:1, pp. 1-10) terms. But Hindu nationalists reject this claim, insisting that Aryan Hindus were the original settlers (Oommen, 1994:459).

[16] The administrative state

[17] The linguistic group

[18] The religious group

[19] The caste group

References

Allen, R. C. (1987). Talking about television. In R. C. Allen (Ed.), *Channels of discourse: Television and contemporary criticism.* London: Methuen.

Anderson, B. (1983). *Imagined communities: Reflections on the origin and spread of nationalism.* London: Verso.

Ang, I. (1985). *The melodramatic imagination.* London: Methuen.

Bennet, & Blundell. (1995). "First Peoples." *Cultural Studies,* 9:1, pp. 1-10.

Chan, J.M. (1994). National responses and accessibility to STAR TV in Asia. *Journal of Communication, 44*(3), 113-131.

Connor, W. (1993, July). Beyond reason: The nature of the ethnonational bond. *Ethnic and Racial Studies, 16*(3), pp.373-389.

Das, S., & Harindranath, R. (1995). *Nation-state, national identity and the media.* Leicester: Centre for Mass Communication Research.

Deshpande, G. P. (1994, July 16). 'The kingdome of darknesse' or the problem of culture. *Economic and Political Weekly,* pp.1864-1867.

Dowmunt, T. (Ed.). (1993). *Channels of resistance.* London: Channel Four Television.

Drummond, P. (1993). Introduction: Collective identity, television, and Europe. In P. Drummond (Ed.), *National identity and Europe: The television revolution.* (pp. 1-8). London: BFI.

Garnham, N. (1993). The mass media, cultural identity and the public sphere in the modern world. *Public Culture, 5,* 251-265.

Gellner, E. (1964). *Thought and change.* London: Weidenfield and Nicholson.

Hall, S. (1992). The question of cultural identity. In S. Hall, D. Held, & T. McGrew (Eds.), *Modernity and its futures.* pp. 273-324. Cambridge: Polity Press, in association with Open University Press.

Hall, S. (1994). Encoding/ decoding. In D. Graddol, & O. Boyd-Barrett (Eds.), *Media texts: Authors and readers.* pp. 200-211.

Clevedon: Multilingual Matters, in association with The Open University.

Hall, S. (1995). Negotiating Caribbean identities. *New Left Review, 209,* 3-14.

Hartley, J. (1992). *Tele-ology: Studies in television.* London: Routledge.

Hobsbawm, E., & Ranger, T. (1983). *The invention of tradition.* Cambridge: Cambridge University Press.

Jensen, K. B. (1990). When is meaning? Communication theory, pragmatism, and mass media reception. *Communication Yearbook 14.* London: Sage.

Katz, E., Blumler, J., & Gurevitch, M. (1974). Utilization of Mass Communication by the Individual. In J. Blumler and E. Katz (Eds.), *The uses of mass communication,* pp. 19-32. London: Sage.

Kaviraj, S. (1994). Crisis of the nation-state in India. *Political Studies, 42,* 115-129.

Lerner, D. (1958). *The passing of the traditional society.* New York: Free Press.

Liebes, T., & Katz, E. (1990). *The export of meaning: Cross-cultural interpretations of Dallas.* New York: Oxford University Press.

Lindlof, T. (1995). *Qualitative communication research methods.* Thousand Oaks: Sage.

Market diary. (1994, December 21). *Economic Times,* p. 7.

Marr, J. P. (1975). The early Dravidians. In A. L. Basham (Ed.), *A cultural history of India.* Oxford: Clarendon Press.

Martin-Barbero, J. (1993). *Communication, culture and hegemony: From the media to mediations.* London: Sage.

Mathew, M. (Ed.). (1995). *Manorama yearbook 1995.* Kottayam: Malayala Manorama Company Limited.

Morley, D. (1980). *The nationwide audience.* London: British Film Institute.

Oommen, T. K. (1990). *State and society in India: Studies in nation-building.* New Delhi: Sage.

Oommen, T. K. (1992). Contradictions in language policies in independent India. *Media Development, 1,* 19-21.

Oommen, T. K. (1994). Religious nationalism and democratic polity: The Indian case. *Sociology of Religion, 55*(4), 455-472.

Pandey, G. (1994a, June 18). "Modes of History Writing: New Hindu History of Ayodhya." *Economic and Political Weekly,* pp. 1523- 1528.

Pandey, G. (1994b). "The New Hindu History." *South Asia,* Vol XVII, Special Issue, pp. 97-112.

Philo, G. (1990). *Seeing and believing: The influences of television.* London: Routledge.

Pool, I de S. (1983). *Technologies of freedom.* Cambridge: Harvard University Press.

Radway, J. (1984). *Reading the romance.* Chapel Hill: University of North Carolina Press.

Rubin, A.M. (1994). Media uses and effects: A uses-and-gratifications perspective. In J. Bryant & D. Zilman (Eds.). *Media effects: Advances in theory and research* (pp. 417-436). Hillsdale, N.J.: Lawrence Erlbaum Associates.

Schiller, H. (1984) *Information and the crisis economy.* Norwood: Ablex.

Schlesinger, P. (1991). *Media, state and nation: Political violence and collective identities.* London: Sage.

Schramm, W. (1964). *Mass media and national development.* California: Stanford University Press.

Schudson, M. (1994). Culture and the integration of national societies. *International Social Science Journal, 139, 63*-81.

Smith, A. D. (1991). *National identity.* London: Penguin Books.

Srivastava, A. K. (1990). Multilingualism and school education in India: Special features, problems and prospects. In D. P. Pattanayak (Ed.), *Multilingualism in India..*Clevedon: Multilingual Matters.

Sun TV. (1993). *Viewership survey.* Madras: Sun TV.

Television listings. (1996, June 26). *The Hindu,* p. 5.

Tomlinson, J. (1991). *Cultural imperialism.* London: Pinter.

Vijay. (1983). *India is one.* Pondicherry: Shri Aurobindo Society.

Wallerstein, I. (Ed.). (1991). *Unthinking social science: The limits of nineteenth century paradigms.* Cambridge: Polity Press.

Webster, F., & Robins, K. (1986). *Information technology: A luddite answer.* Norwood: Ablex.

White, M. (1987). Ideological analysis and television. In R. C. Allen (Ed.), *Channels of discourse: Television and contemporary criticism*. London: Methuen.

Chapter 9

Use of STAR TV and Doordarshan in India: An Audience-Centered Case Study of Chennai City[1]

Srinivas R. Melkote
B.P. Sanjay
Syed Amjad Ahmed

The growth of STAR viewership has been phenomenal. From a start of 412,000 homes in January 1992 the numbers went up to nearly 1.3 million urban homes by the end of 1992, an increase of nearly 211 percent. This made India the biggest audience in the 38-nation footprint of STAR's four English-language channels ("The New TV," 1992). However, STAR's staggering growth still dwarfs in the face of Doordarshan television's coverage in India. Doordarshan has a total reach of nearly 125 million in urban areas and nearly 75 million in the rural areas. Doordarshan and STAR, the two major television networks available to the urban Indian viewer, represent distinctly different types of ownership pattern and control. Doordarshan, until recently, was state-owned and controlled. It has had a history of being used by the political party in power in New Delhi to further its political agenda. STAR television, on the other hand, represents global market interests and serves as a vehicle for multinational corporations involved in program production and advertising agencies to penetrate into hitherto "protected" areas in the Third World

The popularity of STAR not only threatened the virtual monopoly held by Doordarshan but also started a process of penetration by other satellite-based television networks. STAR television, then, is to be credited with starting India's satellite revolution. Indian audiences starved for "infotainment" programs have responded very well to the novelty of satellite television. *India Today* (November 15, 1992) had this to say:

> In fact, the two STAR Plus re-runs became such a rage with Indian viewers that last May, STAR rescheduled the Sun Belt melodramas to local prime time. More dramatically, both the soaps are sponsored by Indian advertisers. Godrej sponsors *The Bold and the Beautiful* while *Santa Barbara* comes courtesy of Real Value Appliances (p. 24)

What then is the impact of STAR television on Indian viewers? There has been no mass medium that so quickly garnered such huge numbers of viewers and changed the face of television entertainment in India. Most of the media effects research in India has focused on the source or the channel of communication. For example, there is a respectable body of research in the areas of development communication and diffusion of innovations that have investigated the effects of media from the point of view of the source or the medium (See Shingi & Mody, 1976; Rogers, 1983). While a plethora of research exists on the effects of communication, there is a glaring gap in studies examining uses of the mass media from the perspective of the individual media users in India (Yadava & Reddi, 1988). With the exception of a few studies (ex. Reddi, 1985; Yadava & Reddi, 1988) which have examined factors influencing patterns of media use among adolescents and urban populations, most mass media research in India has focused on the media as agents of development (or effects). Other kinds of audience-centered research studies in India are the television viewer profiles periodically conducted by the research divisions of Doordarshan. These studies center chiefly on the popularity of programs, the peak listening hours, and program preferences of viewers. The research studies rarely consider the "emotional, social and physical needs of their audiences" (Doshi & Agrawal, 1989:220). This study is one of a few that attempts to bridge the gap in the area of audience-centered investigations in India. It is in the forefront of investigations in India that examine audience-media relationships chiefly from the perspective of the individual audience member. It attempts to understand why people watch STAR TV and Doordarshan and the gratifications derived from watching these channels. Scholars have studied the uses people make of the media. In the early 1940s, Herta Herzog investigated the radio listening habits of women and examined the satisfaction they derived from daytime radio serials (Herzog, 1944). Another early study used the occasion of a newspaper strike to study why people read the newspaper (Berelson, 1949). These studies were the forerunners of a type of research that was later labeled as the uses and gratifications perspective. This perspective has been employed in this study to provide the theoretical underpinnings for the audience-media interaction. Katz, Blumler, and Gurevitch (1974), Rosengren (1974), and a host of other scholars described the uses and gratification perspective and did seminal work in this area during its initial conceptualization. Rubin (1994) describes the uses and gratifications as "a psychological communication perspective that shifts the focus of inquiry from the mechanistic perspective's interest in direct effects of media on receivers to assessing how people use the media" (p. 418). Rubin (1994) summarizes the work done in the area of uses and gratifications by distilling the main assumptions on which this body of research is grounded:

> (a) Communication behavior, including media selection and use, is goal-directed, purposive, and motivated. People are relatively active communication participants who choose media or content. The behavior is functional and has consequences for people and societies (p. 420);
> (b) People take the initiative in selecting and using communication vehicles to satisfy felt needs or desires. Instead of being used by the media, people use and select media to gratify their needs or wants (Rubin, 1994, p. 420; Katz, Gurevitch, & Haas, 1973).

The uses and gratifications perspective also states that media compete with other types of communication for audience attention (Rubin, 1994). In this study, we use the uses and gratifications theory to specifically examine competition among different channels of television (STAR and Doordarshan) for audience selection, attention, and use to gratify their needs or wants. And, we apply the uses and gratifications perspective to a new population---India's urban television audiences.

The present study has adopted a quantitative, empirical approach to study audience use of media. Within this methodology, there are many strategies that may be employed (Becker, 1979). A commonly used method is one in which the researcher provides the respondents with a list of motivations for media exposure and asks them to select and describe their motivations. It is this methodology that has inspired the growth of various typologies over time, typologies that have been used and refined by scholars working to conceptualize an exhaustive list of motivations (see Katz et al., 1973; McQuail, Blumler & Brown, 1972; Blumler & Katz, 1974; McGuire, 1974; Rubin, 1994).

Hypotheses

Based on a review of uses and gratifications literature and the popularity of STAR programs, several research hypotheses were proposed for this study:

1. There will be a significant difference between the frequency of viewing preferred program types on STAR TV and Doordarshan.
2. There will be a significant difference in the perceptions about the quantity of different program types on STAR and Doordarshan.
3. There will be a significant difference in the satisfaction derived from STAR and Doordarshan programs
4. There will be a significant relationship between motivations for watching television and gratifications derived by watching television for both STAR and Doordarshan.

Operationalization of Variables

Motivations for viewing STAR TV/ Doordarshan

Motivations for watching the two channels were examined by a series of items measured on a four-point scale (strongly agree/ somewhat agree/ somewhat disagree/ strongly disagree). Respondents answered that he/she watched STAR TV/ Doordarshan: to relax; to be entertained; to learn things about oneself and others; to forget the daily routine; for companionship; to spend time usefully; to have a good time; to be able to talk with others about what is on TV; to learn to do things not done before; to learn more about things in India and abroad; to be with friends and family who are watching; to learn about other cultures.

Frequency of viewing preferred program types on STAR TV/ Doordarshan

This was measured by questionnaire items listed below which were measured on a four-point scale (Always/ Sometimes/ Rarely/ Never): Watch serials; watch music and dance programs; watch news; watch educational programs; watch sports programs; watch movies; watch variety programs; watch commercials.

Perception of quantity of different programming genres on STAR TV/ Doordarshan

This was examined by several items in the questionnaire measured on a three-point scale (Too Many/ Adequate/ Too few). The programming types examined were: News, Educational, Sports, Movies, Serials, Variety, Music and Song, and Children's programs.

Satisfaction with programs on STAR TV/ Doordarshan

Respondents were queried on their satisfaction with different programs (Very Satisfied/ Somewhat Satisfied/ Somewhat Dissatisfied/ Very Dissatisfied) such as: Children's shows, Music and Dance, Variety shows, Serials, Movies, Sports, Educational shows, and News.

Gratifications derived from viewing STAR TV/ Doordarshan

Gratifications derived from watching the two channels were examined by a series of items measured on a four-point scale (strongly agree/ somewhat agree/ somewhat disagree/ strongly disagree). Respondents answered that by viewing STAR TV/ Doordarshan he/she: felt relaxed; was entertained; gained new information; escaped monotonous routine; gained companionship; spent time usefully; and, was able to interact with friends and family while watching.

Population and Sample

This study was conducted in Chennai, a large metropolitan city in India. The researchers were interested in examining television viewing behavior of individuals who had access to a television set and viewed both STAR and Doordarshan channels on a regular basis. This population would then consist mostly of middle to upper middle class, the core viewing group for STAR programs. A judgment sample was chosen for the study. To ensure adequate representation, middle class neighborhoods were identified and questionnaires distributed to random households. Any one adult in the household who viewed the two channels regularly and was willing to participate in the survey was given a questionnaire to fill out. A total of 300 questionnaires were distributed.

A structured questionnaire containing all the items described earlier as well as questions requesting demographic information was used by trained interviewers to collect the data. A total of 150 questionnaires were completed and used for the analysis of data.

Data Analysis and Results

Motivations for watching STAR/Doordarshan

Questionnaire items dealing with motivations for watching STAR TV/ Doordarshan programs were subjected separately to principal axis factor analysis using the varimax method for rotation. Tables 9.1 and 9.2 present the results of the factor analysis. The data from Table 9.1 reveal that two motivation factors were extracted for watching STAR: *Learning about new things, places and cultures;* and *Pleasurable and relaxing activity.* Questionnaire items with a minimum loading of .40 on the two factors were included respectively in each of the two scales to constitute a summative index. The higher the score on these two scales, the higher was the agreement with the questionnaire items.

The data from Table 9.2 reveal that two motivation factors were extracted for watching Doordarshan: *Pleasurable and relaxing activity;* and *Learning about new things, places and cultures.* Questionnaire items with a minimum loading of .40 on the two factors were included in the scales to constitute a summative index The higher the score on these two scales, the higher was the agreement with the questionnaire items.

Table 9.1 Rotated Factor Matrix of Motivations for Watching STAR TV

Motivations	Learning about new things, places & cultures (Factor I)	Pleasurable & relaxing activity (Factor II)
Learn about other cultures	.6974	.0904
Learn about myself and others	.6334	.1421
Learn to do new things	.5893	.1355
Learn about India and abroad	.5834	.2020
To be entertained	.0768	.8973
To have a good time (enjoyable pastime)	.1487	.6358
Watch to relax	.1218	.5278
Watch to see interesting shows	.2871	.4375
Eigenvalue	4.37	1.25
Percent of variance explained	33.6	9.6
Reliability(Cronbach alpha)	0.83	0.79

From Tables 9.1 and 9.2, it may be seen that viewers had the same motivations for viewing both STAR and Doordarshan. However, the rank ordering of the motivations differed for the two channels. For STAR, the major motivation for watching the shows (variance explained: 34%) may be grouped under the label of *Learning about new things, places and cultures,* the second group of motivations (variance explained: 10%) falls under the category of *Pleasurable and relaxing activity.* In the case of Doordarshan, this ordering of motivations was reversed. *Pleasurable and relaxing activity* was the major motivation (variance explained: 41%), followed by *Learning about new things, places and cultures* (variance explained: 5%). These results suggest that the viewers viewed the two channels generally to relax and be entertained, while in the case of STAR a major motivation besides the pleasurable nature of the activity was to be informed about new places, things and cultures.

**Table 9. 2 Rotated Factor Matrix of Motivations
for Watching Doordarshan**

Motivations	Pleasurable & Relaxing Activity (Factor I)	Learn about new things, places, & cultures (Factor II)
Watch to be entertained	**.7734**	.3439
Watch to relax	**.7511**	.1508
Watch to have a good time (enjoyable pastime)	**.6108**	.3274
To see interesting shows	**.5750**	.3942
To learn new things	.1356	**.7031**
To learn about myself and others	.2892	**.5692**
To be introduced to other cultures	.3166	**.5314**
To learn about India and abroad	.3770	**.5193**
To talk about what is on	.2343	**.4821**
To be with friends and family	.1595	.3597
Eigenvalue	5.87	1.14
Pct. of variance explained	41.8	5.4
Reliability (Cronbach alpha)	0.88	0.83

Viewing frequency of programs on STAR and Doordarshan

The first hypothesis in this study posited that: There will be a significant difference between the frequency of viewing preferred program types on STAR TV and Doordarshan. To test this hypothesis, the viewing frequency of preferred program types, i.e. serials; music and dance programs; news; educational programs; sports programs; movies; variety programs; and, commercials for STAR and Doordarshan respectively were submitted to a repeated measures multivariate analysis of variance (MANOVA).

Mauchly's sphericity test (W= .02, p < .001) indicated that the dependent variables (i.e. program types) listed above were correlated. This would make it necessary to use the MANOVA instead of individual "t" tests. The MANOVA across the two television channels (see Table 9.3) was significant. Since there were nine dependent variables included simultaneously in this analysis, the significant difference indicated that there was at least one set of corresponding means (among the nine) for the two channels whose difference was greater than can be attributed to random sampling fluctuation.

Thus, the MANOVA indicated significant difference across the two channels' viewing frequency when the nine programming types were considered together. Univariate "F" tests were conducted to identify the individual programs on which there was significant differences between the two channels. Tables 9.3 and 9.4 list the results of the multivariate and the univariate tests.

Table 9. 3 Repeated Measure MANOVA Test Showing Differences Between STAR TV and Doordarshan Programs Viewing Frequency

Test	Value	F-Value (Within Subjects)	Hypoth. DF	Error DF	Significance of 'F'
Pillais	.51	12.71	9.0	109.0	p < .001
Hotelling	1.05	12.71	9.0	109.0	p < .001
Wilks	.49	12.71	9.0	109.0	p < .001

Table 9. 4 Univariate F tests Showing Differences Between Individual STAR TV and Doordarshan Program Viewing Frequency

Program Type	Hypoth. SS	Error SS	Hypoth. MS	Error MS	F
Serials	2.86	81.14	2.86	.69	4.13[C]
Music & Dance	8.97	82.03	8.97	.70	12.79[B]
News	.27	103.73	.27	.89	.31
Educational	6.44	56.06	6.44	.48	13.45[A]
Sports	51.27	72.73	51.27	.62	82.48[A]
Movies	.11	84.39	.11	.72	.15
Variety	17.36	69.44	17.36	.60	29.16[A]
Children's	12.82	59.68	12.82	.51	25.13[A]
Commercials	2.44	60.56	2.44	.52	4.72[C]

[A]$p<.0001$; [B]$p<.001$; [C]$p<.05$

Table 9. 5 Frequency of Viewing Preferred Programming Types on STAR TV & Doordarshan

Program	STAR Mean	Std. Dev	Doordarshan Mean	Std. Dev
Music & Dance	2.69[Aa]	0.91	2.31[Bb]	0.91
Educational	2.61[Aa]	0. 94	2.28[Bb]	0.92
Sports	3.30[Aa]	0.82	2.37[Bb]	1.04
Variety	2.88[Aa]	0.87	2.38[Bb]	0.91
Children's	2.53[Aa]	1.03	2.10[Bb]	1.03
Commercials	2.79[Aa]	0.95	2.61[Ab]	1.04

Note: For every program type in a row, means having different lowercase superscripts differed at the $p<.05$ level by an F test from the other mean in the same row. Similarly, means having different uppercase superscripts differed at the $p<.01$ level from the other mean in that row

Table 9.5 lists the mean scores for STAR and Doordarshan programs on which a significant difference was detected in Table 9.4. The results in Table 9.5 indicate quite clearly that viewers prefer to watch STAR over Doordarshan programs. In all the program categories listed in Table 9.5, i.e. music and dance; educational; sports; variety; children's; and commercials, preference for viewing STAR was significantly higher than Doordarshan. With the exception of the category of "commercials," the difference between STAR and Doordarshan was significant at p=.01; for the category of commercials, the difference was significant at p=.05.

Quantity of different programming types on STAR and Doordarshan

The second hypothesis for this study stated that: there will be a significant difference in the perceptions about the quantity of different program types on STAR and Doordarshan. In order to test this assertion, perceptions about the quantity of several programming types, i.e. News, Educational, Sports, Movies, Serials, Variety, Music and Song, and Children's programs for STAR and Doordarshan respectively were submitted to a repeated measures multivariate analysis of variance (MANOVA).

The Mauchly sphericity test for correlation between the dependent variables (i.e. programming types) was significant (W=.08, p< .0001). The results of the MANOVA are shown in Table 9.6. The MANOVA test across the two television channels was highly significant. The significant difference indicated that there was at least one set of corresponding means (among the eight programming types) for the two channels whose difference was greater than can be attributed to random sampling fluctuation. Thus, the MANOVA indicated significant difference in the perceptions of the quantity of different programming genres across the two channels. Univariate "F" tests were conducted to identify the individual programs on which there was a perception of significant differences in quantity between the two channels. Tables 9.6 and 9.7 list the results of the multivariate and the univariate tests.

Table 9. 6 Repeated Measures MANOVA Test Showing Difference in Perceptions of Quantity of Different Programming Types Between STAR TV and Doordarshan

Test	Value	F-Value (Within Subjects)	Hypoth. DF	Error DF	Significance of 'F'
Pillais	.59	18.85	8.0	106.0	p < .0001
Hotelling	1.42	18.85	8.0	106.0	p < .0001
Wilks	.41	18.85	8.0	106.0	p < .0001

Table 9.8 presents the means scores for respondents' perceptions of which channel presented a greater number of preferred programming types.

Table 9. 7 Univariate F tests Showing Differences in Perceptions of Quantity of Specific STAR TV and Doordarshan Programs

Program Type	Hypoth. SS	Error SS	Hypoth. MS	Error MS	F
News	12.79	27.21	12.79	.24	53.11[A]
Educational	1.12	31.88	1.12	.28	3.98[B]
Sports	35.52	35.47	35.52	.31	113.2[A]
Movies	.63	42.37	.63	.37	1.68
Serials	.355	35.14	.35	.31	1.14
Variety	5.07	38.92	5.07	.34	14.72[A]
Music/Song	7.74	45.23	7.74	.40	19.31[A]
Children's	5.07	24.92	5.07	.22	22.98[A]

[A]$p < .0001$; [B]$p < .05$

The results in Table 9.8 again clearly show that the respondents perceive that STAR channels show significantly more of the preferred programming types than Doordarshan. The mean scores for STAR were significantly higher for most of programming types over Doordarshan at the 1% significance level. The exceptions were educational programs, movies and serials on which there were no significant differences between the two channels.

Table 9. 8 Perception of Quantity of Preferred Programming Types on STAR TV & Doordarshan

Program Type	STAR Mean	Std. Dev	Doordarshan Mean	Std. Dev
News	2.00^{Aa}	0.68	1.54^{Bb}	0.56
Sports	2.44^{Aa}	0.63	1.67^{Bb}	0.61
Variety	2.16^{Aa}	0.66	1.84^{Bb}	0.72
Song & Music	2.23^{Aa}	0.67	1.84^{Bb}	0.71
Children's	1.89^{Aa}	0.74	1.62^{Bb}	0.68

Note: For every program type in a row, means having different lowercase superscripts differed at the p<.05 level by an F test from the other mean in the same row. Similarly, means having different uppercase superscripts differed at the p<.01 level from the other mean in that row.

Satisfaction with STAR and Doordarshan programs

The third hypothesis for this study posited that there would be a significant difference in the satisfaction derived from STAR and Doordarshan programs. Respondents were queried on their satisfaction with different programs such as: Children's shows, Music and Dance, Variety shows, Serials, Movies, Sports, Educational shows, and News. In order to test the hypothesis, these programming types for STAR and Doordarshan were submitted to a repeated measures multivariate analysis of variance (MANOVA).

The Mauchly sphericity test for correlation between the dependent variables (i.e. programming types) was significant (W=.07, p< .0001). The results of the MANOVA are shown in Table 9.9. The MANOVA test across the two television channels was highly significant. The significant difference indicated that there was at least one set of corresponding means (among the eight programming types) for the two channels whose difference was greater than can be attributed to random sampling fluctuation. Thus, the MANOVA indicated significant difference across the two channels for the satisfaction derived from watching preferred programming types. Univariate "F" tests were conducted to identify the individual programs on which there was significant difference between STAR and Doordarshan. Tables 9.9 and 9.10 present the results of the multivariate and univariate tests.

Table 9. 9 Repeated Measures MANOVA Test Showing Difference in Viewer Satisfaction of Preferred Programming Types Between STAR TV and Doordarshan

Test	Value	F-Value (Within Subjects)	Hypoth. DF	Error DF	Significance of 'F'
Pillais	.58	17.79	8.0	103.0	$p < .0001$
Hotelling	1.38	17.79	8.0	103.0	$p < .0001$
Wilks	.42	17.79	8.0	103.0	$p < .0001$

Table 9.11 presents the means for individual programs on Star and Doordarshan thus enabling us to identify which channel provides greater satisfaction to the viewers. The results in Table 9.11 overwhelmingly support the contention that STAR programs are more satisfying to the viewer than Doordarshan programs. On all the programming categories listed in Table 9.11, STAR programs scored significantly higher ($p < .01$) than Doordarshan.

Relationship between motivations and gratifications

The fourth hypothesis looked for significant relationships between motivations for watching and gratifications derived for both STAR and Doordarshan respectively. Table 9.12 lists the results of the correlations for STAR and Doordarshan.

Table 9. 10 Univariate F tests Showing Differences in Satisfaction Derived from Individual STAR TV and Doordarshan Programming Types

Program Type	Hypoth. SS	Error SS	Hypoth. MS	Error MS	F
News	22.07	41.93	22.07	.38	57.91[A]
Educational	4.90	49.59	4.91	.45	10.88[B]
Sports	72.65	58.85	72.65	.53	135.81[A]
Movies	11.26	48.74	11.26	.44	25.42[A]
Serials	11.72	57.78	11.72	.53	22.30[A]
Variety	26.71	61.79	26.71	.56	47.54[A]
Music/Song	24.67	58.33	24.67	.53	46.51[A]
Children's	13.13	46.86	13.13	.43	30.83[A]

[A]$p < .0001$; [B]$p < .001$

Table 9. 11 Mean Scores for Satisfaction Derived from Individual Programming Types on STAR TV & Doordarshan

Program Type	STAR		Doordarshan	
	Mean	Std. Dev	Mean	Std. Dev
News	3.58[Aa]	0.58	3.00[Bb]	0.83
Educational	2.94[Aa]	0.73	2.62[Bb]	0.85
Sports	3.69[Aa]	0.57	2.57[Bb]	0.94
Movies	3.26[Aa]	0.74	2.80[Bb]	0.96
Serials	3.20[Aa]	0.70	2.71[Bb]	0.91
Variety	3.21[Aa]	0.72	2.48[Bb]	0.94
Song & Music	3.19[Aa]	0.72	2.48[Bb]	0.86
Children's	3.04[Aa]	0.82	2.56[Bb]	0.88

Note: For every program type in a row, means having different lowercase superscripts differed at the $p < .05$ level by an F test from the other mean in the same row. Similarly, means having different uppercase superscripts differed at the $p < .01$ level from the other mean in that row.

The results in Table 9.12 clearly show that both Doordarshan and STAR are successful in meeting the desires of their viewers vis-a-vis the motivations for watching these channels. There seems to be a strong correlation between motivations for viewing and gratifications for all categories of programs but the following have relatively higher correlations: to relax (variance explained: about 32%); to be entertained (variance explained: between 30% and 41%); and to pass time (variance explained: between 23% and 36%).

Table 9.12 Correlations Between Motivations for Viewing and Gratifications Derived for STAR and Doordarshan

Gratifications Derived

Motivation	Am Relaxed	Am Entertained	Forget Routine	Companion -ship	I Pass Time	Am with friends & family
To relax	.57 (.59)					
To be entertained		.64 (.54)				
To forget routine			.37 (.36)			
For companion - ship				.37 (.24)		
To pass time					.48 (.60)	
To be with friends and family						.42 (.49)

Correlations in parentheses pertain to Doordarshan. All correlations significant at p= .01 or less

Summary of Main Findings

What are the chief motivations for watching television?
Viewers had definite motivations for watching the two channels. In general, the viewers sought out television shows for entertainment; relaxation; passing time usefully; learning about new things, places and cultures; and to be with family and friends. However, the rank ordering of the motivations differed for the two channels. For STAR, the major motivation for watching the shows may be grouped under the label of *learning about new things, places and cultures;* the second group of motivations fell under the category of *pleasurable and relaxing activity.* In the case of Doordarshan, this ordering of motivations was reversed. *Pleasurable and relaxing activity* was the major motivation, followed by *learning about new things, places and cultures.* These results suggest that the viewers viewed the two channels generally to relax and be entertained while in the case of STAR a major motivation besides the pleasurable nature of the activity was to be informed about new places, things and cultures. This has implications for future programming of Doordarshan programs. Audiences are looking forward to shows on diverse places and things. This finding will be explored further in the next section.

Is there a pattern to viewing frequency of STAR and Doordarshan?
Our study shows that viewers prefer to watch STAR over Doordarshan programs. Whether it was music and dance; educational; sports; variety; children's; or even the commercials, preference for viewing STAR was significantly higher than Doordarshan. Thus, with the exception of serials, news, and movies, where there was no difference in the viewing frequencies, viewers chose STAR programs overwhelmingly over Doordarshan.

How do the viewers feel about the amount of program types on STAR and Doordarshan?

The results in our study clearly showed that the viewers perceived that STAR channels showed significantly more of the preferred programming types than Doordarshan. Examples of these programming types were: news, sports, variety, song and music, and children's shows. This finding reinforces the fact that viewers not only preferred a variety of programs and STAR seemed to be providing them with a wide choice of interesting programs but that STAR was perceived as offering a greater quantity of different programming types over Doordarshan.

How do the viewers perceive their satisfaction with STAR and Doordarshan programs?

The results of our study indicated that STAR programs were more satisfying to the viewer than Doordarshan programs. For every programming type (i.e. news, educational, sports, movies, serials, variety, song and music, and children's) STAR programs scored significantly higher than Doordarshan. This is an important finding and it supports the widespread suspicion that viewers are dissatisfied with Doordarshan programs.

Is there a relationship between motivations for viewing and gratifications derived from viewing television?

Both Doordarshan and STAR were successful in meeting the desires of their viewers vis-a-vis the motivations for watching these channels. There was a strong correlation between motivations for viewing and gratifications for all categories of programs. Doordarshan and STAR did a particularly good job of satisfying motivations such as: to relax, to be entertained, and to pass time.

Discussion

Since its arrival in India in early 1992, STAR has seen a phenomenal growth in terms of viewer subscriptions. Cable hookups of STAR programs have been increasing at the rate of 20% per year (Burch & Straubhaar, 1995). Some accounts put the growth of cable and satellite programming through STAR at about 310 percent (Kishore, 1994). This puts STAR as the fastest growing "infotainment" channel in India in recent history. While the number of viewers reached is still small relative to the coverage of Doordarshan, the impact of STAR has been significant in terms of the changes that it has ushered in television/satellite entertainment in India. As suggested earlier in this chapter, most of the media effects research studies in the past have focused on source and medium-related variables. This study has deliberately put its focus on the audience. Thus, the audience members are looked upon as active with definite reasons for their choice of media programs and their frequency of viewing. Our study has showed conclusively that audiences are interested in 'infotainment.' They like to be entertained with enjoyable and interesting programs on a variety of topics so that they may relax and pass time with family members or close friends in a useful way. Viewers would also like to learn new facts about India and the world around them. Both Doordarshan and STAR were successful in attracting viewers but STAR was perceived as the channel of choice for viewing a variety of shows and learning about new things and places. This was not a surprising finding because at the time data was collected for our study, STAR offered five channels of interesting programs to Doordarshan's single channel. Subsequently, and most probably due to the pressure from STAR, Doordarshan increased its programming fare to include more channels such as the metro channels in major Indian cities.

Our study findings also indicate that viewers more frequently viewed STAR programs, felt that STAR provided more diverse programs, and that viewers derived significantly greater satisfaction from its programs relative to that of Doordarshan. This confirms the speculation in recent literature (Kishore, 1994; Chan, 1994) that audiences viewed the programs of Doordarshan to be dull in content and narrow in the range of topics or areas covered.

The number of subscribers to STAR in India as per recent estimates (Burch & Straubhaar, 1995) is only about 7.5 million homes. This puts India in the second spot (after P.R. China) among the countries served by STAR. While the number of people reached may be much greater than 7.5 million (probably by a factor of 4), it still dwarfs in the face of Doordarshan's penetration in India that goes beyond 80 million homes. However, the impact of STAR may be much greater than what its viewership numbers may suggest since most of its viewers are influential urban and middle to upper middle class Indians. India has a huge middle class next only to the US and the former Soviet Union and the fact that a "foreign" channel effectively reaches most of the middle class and also has a significant impact on them makes India a very interesting case study. It should also be noted that while India trails P.R. China in the number of viewers, India is number one for STAR's English language programs in Asia. This has very serious implications for transnational advertising organizations and program production companies looking for lucrative markets both for consumer goods and English entertainment programs.

The popularity of STAR in India in spite of most of its programs being in English deserves special mention. India is a country of diverse cultures and languages, yet the state has taken upon itself to define and showcase Indian culture through Doordarshan. Doordarshan's objective has been to not only integrate the various parts of the country with programs that show a "pan-Indian" culture but at the same time provide a showcase for its Hindi language shows. Prior to the advent of STAR, the prime-time national programs were dominated by Hindi programs and English programs were increasingly pushed aside. This matched the rhetoric of politicians in New Delhi who constantly reminded Indians that English was a "foreign" language and Hindi was the national language of the country. However, the phenomenal success of STAR programs, especially soaps such as *Santa Barbara* and *The Bold and the Beautiful*, all over India clearly indicated that Indians turn to television for entertainment and not for lessons on national integration. If a certain program is enjoyable and gratifying, it would be watched even if it was in English. In fact, the rhetoric about the insignificance of English has been overplayed. Almost all of the urban and middle to upper middle class Indians understand and can communicate effectively in English. So, our study also raises questions about the efficacy of the role of the government using an entertainment medium (such as Doordarshan) to prescribe a certain pan-Indian culture and language.

Another consequence of Doordarshan's policy of favoring Hindi language programs has put other Indian languages at a disadvantage. Languages such as Telugu, Tamil, Bengali, Kannada, and Malayalam have had vibrant film industries that date back to the 1920's. The fan following for movies in these languages is phenomenal and rival that of the Hindi films. Yet, Doordarshan reserved its prime time for Hindi programs and the quality of the regional Indian language television programs was generally quite poor. The advent of STAR and its popularity has had the interesting outcome of Doordarshan strengthening its other Indian language programs in its bid to compete with STAR. STAR, on the other hand, has been experimenting with the idea of offering more Hindi programs besides its own Zee channel.

Also, several other satellite-based channels have sprung up in several parts of the country providing diverse and high quality programs in Telugu, Tamil, Malayalam, Kannada, etc. All of these developments raise interesting questions about the future of one national culture and one national language in a country with a rich diversity of cultures and languages.

As far as television is considered, the lessons learnt are quite clear. In the end it is the audiences who will decide what they want. The role of the government tightly controlling the information/ entertainment scene and also playing the role of the cultural guardian through its selection of specific language or program types may not win too many viewers especially given the rich diversity of languages in the country and the fierce competition from national and international commercial networks to provide interesting and diverse types of programs.

Notes

[1]We wish to thank the following persons and institutions for helping us collect data for this study and other such studies in south India: students and staff in the departments of communication at the University of Hyderabad, University of Madras, and the University of Calicut, India.

References

Becker, L.B. (1979). Measurement of Gratifications. *Communication Research.* 6 (1), 54-73.

Berelson, B. (1949). What 'missing the newspaper' means. In P.F Lazarsfeld & F.N. Stanton (Eds.). *Communications Research 1948-1949* (pp. 111-129). New York: Harper.

Blumler, J.G., & E. Katz. (Eds.). (1974). *The Uses of Mass Communication: Current Perspectives on Gratifications Research.* Beverly Hills, CA: Sage Publications.

Burch, E., & J. Straubhaar. (1995). TV Without Borders: DBS and Cable Television Across Asia. Paper presented to the International Communication Division of the Association for Education in Journalism and Mass Communication.

Chan, J.M. 1994. National Responses and Accessibility to STAR TV in Asia. *Journal of Communication* 44 (3), Summer.

Doshi, J.K., & B.C. Agrawal. (1989). Audience Profiles and Evaluation Research. In R.E. Ostman (ed.). *Communication and Indian Agriculture.* (pp. 217-24). New Delhi: Sage

Herzog, H. (1944). What do we really know about daytime serial listeners? In P.F Lazarsfeld & F.N. Stanton (Eds.). *Radio Research 1942-1943* (pp. 3-33). New York: Duell, Sloan & Pearce.

Katz, E., Blumler, J.G., & Gurevitch, M. (1974). Utilization of mass communication by the individual. In J.G. Blumler & E. Katz (Eds.)., *The uses of mass communications: Current perspectives on gratifications research* (pp. 19-32). Beverley Hills, CA: Sage.

Katz, E., Gurevitch, M., & Haas, H. (1973). On the use of the mass media for important things. *American Sociological Review, 38*:164-181.

Kishore, K. (1994). The Advent of STAR TV in India: Emerging Policy Issues. *Media Asia, N*o. 21, No. 2, pp. 96-101.

McGuire, W.J. (1974). Psychological Motives and Communication Gratification. In J.G. Blumer and E. Katz (eds.). *The Uses of Mass Communication. (*pp. 167-96). Beverly Hill, CA: Sage

McQuail, D., Blumler, J.G., & Brown, J.R. (1972). The television audience: A revised perspective. In D. McQuail (Ed.), *Sociology of mass communications* (pp. 135-165). Middlesex, England: Penguin.

Reddi, U.V. (1985). *Factors Influencing Patterns of Mass Media Use and Gratifications among Adolescents in India.* Unpublished doctoral dissertation, University of Poona, India.

Rogers, E.M. (1983). *Diffusion of Innovations,* 3rd Edition. New York: The Free Press.

Rosengren, K.E. (1974). Uses and gratifications: A paradigm outlined. In J.G. Blumler & E. Katz(Eds.)., *The uses of mass communications: Current perspectives on gratifications research* (pp. 269-286). Beverley Hills, CA: Sage.

Rubin, A.M. (1994). Media uses and effects: a uses -and-gratifications perspective. In J. Bryant & D. Zillman (Eds.), *Media effects: Advances in theory and research,* (pp. 417-436). New Jersey: Lawrence Erlbaum.

Shingi, P.M., & Mody, B. (1976). The communications effects gap. In E. Rogers (Ed.), *Communication and development: Critical perspectives,* (pp. 79-98). Beverly Hills, CA: Sage.

'The New TV Superbazaar.' (1992, November 15). *India Today,* pp. 22-36.

Yadava, J.S. & Reddi, U.V. (1988). In the Midst of Diversity: Television in Urban Indian Homes. In J. Lull (Ed.). *World Families Watch Television.* (pp. 25-34). Newbury Park: Sage

Chapter 10

Viewing of Doordarshan By Cable Subscribers in Bangalore, India: Is There A Difference With Non-Subscribers?

Sandhya Rao
Srinivas R. Melkote

Doordarshan was the sole provider of television programs in India for about 30-odd years. When cable entered the country in a small way in 1984 (Rahim, 1994), it did not make much of a difference to viewers in most parts of the country. But, with the liberalization of the Indian economy in the early 1990's and the subsequent deregulation that included the information sector, there has been a rapid diffusion of privately-owned satellite networks. These networks have posed a serious threat to Doordarshan's monopoly of the air waves (Dua, 1992). The Hong Kong-based STAR TV was the prime catalyst in this process. Indian viewers who were used to watching one or two channels on Doordarshan were finally offered a choice of programs and channels. STAR TV initially carried five channels: STAR Plus, MTV, BBC News, STAR Sports and ZEE TV, a Hindi language channel. Zee TV, a private television channel on STAR was launched in 1992 and quickly became popular with its entertaining programs (Karp, 1994). By 1994, viewers could access about 25 channels including CNN, Zee, Jain, Sun, Asianet and ATN (*Manorama Year*

Book, 1995). And, by 1996 most cable subscribers could access about 35 satellite channels.

Doordarshan met the challenge head on by adding its own satellite channels and shifting its programming content from the social goals of development and education to entertainment, mostly for the urban audiences. The restructuring of Doordarshan was seen as a way to retain "up-scale" audiences (N.G. Srinivas, Director Doordarshan, Bangalore, personal communication, July 1996) and the advertisement revenue (Dua, 1992). Doordarshan introduced a number of news related programs, live programming and new entertainment programs earlier considered as 'elitist' (Agarwal, 1994). It also increased the non-Hindi Indian language content on its satellite/cable channels to compete with the popular, privately-owned non-Hindi channels. However, at present, only cable subscribers can access the new and improved Doordarshan programs. Those without cable may only access the National programs and limited regional Indian language (i.e. non-Hindi) programs on Doordarshan's terrestrial network.

Despite being challenged by cable/satellite channels, Doordarshan appears to be doing well. The comparative ratings for Doordarshan and satellite channels in Bangalore, based on all television viewers as reported by the Indian Market Research Bureau, showed that Doordarshan's DD-1 programs including music-based programs such as *Chitrahaar* had ratings ranging from 29.5 to 46.3 per cent, whereas ratings for similar programs on Zee TV and Sun TV (two popular satellite channels) ranged from 1.7 to 6.8 per cent (*Doordarshan '96*). Doordarshan also has "...four times the audience of the satellite webs," (Young, 1996, p.45). Doordarshan has a vast terrestrial network and its primary channel, DD-1 reaches 87 per cent of India's over 950 million people (*Doordarshan 1998*). Another advantage Doordarshan has is the technical capability to provide news immediately, whereas satellite program providers have to ship their programs to Hong Kong or Singapore from where they are uplinked to a satellite before being beamed to India (N.G. Srinivas, personal communication, July 1996).

Cable/satellite channels have come to stay in India and they are attracting large numbers of India's 270-million middle class viewers. Melkote, Sanjay and Ahmed point out in the previous chapter that in 1992 homes converting to cable to watch STAR TV programs jumped up by as much as 211 per cent. Thus, it would be useful to identify factors that may be encouraging viewers to go in for a cable/satellite hook-up. This may best be done by comparing satellite/cable subscribers with non-subscribers. As the non-subscribers may only access Doordarshan's terrestrial programs whereas the cable/satellite subscribers may view all channels including Doordarshan, the comparison between the two groups of viewers may only be based on factors involved with viewing Doordarshan channels. In their study, Melkote, Sanjay and Ahmed have compared the content of Doordarshan and STAR TV in terms of different program attributes and viewer satisfaction sought from both Doordarshan and STAR TV. In this study, the comparison is not between Doordarshan and cable/satellite channels but between individuals who chose to subscribe to cable/satellite hook-up and thus receive the satellite channels and Doordarshan and those who did not and can receive only Doordarshan terrestrial channels.

So, what are the factors that may be encouraging viewers to go in for a cable/satellite hook-up? And, is there a significant difference on these factors between subscribers and non-subscribers? Though a few studies on satellite television have been conducted in other parts of India, this was the first such study conducted in Bangalore, the capital of Karnataka State in south India. In general, most studies on cable television have been concerned with differences between cable and network viewing habits of audiences. In this study, the emphasis was on differences in viewing Doordarshan channels. Because Doordarshan has added several cable/satellite channels to compete with other cable/satellite channels, it was decided to find out whether the perception of Doordarshan among those who had cable channels would be different from those who did not subscribe to cable. In that sense, this was an exploratory study.

Based on the Melkote et al. study described in the previous chapter and other research studies in the uses and gratifications perspective, the main aims of this study were to look for differences between the two groups in terms of: individual characteristics (gender, age, education, income level, etc.); level of viewing Doordarshan; frequency of viewing different program types on Doordarshan; satisfaction derived from watching the different types of programs on Doordarshan; and differences in the extent of ownership of other media (including computers, VCRs, and cellular telephones).

Background

Bangalore, the capital of Karnataka state, is a cosmopolitan city with a population of over 4.5 million. Known as the 'Silicon Valley' of India, Bangalore houses numerous electronic and other high-technology industries including Motorola and Texas Instruments. Doordarshan programs started in Karnataka state in 1975-76 during the Satellite Instruction Television Experiment (SITE) that was conducted in six Indian states to find out how best television could be used for education and development. The city of Bangalore, however, was not covered by SITE. A relay station was established in Bangalore in 1981 and production facilities were introduced with news in Kannada, the state language of Karnataka in 1983. When cable was introduced in 1990, Doordarshan began broadcasting more Kannada programs on cable channel DD-4. In 1994, cable channel DD-9 was introduced. The Bangalore television station has a total program output of 80 hours in Kannada with a minimum production of 30 minutes per week. Regional programs are transmitted for 12 hours per day. Of the 52.3 million television homes in India, 3.5 million are in Karnataka state with an estimated 22.27 million viewers on the whole, including those who view television on community sets (*Doordarshan '96*).

Cable/satellite channels reach 30-40 percent of the television homes in Karnataka. There are more than 800 cable operators in Bangalore city providing an average of about 35 satellite channels including STAR TV, BBC World, CNN International, ZEE, Sony, SUN TV, Udaya TV, Eenadu TV, MTV, etc. Among the Indian language channels, Zee-TV in Hindi, Sun TV in Tamil and Eenadu in Telugu, are ranked the top three. Kannada channels, though Kannada is the local language, are ranked 5th or 6th in preference.

Previous Research

Diffusion of media such as cable, satellite and the VCR has resulted in increased viewing choices for audiences, audience fragmentation, and increased autonomy of audiences (McQuail, 1994). The uses and gratifications approach deals with audience behavior in relation to media. It "...has been centrally concerned with the choice, reception and manner of response of the media audience. A key assumption is that the audience member makes a conscious and motivated choice among channels and content on offer" (McQuail, 1994, p.318). Even though the uses and gratifications approach has been criticized as being too behavioral, "...the last decade has been a period of rather vigorous theoretical growth for the uses and gratifications approach" (Palmgreen, 1984).

Various factors have accounted for increased gratifications from television viewing. Among these are program variety and program quality (Jacobs, 1995). The increased channel offering by cable television has served to take away audiences from network and local broadcast news (Baldwin, Barrett & Bates, 1992). Krugman and Rust (1993) found that the prime-time share of the three US networks, which was 87 percent in 1980, dropped to 62 percent in 1990 mainly due to cable and VCR penetration. Increased choices of programming and viewing times have led to higher viewing satisfaction with cable offerings (Lin, 1994).

Program preferences vary between network television and cable channels. Studies examining differences in viewing news on network and cable channels have found varying results. For example, Baldwin, Barrett and Bates (1992) found that viewers depended more on broadcast networks for news than on cable across all dayparts. However, they also found that CNN was chosen by many in times of national crises. In another study, Henke, Donahue, Cook and Cheung (1984) reported that cable subscribers viewed network news significantly less than did non-subscribers. They also found that they viewed less network news the longer they had cable. Rahim (1994), in a study conducted in Hyderabad, India, did not find a significant difference in the average time spent by audiences watching news programs on Doordarshan and cable channels.

Cable subscribers were found to be better educated and to have higher incomes than non- subscribers (Lin, 1994; Atkin, 1993; & Rahim, 1994). Cable subscribers were likely to be more exposed to mass media and own more media technologies than non-subscribers. For example, newspaper subscription has been found to be associated with cable subscription (Viswanath et. al., 1990). Atkin (1993) found a positive relationship between cable subscribership and ownership of technologies such as the VCR and personal computers.

Hypotheses

Based on previous research, the following hypotheses were posited:

H_1: There will be an association between viewer characteristics (gender, age, education, income level, etc.) and cable subscription.

H_2: The level of viewing exposure to Doordarshan will differ between cable subscribers and non-subscribers.

H_3: The frequency of viewing different program types on Doordarshan will differ between cable subscribers and non-subscribers.

H_4: The level of viewing satisfaction of programs on Doordarshan will differ between cable subscribers and non-subscribers.

H_5: There will be an association between media ownership (including computers and fax machines) and cable subscription.

Definition of Terms

Level of viewing exposure was defined as the total number of hours audiences view television per day. Viewing time for an average weekday, Saturday and Sunday were collapsed and an average computed in order to get a better idea of viewing time per average day.

Doordarshan included Doordarshan's network as well as its cable channels.

Cable/satellite excluded Doordarshan's channels and included all private cable/satellite channels.

Frequency of viewing was measured on a four-point scale ranging from frequently (1) to never (4).

Satisfaction of viewing was measured on a five point scale: Very satisfied (1), satisfied (2), dissatisfied (3) very dissatisfied (4) and not applicable (5).

Program types included 12 categories based on previous research.

Methodology

The sample consisted of 600 television households from 12 representative residential areas based on income levels. The Bangalore City Corporation was divided into 100 areas or wards. In consultation with the municipal authorities, these wards were divided into upper, middle and lower income areas or wards. These groupings were based on property-tax returns. There were 19 upper wards where more than 50 percent of the households had a household income of over Rs. 7,501 (1 USD = Rs. 35 approx.) per month; 38 middle wards with more than 50 per cent of the households earning between Rs. 3,001 to Rs. 7,500 per month; and 43 lower level wards where more than 50 percent of the households earned less than Rs. 3000 a month. The stratified random sampling method was used to draw a sample of 12 areas, with four areas in each socio-economic category. Fifty households (ten clusters of five each) were selected in each category through cluster sampling and the individual households were selected randomly. Quota sampling was used to give representation to income, gender and age in the sample. The male-female ratio in the sample was kept at 40:60 in order to give a higher representation to housewives who constituted a larger percentage of the television viewing public.

The cross-sectional survey method was employed to collect data. A questionnaire was formulated based on previous research. Responses to the items pertaining to some of the variables of the study were measured on a Likert scale. Responses to the demographic items were gathered by asking closed-ended questions. The questionnaire was pretested for comprehension and relevance in Bangalore. Pretesting and administration of the questionnaires were carried out in July-August 1996 with the help of trained research workers from a professional research firm. The questionnaires were administered door to door to ensure completion of all 600 questionnaires. Only those 18 years of age and older were administered the questionnaire. The questionnaires were pre-coded for analysis. The Statistical Package for the Social Sciences, SPSS, was used to analyze data.

Findings

Audience Profile

The audience fell between the ages of 18 and 85 with a mean age of 37 years. Most respondents were under 45 years of age (457) with the largest number (175) in the 26-35 age group (see Figure 10.1). About thirty eight percent (229) of the sample was male and about 62 percent (371) was female. Almost 76 percent of the sample had a household strength ranging from three to six people.

Figure 10.1 Age in Years

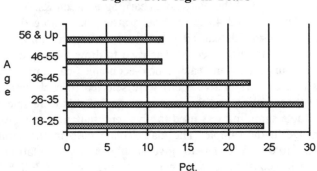

A little over fifty percent of the respondents earned between Rs. 3001 and Rs. 7500 a month and about 40 percent earned Rs. 7501 or higher (see Figure 10.2). About nine percent of the respondents earned less than Rs. 3000 per month. (1 USD= Rs. 35)

Figure 10.2 Monthly Income

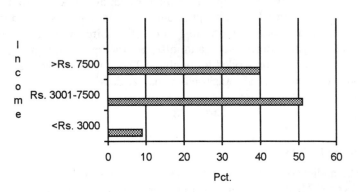

Respondents had occupations that included government service, private sector service, business and farming. However, 43.6 percent of

Figure 10.3 Occupation of Respondents

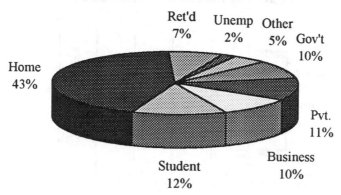

Ret'd 7%   Unemp 2%   Other 5%   Gov't 10%

Home 43%

Pvt. 11%

Business 10%

Student 12%

the respondents were women (mainly because women were deliberately given a larger representation in the sample) who did not work outside the house. The results are reported in Figure 10.3.

The education levels ranged from not completing high school to ostgraduate studies (see Figure 10.4). While 167 (28%) of the respondents had at least an undergraduate degree, 51 (9%) respondents had post-baccalaureate degrees. About 24 percent (143) had completed high school (10th grade), and 17.2 percent (103) percent had studied up to the twelfth grade (or the Pre University level). While 70 (12%) respondents had not completed high school, 22 (4%) had other education (this category included trade school diplomas and certificate courses).

Only households with television were included in the sample. Of the total 600 homes, 398 (66%) had cable and 202 (34%) homes were not hooked up to receive cable/satellite channels (see Figure 10.5).

Kannada was the most widely spoken language at home accounting for almost 45 per cent of the audience (refer to Figure 10.6). While 17.5 percent of the respondents spoke Tamil, 16 percent spoke Telugu. Hindi, Malayalam and other languages were spoken by the others.

Figure 10.4 Education of Respondents

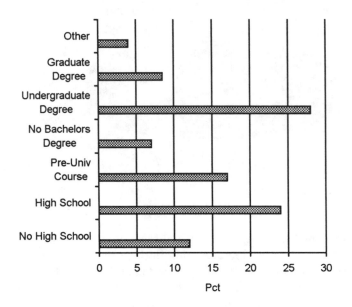

Figure 10.5 Cable Subscribers

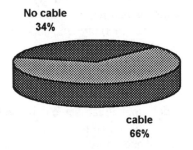

Figure 10.6 Language Spoken at Home

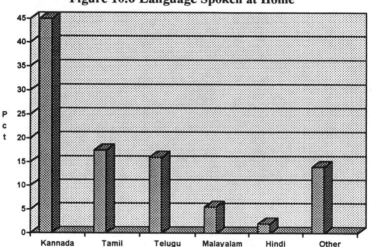

Demographic Characteristics

In order to test the first hypothesis (H_1), chi-square tests were conducted. Table 10.1 shows the results of the tests. As can be seen from Table 10.1, the audience characteristics were significantly different for the income groups. Cable subscribership was associated with higher income levels ($p < .05$). The income category Rs. 3001-7500 was the single largest group. Roughly half the percentage in the two groups earned an income of Rs. 3001-7500 per month. But, the cable group had a far greater percentage of families that earned Rs. 7501 and higher. As far as education was concerned, a larger percentage of cable subscribers had higher education levels such as the bachelor's and master's degrees. But, the differences were not statistically significant.

There were no significant overall differences in age among the two categories. A slightly larger percentage of those in the '46-55 years' and '56 years and above' age groups were in the cable subscriber category. In terms of occupation, over 40 per cent of the audience in

**Table 10.1: Demographic Characteristics of Cable Subscribers
And Non-Subscribers**

	Cable %	Cable F	Non-Cable %	Non-Cable F
Sex				
Male	36.9	147	40.6	82
Female	63.1	251	59.4	120
Age (Years)				
18-25	23.1	92	26.1	54
26-35	29.9	119	27.7	56
36-45	20.6	82	26.7	54
46-55	13.3	53	8.9	18
56 and older	13.1	52	9.9	20
Education				
Not Completed High School	10.3	41	14.4	29
Completed High School	22.4	89	26.9	54
Completed 12th Grade	17.4	69	16.9	34
Not Completed U. Degree	7.3	29	6.5	13
Completed Bachelors Degree	29.2	116	25.4	51
Completed Masters or Higher	9.8	39	6.0	12
Other	3.5	14	4.0	8
Occupation				
Government Service	10.1	40	8.4	17
Private Service	9.6	38	14.9	30
Business	10.1	40	9.9	20
Student	11.3	45	13.9	28
Housewife	44.1	175	42.6	86
Retired	8.1	32	5.0	10
Unemployed	2.5	10	0.5	1
Other	4.3	17	5.0	10
Income[*]				
Below Rs. 3000	6.4	25	14.6	29
Rs. 3001-Rs. 7500	47.1	184	56.6	112
Rs. 7501 and higher	46.5	182	28.8	57

[*] $p < .05$ across cable and non-cable viewers.

both the categories were homemakers. H_1 was supported for only the income variable.

Viewing Levels

H_2 was tested both for the periods before and after cable was introduced in Bangalore. A t-test was conducted to find out whether there was a significant difference in the amount of time cable subscribers and non-subscribers watched Doordarshan before cable was introduced in Bangalore.

The test showed that cable subscribers watched Doordarshan for 3.34 hours and non-subscribers watched Doordarshan for 3.56 hours per average day before cable was introduced. There was no significant difference in the amount of time they viewed television.

Table 10. 2: Results of a T-Test Between Cable Subscribers and Non-Subscribers on Doordarshan (DD) Viewing Level (Hours Per Day)

	Viewing Levels of DD of Cable Subsricbers	Viewing Levels of DD of Non-Subscribers
Before Cable	3.34	3.56
After Cable*	1.34	3.92

*p<.001

In order to test H_2, a t-test was also done to find out whether cable subscribers had a higher level of viewing exposure to Doordarshan than non-subscribers after cable was introduced. As seen in Table 10.2, it was found that cable subscribers watched Doordarshan for an average of 1.34 hours per day and the non-subscribers watched for an average of 3.92 hours a day. That is, those who subscribed to cable considerably reduced the time spent viewing Doordarshan while those who did not have cable continued to spend about the same or a little more time watching Doordarshan. The t-test revealed that the difference was very significant (p <.001) offering support for H_2.

The decrease in Doordarshan viewing time of cable owners by over 50 per cent (from over 3 hours to about 1.5 hours) was amply compensated by watching 4.3 hours of cable per average day.

Frequency of Viewing Program Types

MANOVA was performed to find out whether there were significant differences between the frequency of viewing different types of programs on Doordarshan among cable subscribers and non-subscribers. Results show that whether or not respondents had cable made a significant difference in the frequency with which they viewed different program types on Doordarshan (see Table 10.3). The MANOVA on frequency of viewing different program types across cable subscribers and non-subscribers was significant (Pillai's trace = .19, F=11.21, p<.001). Univariate F-tests also revealed that there were significant differences among cable subscribers and non-subscribers in the frequency of viewing all program types except Western Serials. H3 was supported.

Table 10. 3 Results of MANOVA Between Cable Subscribers and Non-Subscribers on Frequency of Viewing Different Doordarshan Programs

Test	Value	F	Hypoth. DF	Error DF	F
Pillais	.19	11.21	12.00	587.00	.001
Hotellings	.23	11.21	12.00	587.00	.001
Wilks	.81	11.21	12.00	587.00	.001

A post-hoc discriminant analysis was conducted to check for the multivariate dimensions along which the two groups differed. Results are shown in Table 10.4.

One significant discriminant function was obtained (Wilks Lambda = .81, p<.0001, percent of canonical correlation= .43). The canonical discriminant function coefficients showed that the variable 'Movies' loaded the highest (.50) on the discriminant function; 'Indian Serials' loaded at .28 and 'Music Programs' loaded next with .26. This indicated that the significant discriminant function (i.e. Viewing frequency of movies, Indian serials & music programs) best described the multivariate dimension along which the cable subscribers and non-subscribers differed. The plotting of the group means (centroids) of the two groups along this significant discriminant function indicated that the cable group had a higher score of (+.34) than the non-cable group that had a mean group score of (-.67). This indicated that as a group the cable subscribers watched movies, music programs and Indian serials (on Doordarshan) significantly less frequently than did non-subscribers (because frequency of viewing was measured on a scale where a higher score indicated less frequent viewing).

Table 10. 4: Discriminant Function Centroids for Cable Subscribers and Non-Subscribers

Non-Subscribers	Subscribers
-.67	+.34

-2.0	-1.0	0.0	+1.0	+2.0

Discriminant Function 1*: Viewing Frequency of Movies, Indian Serials & Music Programs

---

* DF1: Wilks Lambda=.81, p<.0001, % of canonical correlation = .43.

Standardized canonical discriminant function coefficients for DF1: News (.07), News Magazines (.14), Sports (.15), Movies (.50), Western Serials (-.08), Indian Serials (.28), Indian Soap Operas (.13), Music Programs (.26), Dance and other Cultural Programs (-.15), Talks/interviews (-.00), Educational Programs (-.13), and Documentaries (.17).

Mean scores of the two groups pertaining to individual program types (see Table 10.5) showed that as a group the cable non-subscribers watched all program types on Doordarshan more frequently than cable subscribers with the most difference recorded for Movies, Indian Serials, and Music Programs (Note: higher viewing scores denote lower viewing levels because frequency of viewing was measured on a scale where a higher score indicated less frequent viewing).

Viewing Satisfaction

In order to find out whether significant differences existed between the level of satisfaction of viewing different types of programs on Doordarshan among cable subscribers and non-subscribers (H4), a MANOVA was performed (results are reported in Table 10.6). It was found that the MANOVA of the level of viewing satisfaction of different program types on Doordarshan across cable subscribers and non-subscribers was significant (Pillai's trace =.11, F=6.09, p<.001). Univariate F-tests also revealed that there was a significant difference between the two groups on all program types except the following: Western Serials; and Dance/Cultural Programs. Thus, the hypothesis H4 was supported.

A post hoc discriminant analysis was conducted to check for the multivariate dimensions along which the two groups differed. Results are shown in Table 10.7.

Table 10. 5: Means And Standard Deviation Scores For Frequency Of Viewing Different Types Of Programs On Doordarshan By Cable Subscribers And Non-Subscribers

Program Types on Doordarshan	Cable Subscribers		Non-Subscribers	
	Mean	SD	Mean	SD
News	1.53	0.95	1.12	0.41
News Magazines	2.51	1.23	2.16	1.23
Sports	2.70	1.07	2.23	1.14
Movies	2.23	1.02	1.45	0.70
Western Serials	3.85	0.54	3.84	0.53
Indian Serials	2.12	1.17	1.32	0.70
Indian Soap Operas	2.51	1.24	1.89	1.18
Music Programs	2.09	1.18	1.34	0.76
Dance & Culture	2.95	1.13	2.65	1.21
Talk/Interviews	3.04	1.10	2.72	1.13
Educational Programs	3.04	1.30	2.77	1.08
Documentaries	3.32	0.93	2.95	1.09

Table 10. 6: Results of MANOVA Between Cable Subscribers and Non-Subscribers on Level of Satisfaction of Viewing Different Program Types on Doordarshan

Test	Value	F	Hypoth. DF	Error DF	F
Pillais	.11	6.09	12.00	586.00	.001
Hotellings	.12	6.09	12.00	586.00	.001
Wilks	.89	6.09	12.00	586.00	.001

Table 10.7: Discriminant Function Centroids For Viewing Satisfaction of Doordarshan Program Types By Cable Subscribers and Non-Subscribers

Non-Subscribers   Subscribers
    -.49   +.25

-2.0   -1.0   0.0   +1.0   +2.0

Discriminant Function 1*: Viewing Satisfaction for Music Programs & Indian Serials

*DF1: Wilks Lambda =.89, p<.0001,% of canonical correlation =.33. Standardized canonical discriminant function coefficients for DF1: News (.13), News Magazines (.06), Sports (.09), Movies (-.00), Western Serials (-.15), Indian Serials (.42), Indian Soap Operas (.13), Music Programs (.47), Dance and other Cultural Programs (-.19), Talks/interviews (.02), Educational Programs (.00), and Documentaries (.35).

One significant discriminant function was obtained (Wilks Lambda= .89, p<.0001, percent of canonical correlation =.33). The canonical discriminant function coefficients showed that the program type *Music Programs* loaded the highest (.47) on the discriminant function; *Indian Serials* loaded next with .42. This indicated that the significant discriminant function (i.e. Viewing Satisfaction of Music Programs and Indian Serials) best described the multivariate dimension along which the cable subscribers and non-subscribers differed. The plotting of group means (centroids) along this significant discriminant function indicated that the group that had cable had a higher score of +.25 than the non-cable group that had a group mean of -.49. This indicated that as a group the cable subscribers had a lower level of satisfaction than non-subscribers with *Music Programs and Indian Serials* on Doordarshan (because level of viewing satisfaction was measured on a scale where a higher score indicated lower satisfaction).

Mean scores of the two groups pertaining to individual program types (see Table 10.8) showed that as a group the cable non-subscribers had higher satisfaction levels for all program types on Doordarshan than cable subscribers with the most difference recorded for Music Programs and Indian Serials. (Note: higher mean scores denote lower satisfaction levels because level of viewing satisfaction was measured on a scale where a higher score indicated lower satisfaction).

Table 10.8 Mean Scores for Satisfaction of Viewing Different Types of Programs on Doordarshan for Cable Subscribers and Non-Subscribers.

Program Types on Doordarshan	Cable Subscribers		Non-Subscribers	
	Mean	SD	Mean	SD
News	2.15	1.06	1.81	0.62
News Magazines	2.95	1.51	2.63	1.47
Sports	3.03	1.42	2.58	1.30
Movies	2.52	1.19	2.06	0.78
Western Serials	4.73	0.84	4.71	0.89
Indian Serials	2.62	1.38	1.94	0.86
Indian Soap Operas	2.96	1.55	2.35	1.41
Music Programs	2.57	1.39	1.86	0.96
Dance & Culture	3.39	1.54	3.16	1.52
Talk/Interviews	3.58	1.49	3.19	1.48
Educational Programs	3.55	1.54	3.13	1.50
Documentaries	3.88	1.42	3.30	1.54

Table 10.9 Media Exposure/Ownership of Cable
Subscribers & Non-Subscribers

Media Exposure/ Ownership	Cable %	F	Non-Cable %	F
Newspapers read daily				
One	63	225	62	106
Two	27.2	97	26.9	46
Three	9.8	35	11.1	19
Magazines read monthly				
One	21.4	60	21.2	29
Two	28.1	79	43	31.4
Three	22.8	64	28	20.4
Four	11.0	31	11	8.0
Five or more	16.7	47	19	26
Radio Ownership*				
One	75.4	263	82.6	142
Two	18.9	66	15.7	27
Three	5.7	87	1.7	3
VCR/VCP*				
Yes	28.6	114	14	28
No	71.4	284	86	172
Home Telephone*				
Yes	52.5	209	27.2	55
No	47.5	108	72.8	147
Pager				
Yes	2	8	1	0.5
No	98	390	99.5	201
Answering Machine*				
Yes	3	12	0	0
No	97	386	100	202
Computer*				
Yes	6.5	26	1.5	3
No	93.5	371	98.5	199
Fax				
Yes	0.8	3	0	0
No	99.2	395	100	202

*$p < .05$

Ownership of Media Technologies

In order to test whether cable subscribers owned more media technologies and had a higher exposure to media (H5), chi square tests were conducted. Results are given in Table 10.9. The hypothesis was partially supported. Table 10.9 shows that there were no significant differences between cable subscribers and non-subscribers in their exposure to media such as the newspaper and magazines. However, there were significant differences in the ownership of most media technologies. A significantly larger percentage of cable subscribers owned radio sets, VCR/VCPs, home telephones, answering machines and computers than non-subscribers. A higher percentage of cable subscribers (24.6 percent) owned more than one radio set compared with non-subscribers (17.4 percent). The percentage of cable subscribers that owned VCR/VCPs or telephones was almost twice that of the non-subscribers who owned these media. While 6.5 percent of cable owners owned computers just about 1.5 percent of non-subscribers were computer owners.

Discussion and Conclusion

Doordarshan continues to be a major player in audience reach and ratings despite the increased competition from STAR TV, ZEE, ESPN, TNT, Discovery, or other Indian-owned private satellite channels such as SUN, Eenadu, Asianet, Udaya, etc. Yet, Doordarshan has continued to add new satellite channels and increase its programming time and variety in a bid to thwart the competition. And, in the urban centers of India, there is a proliferation of cable connections especially to the large number of middle class homes. So, how is Doordarshan faring among these viewers? As the cable channels carry all Doordarshan shows (both terrestrial and satellite channels) and the privately-owned satellite channels of its competitors, this study sought to gather preliminary data on key variables such as frequency of viewing specific Doordarshan programs, satisfaction derived from viewing Doordarshan programs, etc. from the cable subscribers and compare it to cable non-subscribers who can view only Doordarshan's terrestrial offerings. This study sought to find out differences among cable subscribers and non-subscribers in Bangalore in terms of demographics, media ownership/exposure, level of viewing, frequency of viewing programs and satisfaction of viewing specific Doordarshan programs.

The finding that cable subscribers watched Doordarshan programs for a significantly lesser amount of time per average day when compared with non-subscribers and the finding that cable subscribers have significantly reduced their viewing time of Doordarshan programs after they subscribed to cable implies that Doordarshan's programs have not made a positive difference in terms of the level of viewing with the urban, cabled viewers. Doordarshan's efforts of adding new cable channels and programs particularly meant for urban audiences on its various cable channels have yet to make a significant positive impact on cable audiences (who have numerous private channels to choose from) at least in terms of the level of viewing.

Past research has indicated that in the United States, one reason for cable audiences' viewing of fewer programs of the major networks is increased program offerings by the cable channels. This study found that cable owners watched Doordarshan channels significantly less frequently than did non-subscribers. They were also significantly less satisfied than cable non-subscribers with Doordarshan's programs. Melkote, Sanjay and Ahmed in their study (in this volume) have indicated that satisfaction with television viewing is associated with program variety and program quality. The finding that cable subscribers were significantly less satisfied with Doordarshan programs compared with cable non-subscribers may be an indication that cable subscribers derive greater satisfaction by viewing programs of the privately-owned satellite channels.

Doordarshan has a considerably larger overall market share than private cable/satellite channels because of its vast terrestrial network. It also has an advantage over dissemination of news because of its control over the uplinking facilities. This study showed that both cable subscribers and non-subscribers watched news on television and were more satisfied with news than with any other program on Doordarshan. Our study supports Melkote et al.'s study in Chennai, India; if the results of these studies also reflect the reality in other urban centers in India, the state-run television has difficult challenges to face especially because cable/satellite channels are diffusing at a rapid pace in India.

When STAR TV first entered India, there was a fear that foreign programs may have an adverse impact on the Indian culture. However, the initial popularity of American soaps such as *Bold and Beautiful* and *Santa Barbara* seems to have waned. In this study, it was found that Western serials were least frequently watched by both cable subscribers and non-subscribers. Both categories of audiences were also least satisfied with Western serials. This finding does question the cultural imperialism thesis that presumes a dominant cultural impact of Western programs in non-Western countries.

As in earlier studies, cable subscribers were found to belong to higher income categories compared with non-subscribers. A larger percentage of cable subscribers were found to have higher education levels. In terms of media ownership, it was found that there was a significant difference among the cable subscribers and non-subscribers. More cable subscribers owned radio sets, VCR/VCPs, home telephones, answering machines and computers than non-subscribers.

The findings regarding program preferences in terms of frequency of viewing and level of satisfaction may be useful for advertisers and program producers of Doordarshan and private cable channels. Understanding audience fragmentation in terms of cable subscribers and non-subscribers would also be useful for program producers and advertisers.

This is one of the first studies comparing cabled with the non-cabled homes in India. It is, therefore, an exploratory study . As cable television is a fairly new phenomenon in India and is showing the potential of growing into a major industry, there is a need for more studies such as this to be conducted in India.

References

Agarwal, A. (April 15, 1994). Opening up at last. *India Today*, 108-119.

Atkin, D. (1993). Adoption of Cable Amidst a Multimedia Environment. *Telematics and Informatics*, 10 (*1*), 51-58.

Baldwin, T. F., Barrett, M, and Bates, B. (1992). Uses and values for news on cable television. *Journal of Broadcasting & Electronic Media*, 36 (*2*), pp. 225-233.

Doordarshan '96. Annual report of the Audience Research Unit of Doordarshan, New Delhi.

Doordarshan, 1998. Home page of the government-run television in India at http://www.ddindia.net

Dua, M.R.. (June 15, 1992). No way to put the clock back. *Deccan Herald.*

Henke, L.L., Donohue, T.R., Cook, C., & Cheung, D. (Spring, 1984). Impact of cable on traditional news viewing. *Journalism Quarterly*, 61(1), 174-178.

Jacobs, R. (1995). Exploring the determinants of cable television subscriber satisfaction. *Journal of Broadcasting & Electronic Media.*, 39, 262-274.

Karp, J. (1994). "TV Times," *Far Eastern Economic Review*, 157 (50).

Krugman, D. M. & Rust, R.T. (January/February, 1993). The impact of cable and VCR penetration on network viewing: Assessing the decade. *Journal of Advertising Research*, 67-73.

Lin, C.A. (November/December, 1994). Audience fragmentation in a competitive video marketplace. *Journal of Advertising Research.*

Manorama Year Book. (1995). Kottayam, India: Malayala Manorama.

McQuail, D. (1994). *Mass Communication Theory--An Introduction*, (3rd ed.). London: Sage Publications.

Palmgreen, P. (1984). Uses and gratifications: A theoretical perspective. In R.N. Bostrom (Ed.). *Communication Year Book*, 8: 20-55. Beverly Hills, CA: Sage.

Rahim, A. (1994). Impact of cable TV on television and video viewing in Hyderabad: A survey. *Media Asia*, 21(1), 15-20.

Viswanath, K; Finnegan, J.R., Jr.; Rooney, B; & Potter, J. (1990). Community ties in a rural midwest community and use of newspapers and cable TV. *Journalism Quarterly*, 67(4), 899-911.

Young, D. (February 19,1996). In India, it's Bombay-watch. *Variety.*

PART II

Critical Issues in the Asian Context

Chapter 11

Culture as a 'Market Force': Corporate Strategies in Asian Skies[1]

John Sinclair

"The advances in the technology of telecommunications have proved an unambiguous threat to totalitarian regimes everywhere" (Murdoch, quoted in Hutcheon, 1995). Rupert Murdoch's challenging claim for the liberating force of international television satellite broadcasting, issued in his famous Banqueting House broadcast from London shortly after he had acquired a controlling interest in the pan-Asian STAR TV system in 1993, seems a fair characterisation of the attitude with which several national leaders in the erstwhile Third World regarded this new technology during the 1970s and 1980s. Yet it has proved a hollow threat to the extent that Murdoch has worked hard since to appease the leadership of some of those 'totalitarian' regimes, and undertaken negotiations with them to tailor STAR's mode of delivery and content to their requirements, so as to do business in the national markets of which they clearly are still in effective control (Atkins, 1995). This chapter is about these national political but also cultural barriers which have asserted themselves in relation to the globalising forces within Asian television, and so prevented the realisation of both the hopes and the fears of the 'borderless' television future for Asia which international satellite television broadcasting has seemed to portend.

Old Issues and New Technologies

Because the international satellite system set up by Intelsat in the Asia-Pacific in the late 1960s was based on government co-operation at the global level, and since it was intended predominantly for telephony rather than television, national governments were unprepared for the phenomenon of satellite television signal spillover when, in the 1980s, many countries joined in a trend toward domestic satellite systems, and some television broadcasting migrated to satellite delivery. The challenge to national sovereignty seemed clear, and countries such as Indonesia, although the first country in the region to mount its own satellite system, had to deal with unwanted spillover transmissions being received from neighbouring countries, as well as face the contradiction that domestic audiences could legally watch the Thai and Malaysian channels which were leasing transponders on the Indonesian satellite, Palapa (Kitley, 1994).

In addition to unwanted transborder reception, competition for scarce satellite capacity and for orbital space slots became issues which were fought out in international forums, notably UNESCO and the ITU, throughout the 1970s and 1980s. The dominance of the world satellite business by corporations based in Western nations was contrasted against the communication infrastructure difficulties faced by what were then called 'Third World' nations, and satellite issues were thus incorporated into their whole rhetoric of 'cultural imperialism' and the demands for a New World Information and Communication Order (NWICO). In this context, the 'alien' ways of life and values represented in Western news, entertainment and advertising on television were seen as a deliberate strategy to undermine national sovereignty and cultural integrity.

In the West, the critics of cultural imperialism have become more subdued if not repentant in the 1990s (Schiller, 1991), as the complexities of international cultural influence have become more apparent (Tomlinson, 1991). However, in what are now called the 'newly industrialising' countries, 'cultural imperialism' remains potent as an ideological defence of national governments against mediated cultural influence from the West, perceived as a strategic threat to their control over communication and information flows within their countries. Thus, for example, the Malaysian Prime Minister Mahathir's reaction to Murdoch's initial venture into STAR

TV: "Why has Mr Rupert Murdoch bought 64% stake in STARTV for US $500 million? If he is not going to control news that we are going to receive, then what is it?" (quoted in Atkins, 1995, p. 54).

At the same time as Asian leaders have shown such concern over the apparent penetration of their societies by Western influences, there has been an assertion of 'Asian values'. This is the concept that, despite all their differences, Asian countries when compared to the West have a common core of values which provides the basis for cultural resistance. In practice, rather than an abstract set of essential beliefs and behaviours, 'Asian values' tend to reflect the priorities of different national governments and the more conservative organisations which support them; hence the official codes of *Rukunegara* in Malaysia, *Pancasila* in Indonesia, and Confucianism in Singapore (Karthigesu, 1994). Chenard (1995) noted:

> Especially popular with the Malaysian, Indonesian and Singaporean authorities, the idea is that Asians may not live in multi-party democracies and have unchecked freedom of expression, but they are demonstrably happier and better off than the westerners seen on CNN. (p. 52)

The image of Murdoch and other Western satellite service providers such as Ted Turner, Time-Warner and Disney all positioning themselves to undermine the national cultures of Asia rests upon an anachronistic 1980s rhetoric. With the digital compression and signal encryption capabilities of the coming generation of satellites in Asia, their most striking and consequential characteristic will be their responsiveness to the quite specific political, cultural and linguistic demands of each particular country under their enormous footprints. That is, although the international reach of broadcast satellites might suggest at first sight that their intrinsic advantage is in the economies of scale with which they can reach a dispersed, pan-Asian audience with blanket coverage, experience is showing that the political and cultural-linguistic realities of national markets in Asia requires a country-by-country approach. Contemporary satellite technologies are well placed to meet this alternative purpose, and Western broadcasters are beginning to adopt strategies which use technological solutions to deal with national differences within the region, and the perennial concerns with cultural imperialism.

The Case of Star TV

The history of STAR TV is exemplary in this regard. It began in December 1991, at the initiative of HutchVision, a broadcasting arm of Hutchison Whampoa of Hong Kong, broadcasting five free-to-air advertiser-supported channels over AsiaSat 1. Part-owned by Hutchison Whampoa, in conjunction with Cable & Wireless and a Chinese investment trust, and controlled by the Li Ka-shing family, AsiaSat 1 was the first commercial satellite system to provide blanket regional coverage, and the STAR service immediately provoked anxieties in the People's Republic of China (PRC) and Southeast Asia (Scott, 1991; Hawkes, 1995). When Rupert Murdoch's News Corporation acquired 64% of STAR TV in July 1993, STAR TV was estimating its audience at 45 million, spread over 38 countries (Manasco, 1993). However, four of the five channels were in English (news, entertainment, sports, and music), and the other in Mandarin (Gautier, 1995). Mandarin is the language of the PRC rather than Hong Kong, but this huge potential market already had been proving difficult to HutchVision (Atkins, 1995, 57), and Murdoch's Banqueting House challenge to 'authoritarian regimes' in September 1993 only confirmed Beijing's determination to ban the private ownership of satellite dishes, and so freeze-out STAR (Hutcheon, 1995).

Murdoch soon began implementing a regionalisation strategy of 'going local'. The beam was split into a northern beam for 'Greater China' (Hong Kong, Taiwan and the PRC), and a southern beam for the Indian subcontinent, Southeast Asia, and the Middle East. A significant move came in April 1994, at the stage at which Murdoch was claiming to have built the audience to 173 million and was taking his strategy to regional partners. In the course of 'upgrading' the Chinese service, Murdoch also dropped the BBC World Service Television news channel from STAR. Although STAR has continued to maintain that this was a commercial decision, it is privately conceded that it was political, specifically a response to a direct request from the PRC to drop the service following a frank documentary on Mao Zedong and the use of file footage from Tiananmen Square. Other quite blatant attempts by Murdoch to appease the Chinese hierarchy have followed (Atkins, 1995; Brenchley, 1994; Hutcheon, 1995).

While Murdoch has continued to deal with the PRC as a political problem, other regions have been taken more as cultural and linguistic problems. In addition to its own customised (but still in English) range of channels currently broadcast into India, STAR has acquired a minority half-share in Zee Telefilms which supplies programs to Zee TV and EL TV, in which STAR has a similar stake. Zee TV, in Hindi, is the most popular channel to emerge in India since 1991-92, when satellite-to-cable systems began to proliferate, and undermine the former monopoly of the national public network, Doordarshan. It captures 20% of advertising revenue spent on television, and 25% of the audience, compared to STAR's 5%. This highlights both the minority status of English in India, and the limitations STAR still experienced so long as it carried just a regional blanket of Western programs in English, because a good part of the success of Zee and EL is based on the fact that they produce the bulk of their own programming in popular genres through Zee Telefilms (Ray and Jacka, 1996). Thus, the Indian case has demonstrated that it is not just language which forms a 'natural' cultural barrier against Western content, but that the cultural content of the programs themselves is an issue.

Going Local

Murdoch seems to have grasped these points much more readily than his critics who thought that STAR TV would homogenise Asia with Western culture, and so misread the economic imperative which was motivating his moves. Within six months of acquiring STAR, the declared strategy was to "develop a regional focus---each major market to have a tailored package of both international and local language channels" (quoted in Brenchley, 1994). Noting how in several major Asian markets, 90% to 100% of the top 20 programs were locally produced, STAR affirmed that its acquisition of Zee TV and its 'upgrade' of the Chinese channel were consistent with achieving such a desirable mix of local and international programming, and further announced its intention to mount channels in Hindi, Arabic and Bahasa Indonesia (Brenchley, 1994). As STAR's Director of Corporate Affairs has explained, this strategy of 'going local' meant:

(a) observing the local language, recognising the local culture, local sensitivities and local market conditions;
(b) people want to watch television shows in their own languages that reflect circumstances they can 'identify' with or 'relate to' (Gautier, 1995, p. 2).

The implementation of this strategy has involved a number of deliberate steps. There is the creation of a program production base in the major markets of the region, either by direct investment (as in the case with Zee in India), or by co-production arrangements, such as STAR has established with Taiwan, Hong Kong, and the Philippines (Brenchley, 1994; Gautier, 1995). At the same time, there is ever more devolution of management and programming functions out of Hong Kong and into the major markets. STAR can now boast:

(a) in India we have complete facilities for all STAR TV activities in the country: specifically---production, pay-TV marketing and distribution, subscriber management and customer service, programme publicity, advertising sales, pay TV marketing and distribution, and administrative support. The people making the decisions about which programming and services go to India are based there---on the ground and able to respond quickly to the demands of our viewers;
(b) STAR TV operations for Taiwan and the Middle East (centred in Dubai) and our newly-established headquarters for Southeast Asia (centred in Jakarta) are structured similarly.
(c) Wherever we enter into co-production agreements for new Asia-language material, we devolve as much creative input as possible to our local partners (Gautier, 1995, p. 7).

Technological Solutions

There is a significant technological dimension to STAR's Asian strategies---in fact, as they become available, technological solutions are being applied to deal with the political and cultural barriers which divide the Asian region. First, there is the use of signal encryption, which is used to separate pay services from free-to-air on STAR, and now also is being developed to manage the sensitive problem of unwanted spillover across borders. Controls on the signal can be achieved not just through scrambled transmission, but at the point at which it is re-broadcast through a second satellite and/or cable distribution system. Most so-called 'satellite' and 'cable' television services in the home are in fact delivered by satellite-to-cable systems, and there is relatively little unencoded direct-to-home (DTH) reception of regional (as distinct from national) services in Asia (Atkins, 1995, p. 56). Furthermore, control is also possible with the design of the set-top receiver/decoder box, a business in which Murdoch also has an interest. 'ASIC' technology (application specific integrated circuitry) is bringing down the cost of set-top boxes (van der Heyden, 1995), while News Datacom is developing a 'smart card' conditional access system for DTH reception (Brenchley, 1994, 1995). Thus, News is not only prepared to adapt STAR's delivery system to meet the concerns of particular national governments, it is poised to turn that liability into an asset, by creating immense national markets for its decoders. The digital compression available on the new generation of satellites, notably AsiaSat 2, launched late in 1995 with 32 STAR channels, gives broadcasters great scope to meet the demands of particular national governments as well as catering for the different languages and cultures under the footprint (Cane, 1995; "Star TV Grounded", 1995).

Perhaps the key link in the implementation of all these strategies is Murdoch's direct bilateral negotiations with the leaders of the most difficult countries. The cultivation of 'high level government contacts' with 'Rupert Murdoch visits' was adopted as an arm of News Corporation strategy in 1993, and it has already been noted how far steps have since been taken to resolve the problems News has faced in the PRC (Brenchley, 1994).

Nevertheless, and in spite of widespread evasion, the PRC's ban on satellite dishes remains, and STAR is therefore still locked-out of its largest potential market. However, according to reports from Hong Kong, negotiations are continuing about the prospect of China being able to censor and re-broadcast STAR on its own satellite-to-cable systems (Brenchley, 1995). This would represent a similar solution to that which Murdoch negotiated in person with Prime Minister Mahathir in Malaysia, which reportedly gives the government control over a master switch able to veto programs: re-broadcasting in effect. On the basis of this 'friendly and useful' arrangement, it is now possible that STAR will be carried on Measat, Malaysia's domestic satellite launched in January 1996, with an encrypted DTH service due to be operational around mid-year (Richardson, 1996). This strategy also has the advantage of dealing with the potential competition which the coming generation of other domestic satellite systems in Asia might otherwise present (Atkins, 1995). Formerly, Malaysia has been one of STAR's most vocal opponents. It was Malaysian Prime Minister Mahathir who told the UN General Assembly as recently as 1994, that "Today they broadcast slanted news. Tomorrow they will broadcast raw pornography to corrupt our children and destroy our culture" (Quoted in "Global TV: A Dying Concept", 1994, p. 15).

Cultural Imperialism Not Profitable

Yet, as a Murdoch executive recently observed, "there's no money to be made in cultural imperialism" (Gautier, 1995). STAR sees its interests served by meeting the different demands of its various national markets, not provoking them with the same Western programming which works for News in its other markets, such as with Fox in the US or even BSkyB in Europe. In addition to Murdoch's unilateral deals with Asia's most resistant leaders, the STAR organisation itself is set-up to take care not to offend the considerable political sensitivities and cultural differences within and between the 53 nations under its footprint. STAR claims that it is careful to observe the conditions of its Hong Kong licence, that its 'Standards and Practices Department' vets and self-censors all programming and advertisements, and maintains liaison with national regulatory agencies throughout the region to advise it in doing so, and that it classifies films and provides advance program information for viewers' guidance (Gautier, 1995).

Thus, although STAR has the technological capacity and access to programming which would enable it to rain down the same service right across Asia, 'from Beirut to Beijing', this has been found not to make commercial sense. While there might be notional economies of scale, a service of this kind is not attractive to the broad audiences it seeks, nor therefore to advertisers. It is important to remember that STAR is yet to make a profit: indeed, for the 1994-95 year, STAR lost US $45 million, and expects to lose US $80 million in 1995-6 ("STAR TV Would Lose US $80M", 1995). However, News is well-placed to continue to subsidise STAR from its other ventures (Brewster, 1995), and Murdoch has in the past shown himself prepared to sustain years of heavy losses where he believes that ultimately profit will follow, as was the case with Sky in Europe. News Corporation's commitment to STAR was consolidated in 1995, in fact, with the buying out of the outstanding 36.4% of STAR from the Li Ka-shing family corporations, Hutchison Whampoa and Genza Investment, for US $299 million, giving News full ownership (Frith, 1995).

The 'going local' strategies outlined above constitute a calculated game-plan based on analysis of the limitations and losses of STAR as it was operated when News first acquired its share in 1993. In a play on the aphorism, 'think global, act local', STAR is integrated into Murdoch's global structure, and could deliver just one pan-Asian, regional service, but instead is treating each national market on a case-by-case basis, as we have seen. Also known as 'multilocalism', 'global localism' and even 'glocalisation' (Atkins, 1995), 'going local' emerged in the 1980s as a corporate response to the contradiction between the increasingly globalised nature of production and the localised character of consumption.

This was exemplified in consumer goods marketing, when the British-based global advertising agency Saatchi & Saatchi urged their clients to adopt standardised international advertising campaigns, the 'one sight, one sound, one sell' approach of 'global brands' to fit the new era of global media. On the other hand, other international agencies advocated instead a 'multidomestic' approach, in which their global corporate clients were urged to tailor their marketing in accordance with the cultural and other differences found in their various national markets. In the long run, a few 'global brands' have been successful, but there have been rather spectacular failures, and several international advertising agencies have reorganised themselves to serve global clients on a much more decentralised, regionalised, 'Fordist' mode of operation (Sinclair, 1987, p. 115-119; Mattelart, 1991, p. 48-60). The evidence to resolve this dispute over global marketing strategies will never all be in, but it would appear that intrinsically international goods and services such as credit card systems and airlines lend themselves to a global brands approach, while the great bulk of everyday consumer goods and services are much more successful with a localised approach.

To the extent that the liberalisation of broadcasting and its subsequent sensitivity to 'market forces' makes it analogous to consumer goods marketing, and its attendant strategies of positioning, branding and targeting based on market research, we can say that

News' strategy since 1993 has been to shift STAR TV from a 'global brand' to a 'multidomestic' one. In this process, the use of the languages of the region instead of English, and the fostering of local production for content, are crucial in eliminating the 'cultural discount' which the Asian mass audiences apply to Western programs in English (Hoskins and Mirus, 1988), and also creates its own economies through the vertical integration of production and distribution within the various sub-regional/national markets. At the same time, from the advertisers' point of view, STAR is able to offer a pan-Asian audience to global and regional advertisers, and sub-regional/national audiences advertisers seeking access to audiences at those more limited levels, with each audience being addressed in its own language and cultural terms.

Other Services from the West

If STAR has 'gone local' in these ways, where does that leave the other western-based satellite services in Asia? Both the US-based international television services CNN (owned by Turner Broadcasting Services) and ESPN (the sports service owned by Capital Cities/ABC in the US, which was acquired by Disney) were launched in Asia within a few months of STAR, and carried by Indonesia's Palapa satellite system. Now in its third generation, Palapa is owned by a privatised Indonesian consortium and broadcasts over the ASEAN countries, as well as serving as Indonesia's domestic satellite. It also carries ATV, the international service of the Australian Broadcasting Commission (ABC).

Like STAR, CNN has sought to obtain local programming (Kushu, 1994), and Ted Turner has declared that program schedules dominated by Western material will fail in Asia ("Global TV", 1994), but does not appear to be localising to anywhere near the same extent as STAR (Schuerholz, 1995). CNN and ESPN are now aired on an encrypted, subscription-based arrangement through Indovision, a private Indonesian DTH operation, along with HBO Pacific (owned by Time-Warner); the US Discovery channel; the other Turner channels, TNT and Cartoon Network; and 15 STAR channels, including some specifically designed for Indonesian audiences (Thomas, 1995; 'Briefs', 1995). With its encrypted, pay-TV mode of delivery and Suharto family connections, Indovision represents an Indonesian solution to the problem of national sovereignty over satellite broadcasting, providing both private economic benefit as well as state control (Atkins, 1995).

Although the new Palapa C-1 satellite launched in February 1996 has a wider regional coverage, CNN, ESPN, HBO and Discovery are all more interested in broadcasting into the PRC market, and so have leased space with APT, a consortium of three Chinese government companies and a Thai concern, which owns the APStar satellite system operated out of Hong Kong. However, these and other members of what once could be called the 'Gang of Five', namely MTV (also Channel V in Asia, owned by Viacom of the US); TVBI (Hong Kong's dominant terrestrial broadcaster, and the world's largest producer and distributor of Chinese-language programming); and the Australian ATV service, have all been dealt a serious blow with the destruction of APStar 2 on the launchpad in January 1995 (Hawkes, 1995). Although a replacement is to be launched, and some members of the 'Gang of Five' have transponders on the existing APStar 1, the failure of APStar 2 means a continuing shortage of transponder space going into the PRC---it was to offer abundant channels through digital compression.

However, for STAR TV, the delay in replacing APStar 2 maintains its dominance for the present over the satellite capacity which can broadcast into the PRC, and as well, buys time in which to negotiate the mode of STAR's entry into the prized China market (Atkins, 1995). At present, STAR is continuing to benefit from the Li Ka-shings' original strategy of controlling the entry of competitors by also controlling satellite transponder space. STAR shares Asiasat 1 with China's national broadcaster, China Central Television, which beams to all of the PRC, including Mongolia, Hong Kong, Macao and Taiwan; STAR maintains services to Myanmar and Pakistan, with none of its commercial competitors from the West on Asiasat 1 (Manasco, 1994; Thomas, 1995). Thus, while STAR's position will continue to be advantageous, it will have to deal with competition from however many rival services the 'Gang of Five' will have grown to within the next few years.

Given the trend which STAR is setting towards local languages and content in Asia, the Australian service ATV provides quite an interesting contrast. First established in February 1993, ATV is in the untenable position of being expected to operate as an arm of

Australian cultural diplomacy and national marketing to the region, but having to achieve that on a commercial basis. As one government advocates sees it, "ATV should provide a kind of snap-shot of contemporary Australia and help bury lingering Asian perceptions of an exclusively Anglo-Saxon, agricultural/mining community" (Simper, 1995a). Although never intended as a full commercial service, it is supposed to attract sufficient advertising and sponsorship to fund itself. "We're not competing with STAR for mass audience. We're looking to the niche at the top of the decision-making pole", its Chief Executive still maintains (Mann, quoted in Simper, 1995b). However, even with its restricted target audience, the appropriateness of its programming has been widely questioned, its audience research ridiculed ("Global TV", 1994), and it has not achieved anywhere near the levels of financial support it needs---by 1995, it was nearly US $6 million in debt.

A more positive recent development for ATV has been its inclusion in the package of channels which Singapore CableVision has selected for the new cable service to be delivered over the fibre-optic network now being laid throughout the island. Under its arrangement with SCV (a consortium of Singapore companies with Continental Cablevision of the US), ATV will be able to re-broadcast all of its programs, including the commercial messages, eventually reaching an audience of nearly 3 million when the rollout is completed in 1999. This should make ATV much more attractive to Australian advertisers, and perhaps some Asian ones as well, although this will be quite competitive. Also on the SCV system are STAR Plus; the BBC World Service; Asia Business News; TVB; the Turner channels, CNN, TNT and Cartoon Network; MTV Asia/MTV Mandarin/ Channel V; ESPN; Discovery; and others (Howard, 1995).

National Barriers

Singapore's position with regard to the region's anxieties about cross-border satellite broadcasting is worth noting. Because of its size and perhaps also the relatively strict regimen of social control to which it is accustomed, Singapore has been successful in maintaining a ban on the possession of satellite dishes, while at the same time offering domestic cable instead---a UHF cable system has been available in Singapore since 1992, although with only 25,000 subscribers

(Chenard, 1995; Howard, 1995). In this sense, Singapore arrived at its own counterpart to the controlled satellite-to-cable solution which Murdoch has negotiated with Malaysia and has on the table in China. However, consistent with its drive to establish itself as an information/ communications hub within the region, Singapore has also become active in attracting satellite service providers to locate their regional operations in Singapore, including Asia Business News and the US-based HBO, ESPN, MTV and Discovery Channels. These services uplink to satellites from Singapore, but they may not transmit into it, although most of them are available there on cable. Singapore's rivalry over Hong Kong in this regard has been greatly assisted by Hong Kong's more restrictive regulations and also the Chinese government's decision not to approve Hong Kong's granting of any more uplink licences (like STAR's) in the leadup to the 1997 unification ("Asians Spoilt", 1995). According to one recent report, "Singapore believes it can provide a liberal operating base for electronic media groups without compromising its tight control over local broadcasting or eroding prevailing conservative values" (Richardson, 1995).

A Regional Perspective

STAR's strategy of 'going local' shows how much language and culture have emerged as tangible 'market forces' which global broadcasters, in pursuit of their self-interest, must come to terms with sooner or later. We have seen how the carefully demarcated differences between (and within) Asian nations and their various languages and cultures have favoured the application of technological solutions which have sealed-off each nation from the others, but created a finite aperture for global services such as STAR to enter. If this situation is set in a comparative, world-regional perspective, it provides an instructive contrast to Latin America, where international satellite television is established longer and has become a powerful force for regional cultural integration.

Whereas the several distinct languages and cultures of Asia are barriers to a regional identity, in Latin America, the prevalence of the Spanish language in nearly every nation, even with the significant exception of Portuguese-speaking Brazil, provides the basis for broadcast services and program markets to have developed not just on a continental, but on an intercontinental scale, bridging North as well as South and Central America. Television everywhere continues to perform its traditional nation-binding role in conjunction with the forces of globalisation, but in Latin America, linguistic-cultural similarities enables a level of regional integration not possible in Asia.

Benedict Anderson's (1983) concept of 'imagined communities' has been one of the most influential tropes in theories of national consciousness for more than a decade, but as satellite television distribution transcends the borders of the nation-state, there is still some value in applying it to the new audience entities which that process creates: the imagined communities of speakers of the same language and participants in similar cultures which form 'geolinguistic' regions. The concept of region can be therefore understood as mere contiguous international physical space, as in 'the Asian region'; alternatively, and in more techno-cultural terms, the concept of region can be understood as the imagined community of Spanish-speakers, dispersed in a score of nations on three continents, but united by satellite television in a way that Asia's barriers to STAR make clear that it is not.

Just as the United States for so long has dominated television program schedules in the geolinguistic region of the English-speaking world by virtue of being the largest producer in that language, Mexico dominates the Spanish-speaking world, and Brazil the Portuguese. More particularly, the private media conglomerates Televisa in Mexico and Globo in Brazil predominate in their respective domestic markets, based largely on their vertical integration of production and distribution, not unlike what STAR is achieving with Zee in India. Televisa and Globo have used their market power to go on to develop international operations in program exports, and acquire direct shares in foreign networks. Televisa as well provides international services via satellite to Latin America, the United States and Spain, and is a half-owner in PanAmSat, the world's first privately-owned satellite system, which now has been extended across the globe (Sinclair, 1996). PanAmSat not only covers the Americas and Europe, but has one satellite covering the Asian region (including Australia, where it has its regional office), and another over the Indian Ocean region (Hawkes, 1995; "Summer Launches", 1995).

The international dimensions and activities of Televisa and Globo have not been well known outside of the Latin world, but of course they have not escaped Rupert Murdoch's attention. One of the less-publicised announcements in the Banqueting House speech was a joint venture between Fox and Televisa to produce 500 hours of multilingual popular drama (Amdur, 1993). This year News announced a partnership with Globo to operate a DTH service over Latin America and the Caribbean Basin, this in addition to the Fox Latin America cable channel already operated by News, which has 3.3 million subscribers and partnerships with several sub-regional channels in Latin America ('News, Globo Link', 1995). Although there has been enormous expansion in cable services throughout Latin America over the last decade, the choice of cable as a means of delivery has been commercially driven rather than the political expedient it has been in parts of Asia. Now, DTH seems set to overcome cable, particularly as major global system providers such as PanAmSat and Hughes are committed to DTH development in the region (Foley, 1995). As we have seen, Indonesia and Malaysia have also opted for encrypted DTH systems, but although there are commercial benefits for the systems' owners, the choice of DTH in those countries seems to have been much influenced by the desire of governments to control and limit access to foreign television services.

A related aspect of the unified market which Latin America presents, relative to Asia's differences, is the opportunity which it affords to US-based broadcasters who are already offering services or producing in Spanish for the US Spanish-speaking population of up to 20 million, or who find economies of scale in doing so for the approximately 300 million of Latin America. In addition to Fox, these include several of the same Gang of Five US cable companies which have been competing in Asia: Turner's CNN, TNT and Cartoon Network; Disney's ESPN; Time-Warner's HBO ('Ole'); and Viacom's MTV. PanAmSat has been the carrier for most of these. As one of the trade journalists puts it, Latin America's attractions for foreign investors and programmers are: 'proximity to North America, minimal language variations, cultural affinity with one of America's largest and fastest-growing populations, increasing consumer spending power and, of course, a proven appetite for TV' (Amdur, 1995). Clearly, the linguistic-cultural cohesion of the Americas gives the US a point of entry to the Latin American region for which there is no counterpart in Asia, not for the US nor any other prospective cultural imperialist, as the experience of ATV and even STAR shows. For foreign program and service providers, international satellite broadcasting has not turned Asia's political and linguistic-cultural barriers into bridges, while for Asia, the successful determination of key national governments to subordinate the medium to their control has constrained whatever potential it might have held for a sense of identity as a region.

Conclusion

Given the arrangements now in place to redistribute foreign satellite television---Singapore's cable network, Indonesia's DTH system, Malaysia's master switch and a similar prospective solution in the PRC---what are we to think of the 'cultural imperialism' rhetoric and its image of Western-based global media spilling their signals across one border after another throughout the entire Asian region, undermining national sovereignty, dissipating traditional cultures, and corrupting moral values? The alternative view which emerges from the present analysis is that the regimes in control of the leading nation-states in the region not only have successfully withstood the considerable forces of globalisation, but negotiated arrangements which actually reinforce their power and secure privileges in the communication industries for both state and private interests. Moreover, they have done so with 'cultural imperialism' as their ideological rationale. Even more striking is the conclusion that cultural and linguistic differences have in themselves proved to be much more substantial barriers to foreign programming than the theory of cultural imperialism would have predicted, and that the global service providers have had to accede to the demand for popular programming in the languages of the region.

Notes

[1] An earlier version of this essay appeared under the title, "The Business of Broadcasting: Cultural Bridges and Barriers" in the *Asian Journal of Communication*, Volume 7, No. 1, 1997. Reprinted with permission.

References

Amdur, M. (1993, October). Latin America: TV's Next Frontier? *Broadcasting & Cable International*, 52-60.

Anderson, B. (1983). *Imagined communities: Reflections on the origin and spread of nationalism.* London: Verso.

Asians Spoilt for TV Choice. (1995, May 5). *Ad News*, 30.

Atkins, W. (1995, August). "Friendly and useful": Rupert Murdoch and the politics of television in Southeast Asia, 1993-1995. *Media International Australia, 77,* 54-64.

Brenchley, F. (1994, April 20). Revealed: Murdoch's Star Wars strategy. *Australian Financial Review.*

Brenchley, F. (1995, January 31). Murdoch back-pedals on high ideals to make luck in China. *Australian Financial Review.*

Brewster, D. (1995, August 23). $1.34 bn profit a news record. *The Australian.*

Briefs. (1995, March 23). *Telenews Asia*, 3.

Cane, A. (1995, December 5). Historic AsiaSat-2 heralds long march. *The Australian.*

Chan, J. M. (1996). Television in Greater China: Structure, exports and market formation. In J. Sinclair, E. Jacka, & S. Cunningham (Eds), *New patterns in global television: Peripheral vision* (pp. 126-160). Oxford: Oxford University Press.

Chenard, S. (1995, March). Censorship of satellite TV in Asia: A commentary. *Via Satellite*, 48-56.

Foley, T. (1995, February). The Latin American gold rush: Prospecting for DTH viewers. *Via Satellite*, 40-47.

Frith, J. (1995, July 19). News takes full control of Star TV. *The Australian.*

Gautier, D. (1995). Borderless Communications and Cultural Concerns in Asia: Real or Exaggerated? Paper presented to Asian Mass Communication and Information Research Centre (AMIC) conference on Communications, Culture and Development, Jakarta, 22-4 June.

Global TV: A dying concept. (1994, April). *Communications Update*, 15.

Hawkes, R. (1995, June). Asia's slice of space. *Asian Communications*, 29-32.

Hoskins, C., & Mirus, R. (1988). Reasons for the US dominance of the international trade in television programmes. *Media, Culture and Society, 10* (4), 499-515.

Howard, J. (1995, June 13). ABC wins cable slot in Singapore. *The Australian*.

Hutcheon, S. (1995, January 27). Murdoch makes amends. *The Age*.

Karthigesu, R. (1994, August). Television in the Asian cultural map. *Media Information Australia, 73,* 90-96.

Kitley, P. (1994). Fine tuning control: Commercial television in Indonesia. *Continuum, 8* (2),103-123.

Knapp, G. (1994, February 3-16). PanAmSat focuses on Australian cities', *Encore*, 14-15.

Kushu, O. P. (1994). Satellite communications in Asia: An Overview. *Media Asia, 20* (1), 3-9.

Manasco, B. (1993, November). Reflections on the News Corp./Star TV Deal. *Via Satellite*, 20-22.

Manasco, B. (1994, January). The last empire: APT Satellite prepares to conquer Asia. *Via Satellite*, 62-64.

Mattelart, A. (1991). *Advertising international: The privatisation of public space*. London and New York: Comedia.

News, Globo Link in Latin American Satellite Venture. (1995, July 12). *The Australian*.

Ray, M., & Jacka, E. (1996). Indian television: An emerging regional force. In J. Sinclair, E. Jacka, & S. Cunningham (Eds.), *New patterns in global television: Peripheral vision* (pp. 83-100). Oxford: Oxford University Press.

Richardson, M. (1995, September 5). Obstructive Chinese drive broadcasters into Singapore. *The Australian*.

Richardson, M. (1996, January 19). New satellite puts Pay TV war into orbit in Malaysia. *The Australian*.

Schiller, H. (1991). Not yet the post-imperialist Era. *Critical Studies in Mass Communication, 8,* 13-28.

Simper, E. (1995a, September 11). DFAT urges funding instead of ads for Asia TV. *The Australian*.

Simper, E. (1995b, June 12). Signal failure. *The Australian*.

Sinclair, J. (1987). *Images incorporated: Advertising as industry and ideology*. London and Sydney: Croom Helm and Methuen.

Sinclair, J. (1996). Mexico, Brazil, and the Latin World. In J. Sinclair, E. Jacka, & S. Cunningham (Eds.), *New patterns in global television: Peripheral vision* (pp. 33-66). Oxford: Oxford University Press.

Schuerholz, K. (1995, September). Worldwide programming. *Via Satellite*, 44-57.

Scott, M. (1991, November 28). News from nowhere. *Far Eastern Economic Review*, 32-34.

Star TV grounded by satellite glitch. (1995, March 17). *The Australian*.

STAR TV "would lose US $80 M". (1995, October). *Asia-Pacific Broadcasting*, 2.

Summer launches. (1995, September). *Asian Communications*, 99-101.

Thomas, A. (1995, February). ASEAN television and Pan-Asian broadcast satellites: Terrestrials encounter the extra-terrestrial. *Media Information Australia, 75,* 123-129.

Tomlinson, J. (1991). *Cultural imperialism: A critical introduction.* Baltimore: Johns Hopkins University Press.

van der Heyden, T. (1995). The Impact of New Communication Technologies on the Broadcasting Environment in Asia. Paper presented to Asian Mass Communication and Information Research Centre (AMIC) conference on Communications, Culture and Development, Jakarta, 22-4 June.

Chapter 12

Local Consumption of Global Television: Satellite Television in East Java

Hart Cohen

This chapter summarizes research undertaken in July 1995 in which a sample of television viewers in Surabaya was surveyed on the use of satellite television.[1] The study provides base-line data on the local consumption of global television. It was executed as a pilot project with a sample size of 150 persons. The respondents were selected using the random probability method and questioned on their use of television delivered by a parabolic device.

This study raised a number of issues: (a) the relationship of satellite television to the mediascape of Indonesian society, (b) contemporary media's relationship to older Indonesian cultural and political formations, and (c) satellite broadcasting in Indonesia in the historical and current context of global satellite broadcasting.

The study concludes that tensions are evident in the debate concerning the future of broadcast media in Indonesia. This debate concerns the challenge of assessing the changing cultural values in the local/global nexus of satellite broadcasting in Indonesia.

The chapter consists of four main sections: (1) a review of the study of satellite television, (2) a history of satellite television in Indonesia, (3) an introduction to the key issues surrounding the analysis of satellite television in Indonesia, and (4) a data analysis from a quantitative survey of the use of satellite channels in Surabaya, East Java.[2] This research sampled a segment of the satellite television audience in Surabaya, East Java. While there are many ways to develop the results of this research, this chapter is primarily about the relationship of satellite channels in Indonesia to the audience use of television, both local and global, that is available.

Study of Satellite Television Broadcasting

Research into satellite television has been on the ascendancy for the last five years. In 1990, the Asian Mass Communication Research and Information Centre (AMIC) held its annual conference on the theme of satellites: "Socioeconomic Impact of Broadcast Satellites in Asia and the Pacific." This was closely followed by another conference on satellites sponsored by the Asian Pacific Broadcasting Union. Despite this, the understanding of satellite television's audience is in its infancy. Ask any satellite broadcaster about audience reach and the numbers mentioned bear little resemblance to those associated with home-market consumption. Eyes may enlarge and look upward in a metaphoric gaze of a "sky's the limit" look. But few studies of satellite audiences have admitted to confirming anything but a projected audience based on the statistical projections related to hardware access. What audiences are doing or thinking about with global images is yet to be comprehensively ascertained (Goonasekera, 1995).

To construct the larger picture of international television usage consider that between 1987 and 1991 the average weekly output of international television around the world increased by 42.2%. In 225 of the countries surveyed, total output doubled and in Indonesia, mentioned specifically in this report, it increased by 424%.[3] Between time-binding communication technologies and space-binding ones, a distinction made popular by Harold Innis (1951, 1994), satellite technology is space-binding.

Satellites are said to extend the useful range of the radio frequency spectrum, weaken cost-distance inter-relationships, and economically establish point-to-multipoint (broadcasting) as well as point-to-point (telecommunications) communications across wide geographic areas (Collins, 1990). They have been touted as extending choice, enhancing competition in established communication markets and re-fashioning new relationships out of established communities and markets.

Local-Global Nexus

Foreign satellite television companies are the effective competitors for this television audience and the chief alternative to domestic television in the communication of cultural values. Our research has corroborated earlier surveys (Wang, 1993), however, to show that increased access to foreign-language programming has had only mixed results in relation to the lowering of consumption of locally-produced programming. The trend towards a preference for domestic product over imported television is evident. In an account of the trend towards local programming, Michael Tracey points to a recent study of nine Asian countries; of the 34 networks in these nine Asian countries (Hong Kong, Indonesia, Thailand, Taiwan, Japan, Korea, Malaysia, Philippines, Singapore), the author concluded that a majority of television hours in each of the countries was domestically produced with the exception of Malaysia and Singapore. This ascribes real potency to national, regional and ethnic commitments and sentiments. The trend towards syncretism of television programming allows for the crossover of cultural values. Regional responses may play a large role in how global television is accepted and used.

Brazilian Soap Opera and MTV Asia

The Indonesian commercial television sphere is a complex mix of international and local programs, the most popular being Brazilian soap opera. Why Brazilian soap opera? Brazil has the sixth largest television market in the world. Its main channel, *TV Globo* captures between 60% and 80% of the television audience. In prime time, 84% of its programs are locally produced. In 1983, the top ten were all *TV Globo* productions. As pointed out by Richard Paterson (1982), Brazilian television is devoted to national culture. *TV Globo* has fully utilised the possibilities created by these circumstances to develop a different sort of television and puts into question the thesis about the inevitability of traditional drama retreating before the likes of *Peyton Place* and *Bonanza*. The success of *TV Globo* is massive and it exports to 100 countries. It appears that an example of a developing country such as Brazil will resonate more strongly with a country like Indonesia than countries in the west.

Another area of successful transnational communication occurs in the world of music television. Our study showed that MTV Asia was the most popular channel watched in Surabaya. MTV is very popular across the satellite spectrum and travels well across national borders. Taste cultures which replace national or regional-specific cultural constraint may allow for this ease of exchange across national boundaries.

As noted earlier, language is a barrier but not an absolute one. Speaking and understanding are different skills---television can be watched and understood with sometimes a minimum of language skills. "Reversioning" ensures that language and cultural specificity may be served---for example, a *Neighbours* script might be recast with Russian actors and set in Moscow. In this way the preference for local television is partially served in conjunction with foreign scripts.

Promises and Threats of Satellite Television

Currently, satellite television works through the downlinks and uplinks which permit local broadcasters to cut in and out of particular services. In looking at Australian television, for example, the preferences of local broadcasters may vary the service according to the perceived desires of their audience: Laos takes news, Guandong in China prefers sports, documentaries and music, Vietnam tunes in to science features (Fell, 1995). The target audience is achieved with a cable roll-out for the redistribution of satellite signals. The absence of this redistribution greatly hampers the growth of a satellite audience. The geospatial conditions of any country may or may not favour this technology. Singapore, for instance will be completely cabled in a relatively short amount of time. Indonesia will take much longer.

In a study published in the early part of this decade, Richard Collins (1990) suggested that satellites promised to lower costs of telecommunications and create new stratifications of the television audience; make viable specialised channels for specific publics, eg., children, domestic users, and business. New groupings or "global communities" would replace the national. In Europe, satellite was touted as a means of fostering a European identity---a mass audience and public with a European consciousness and European identity. These promises are also potential threats. Satellite may threaten traditional communication markets pricing former viewers out of the market. New distinctions will emerge between information-rich and poor along new class lines. European cultural interests may be jeopardised by "coca-cola satellites"---the dominance of American pop culture. The older media imperialism thesis finds favour once again. At a UNESCO meeting in Mexico in July 1982, the then French Minister of Culture, Jack Lang, identified the American TV soap, *Dallas* as a threat to the national culture of France. Lang called for a crusade "against financial and intellectual imperialism that no longer grabs territory or rarely, but grabs consciousness, ways of thinking, ways of living...".[4]

These threats and promises are tempered, according to Collins (1990), by an important filter: language. A language community will tend to prefer information content encoded in its own language. But other factors may mitigate this seemingly common sense rule of global television consumption. The size of the market is one such factor as is the variation of languages spoken within a national framework. English programming is frequently finding its way into non-Anglophone markets rather than the other way round. There are a number of comparative advantages which Anglophone producers enjoy. But these advantages do not guarantee open-ended access to non-English markets.

Other important filters are cultural and political in nature. At the moment, satellite service providers are said to bypass national regulatory agencies, they are found to bend quickly when confronted with a potentially lost market. Murdoch's STAR TV is a case in point in the context of India, Malaysia and China. The Chinese objected to the BBC world service news and heeded Murdoch's unusually loose remarks about "satellite television making problems for totalitarian regimes". But should the Chinese government have had anything to worry about? Studies have revealed that global news values are incredibly diverse (Chapman, 1992). In a study by the International Institute of Communications, an analysis of one day's (November 19, 1991) news stories by almost every major television system in the world was carried out. The results were fascinating. Graham Chapman (1992), a geographer, noted:

> As a broad statement there were several stories that reached fairly wide---the meeting of G77 countries in Teheran, a subject wholly ignored by the developed world; the Francophone nations summit held in Paris ignored by the English world except in Canada (bilingual); follow ups on East Timor massacre well reported in Asia but hardly outside it;...appointment of Shevernadze as Foreign Minister for the USSR; conflict in Yugoslavia between

Croats and Serbs; the release of hostages Waite and Sutherland was not mentioned in Korea and by only one station in Japan.

Chapman (1992) concluded that news was very local and frequently did not travel outside national boundaries. Some news traveled but it was predominantly of interest to Western networks. Local concerns predominated..."What it is the world chose to know about itself on this one night is myriad, diffuse, disconnected. It seems there are many world's on this one earth...and that mostly they stay next door, minding their own business." And in the words of another researcher, "The story here is that news doesn't flow very far at all..." (Dennis, E, 1992)

The problems of audience-draw for satellites, then, are many: language and cultural filters, the lack of redistribution technology, competing services for especially local terrestrial "free-to-air" television, and the difficulties of satisfying different audience tastes which vary from country to country and even within countries.

Satellite Television in Indonesia: A Brief History

Indonesia was a pioneer in satellite television adoption and launched its first satellite in 1976. Palapa 1 was seen as a potential development tool, an educating tool, a tool for national unity and fully in line with New Order political values. Little was anticipated of the current global revolution. With third generation satellites launched, Indonesia has continued at the forefront of this form of media but the government is now confronted with a media and public sphere that is considerably more complex than in the era of Palapa 1. This complexity has been analysed as a set of challenges posed by the commercial media sector to what has been a government-controlled industry (Shoesmith, 1993); this may indicate the waning of older ideological schemes (nationalist discourses) in favour of commercial values.

"Open Skies" Vs. "New Order Skies"

In the realm of satellite television, Indonesia is said to pursue an open skies policy. No interference in the coverage of foreign events is supposed to take place. The local channels are rapidly expanding in

Indonesia. TVRI channel was introduced in 1962 but only reached a national audience with the launch of the satellite in 1976. Suharto banned advertising in 1981 because he claimed it would create envy and consumerism. Increasingly, television became a government mouthpiece. By 1989, TVRI was in decline though it is still the sole provider of domestic news while continuing its stated mission of assisting with national development. In 1983, the B generation of Palapa satellites were launched with the possibility of smaller antenna sizes to receive programs. By 1986 significant numbers of Indonesians began receiving television programs directly by satellite. The first commercial station was finally opened in 1987---a licence granted to a company owned by Suharto's son. A second station in the Surabaya region was granted in 1990 to Suharto's cousin. Three further commercial licences have been granted. TPI was granted a licence in August 1990. This channel is owned by Suharto's eldest daughter. The two other channels are owned by close associates of Suharto. The "open skies" of Indonesian television are in reality "New Order skies".

It is doubtful that the nationalist agenda advanced by the government is any longer a viable narrative. Party political purposes prevail in the maintenance of current structures buttressed by military acquiescence. The oscillation between the national and the global forces is much more an encounter between oligarchic forces incorporating the commercial sector and government identities defining a relatively small base of control in the context of global pressures.

Key Issues in the Analyses of Indonesian Satellite Television

The study of global television is also the study of contemporary mediations of cultural values. For Indonesia, the dynamics of cultural practices are mediated by their placement within a social formation crossed by the hybridity of multiple cultural formations within a single state. Questions of media values may be posed and answered as part of a critical assessment of the media in Indonesia as a public discourse. There is a juxtaposition of diverse media activities in the context of a changing mediascape and public sphere. The context of globalisation makes understanding the cultural values of Indonesian media one of cross-cultural understanding and assessment.

Some Definitions

Media. This can refer to the many forms through which a public discourse may be constructed. Print (press, magazines, books), television, radio, film, and music are joined by CD-ROM, the internet and the more recent applications of telecommunications related to information services. This definition of media may also include the traditional work of healers, magicians or tribal elders. Media here might be fire, water, special foods, herbs etc. Our selected media for this research is primarily television (particularly the available television delivered by a parabolic device or satellite) and secondarily, the press and radio.

Guided Democracy and the New Order. "Guided Democracy" is a term coined to describe a period in Indonesian political history. It specifically refers to the period of Sukarno's regime from 1959-1966. The background to this political development in Sukarno's reign is important from the standpoint of linking this period to the current regime known as the "New Order" under Suharto. Suharto began a retrenching of democratic practices---a constraining of the very public debates that had occurred during Sukarno's reign regarding the political direction of the country. The overthrow of Sukarno in 1966 and the installation of Suharto as his successor was a bloody affair.

The idea of a "guided democracy" was retained under Suharto though with a different emphasis. There is a parliament and regular elections in Indonesia but the political culture remains a command culture, strongly centralised with careful constraining and use of interest groups (the army, the Islamic movement) to concentrate power. So in effect, to examine the cultural values of Indonesian media, the larger context of political values which constrain the media in Indonesia must be a part of that examination.

Press Censorship

Paul Tickell (1993) argues that in the context of the press, the current mechanisms of control over the Indonesian press under Suharto's New Order have their roots in Sukarno's Guided Democracy statutes of the 1960's. The Basic Press Law of 1966, for example, was amended in 1982; though the relationship between state and press was left intact. This suggests a greater affinity between the Sukarno and Suharto regimes with regard to press freedom than would have normally been assumed on the basis of other differences (eg., in ideology, political practices). These political values in turn are influenced by the changing scene of global media and the adoption of new communication technologies. For Indonesia with a command political culture and centralised political purposes, this may pose substantial problems. It is well-known, for example, how the different regions create particular political tensions in Indonesia and have done so for some time. It is precisely the fostering of regional identities which global media can influence by bypassing physical borders and engaging in various exchanges from culture to commerce. It is communication processes which are at the focal point where the spheres of culture and commerce cross.

National, International, Global, Local

It is in this context that the terms *national, international, global* and *local* need to be carefully considered. The national in the context of Indonesia is a term related to what could be called its most significant identity-narrative, i.e., the story of Indonesia's independence from a long period of colonisation by the Dutch. The anti-colonial story is the story of the "national"---of Indonesia becoming a nation. (The salient example of Indonesia's success at enacting this story on the world stage climaxed in Bandung in 1956 when Sukarno led a meeting of non-aligned nations. It was at this conference that the term "Third World" was coined as a referent for non-aligned nations). The "national" in Indonesia has had a paradoxical relationship to the "international"---to have forms of internationalism presupposes the existence of nations and nationalism.[5]

The idea of the "global" displaces both the national and the international. Edge cities and regions become centres of potential engagement. As Harold Innis (1986) pointed out, it is on the margins of the various empires where the most significant political events may occur.[6] Innis claimed that particular media could have consequences for centre-margin relationships and attached importance to the assertion of particularism among groups. In this respect, Innis anticipated contemporary arguments about the increasing manifestation of localist assertions in the face of global information systems.

The idea of the "local" is central to contemporary arguments about cultural and political autonomy in the "margins". Local consumption of media implies links to a "centre" but from a local base of "...administrative, cultural, economic and social interest..."[7] and of the possibility of global information and communication systems which may link these "margins" to other margins and other centres. In this regard, it is critical to distinguish the local from the national even as the "national" may operate as an ideological buffer to globalisation. It drives home the point made by Sreberny-Mohammadi (1996) that the cultural hybridity of modern nations produces not a uniform "imagined community" but a community with multiple identifications and affiliations.

Press and the Meta-Narrative of the "National" in Indonesia

National borders do exist and are carefully policed. But increasingly they are bypassed by the forms of global activities in the realms of culture, commerce and communications. The crucial question for the Indonesian media is continuity of its cultural and political values given (a) its close links to the older nationalist movements and contemporary national imaginings in the face of global pressures for fragmentation and (b) the current tensions within localist political and regional formations. This tension has an earlier motif in the development of the press in Indonesian modern history. One of the salient features of the Indonesian press through the period of its nationalist ascendancy was the close relationship between the nationalist groupings, political parties and the press---the various newspaper initiatives from early this century to form the "intellectual vanguard of Indonesian nationalism" (Tickell, 1993, p. 4). This view of the press may be tempered by the former existence of Sino-Malay, Eurasian, and Dutch language press though the disappearance of many of these is an index of the dominance of the anti-colonial, nationalist press. The press in the period immediately after independence (1950-58) was pluralistic and democratic in that there were few instances of censorship. The move to the period of Guided Democracy under Sukarno and the subsequent principles of *Pancasila* under Suharto's New Order saw a considerable tightening of controls on extra-parliamentary groups and an escalation of restrictions on the press.

This was and is evidenced by increased examples of censorship, and the installation of a system of press permits coupled with defamation laws which in formal and institutional terms work to influence the role of the press in a manner that could be seen as anti-democratic (Tickell, 1993).

Anura Goonasekera (1993) has argued that Pancasila is the "...indigenous philosophical foundation of the (Indonesian) nation...." In this context, "...all social institutions are shaped in its image. The press is no exception...The press in Indonesia is a partner in nation-building. It is, therefore, an instrument of the government policy of Pancasila..." This argument seeks to establish a case for the specificity of cultural values within a given ideological framework. *Pancasila* is assumed to be the code for nation-building rather than the ideological framework in use by the current regime. This argument ignores an important historical period in Indonesia's anti-colonial struggle in which the press played a critical role.[8] Holaday (1996) has asserted that earlier studies of satellite television failed to include key aspects of historical context and economic and social organisation, eg., land tenure, agrarian reform, distribution of international loans, etc. These are micro-historical and localist concerns posing culturally specific constraints on media consumption and production and critical to the larger picture of the use of satellite television. Satellite television may be examined in light of these assessments of the institution of the press and the contemporary role of the media. Against the meta-narrative of the "national" which defines the limits of democracy in the mainstream press, may be posed the conflict between the "local" and the "global", whose potential and contradictory effects are evidenced in the local consumption of global media.

Survey of the Use of Satellite Channels in East Java

Local Consumption of Global Television

In turning towards the example of satellite broadcasting in Indonesia, the current moment is a vortex of ideologies, technologies and diversely-held communication values. Adapting Collins' (1990) hardware-software model, "hardware" dimension refers to satellite television's convergence of media and message while the "software" refers to local language and culture. This is analogous to the earlier reference to the encounter between a nationalist press and its global competitors. Because of the potential threats and promises of satellite television and related global communications, a careful assessment of the consequences for the public interest is crucial. There is a need to understand how global television not only stratifies audiences but also how it affects consciousness in the formation of cultural identities and values.

Methodologically, the critical concern of ethnocentrism---the imposition of subjective cultural values on the problems and practices under investigation---has been partially addressed by the involvement of Indonesian research partners in East Java. The Indonesian research team members have been particularly effective in correcting errors in the design of the sample questionnaire. They have informed the study with correct protocols for the execution of research. We have chosen not to avoid the fact of ethnocentrism, necessary in every cross-cultural project, but to treat it as an "objective" bias---as a constraint of knowledge production in this domain. Any interpretative moves of a cross-cultural kind, however, are made in relation to the re-construction of our own cultural processes. In this sense, our "outsiderness" is mirrored and doubled---and the insights obtained are both about Indonesian cultural practices as well as our own.

Looking at the specific results of the survey will allow for a partial account of the current status of the local consumption of satellite television in East Java. The study begins with a survey of "hardware" use. It found in the sample a much higher incidence of ownership of expensive communications hardware than would be expected in this social context.

Demographics

The study was conducted through a random rather than quota sampling method.   It is therefore significant that the sample maintained an earlier suspected bias towards highly educated and wealthy Indonesians in the ownership of satellite dishes, most of whom watch satellite television in their own homes. This trend is confirmed by earlier studies (see Holaday, 1996).

In terms of language, the overwhelming responses were restricted to Bahasa Indonesia and Javanese with the largest second language grouping being Mandarin. The small percentage of declared English speakers suggests that this is not a positive indicator of satellite television usage. In relation to regional affiliation, the sample split between East Java including Surabaya (58%) and other regions (41%). This confirms the hybridity and fluidity of the population suggesting multiple identifications within this particular cultural formation.

Viewing and Listening Frequencies

With close to 50% of respondents reporting that they watch more than 4 hours of television daily, the use of television is substantial. This compares with 32% reported as viewing 3-4 hours daily in an earlier study conducted in 1982 (see Chu, Alfian & Schramm, 1991). However, in 1982, broadcast hours were limited to between 6 and 10 pm with only domestic stations available. Radio listening on a daily basis involved 42% of those surveyed compared with 46% reporting radio as their favoured spare time activity in 1982. Our survey suggests that there is a slight diminished use of radio with increased choice and frequency of television access via satellite. This is less than what is usually predicted by those who propose that television is a more likely medium for the future than radio. It suggests that television and radio are used differently by different media constituencies.[9]

Our survey reports an average of two television sets per household similar to Western averages reflecting the slant toward high-income demographics. Other high percentages were reported for ownership of stereo systems, personal computers and video cassette players, suggesting that those with higher incomes may own more communication technologies (in follow-up studies we found about 10% of those surveyed had an internet connection).

The majority of the group sample owned their own satellite dish (96%) rather than sharing a dish. The purchase of satellite dishes peaked in 1990 for this group of satellite television users. This coincided with the introduction of three new commercial stations in Indonesia. In this regard, Indonesia is somewhat unique in that a majority of domestic television is delivered by satellite. The main reason reported for purchase, however, was to access overseas stations (87%). Familiarity with satellite television may have provided a basis for acceptance of overseas broadcasts despite a reported strong satisfaction with local programming. Other factors may include "perceived" advantages in maintaining contact with the West and the prominence of television as a means of cultural connections within Indonesian society.

Program Interests

News is given high preference ratings here (over 45%), while rock music is rated relatively low (32%). This is contradicted by viewing patterns in which MTV Asia is the highest rated channel. Viewers may be inclined to state what "ought " to be valued but reveal a different pattern of actual consumption. Viewing patterns of overseas television place TV 3 Malaysia and MTV Asia at the top of the list. The highest ranking English language service is CNN. Australia Television is also strongly placed with almost equal access numbers though with lower consumption numbers than other English language stations. There is considerable access and popularity when considered against the available English-language stations. Follow-up studies place CNN, STAR TV, MTV Asia, and Australia Television in the top channel placings (STAR TV includes its "bundle" of channels: STAR Plus, STAR Sports, STAR Chinese Channel, and STAR 'V' Channel). A difficulty in analysing global television in this viewing context is defining precisely what global television is. CNN is deemed a global channel reaching around the globe but targeting certain regions with specific programming. Australia Television is "regional" reaching southeast and northeast Asia and parts of Asia Pacific. Indonesians also access Malaysian TV through satellite services and see it as a part of the "domestic" services. This suggests that from the perspective of consumption, the definition of "global" is a fluid one which may or may not conform to the manner in which a satellite broadcaster is mapping the delivery of programs.

The average daily viewing of overseas programming is just over 2 hours a day. Because 50% of those surveyed watch 4 hours a day, we can conclude that approximately 50% of television watched by this survey group is made up of overseas programming. This is quite high and may reflect the demographic bias of this sample group.

Program Genres Watched

With music (52%) and movies (50%) constituting the leading categories of consumption, the survey establishes "entertainment" as the chief cultural value of television. News is accorded some importance though it is a weaker category compared to the entertainment categories.

In follow-up focus group interviews, individuals expressed a strong interest in the news broadcasts which referred to domestic Indonesian events. In times of crisis, 20% of those sampled said they increased their radio listening. The "perceived" independence of networks like CNN and Australia Television is a strong incentive for viewing these channels for viewers who sense the constraints placed on their domestic media. This is accompanied by a substantial scepticism that these global networks present either a full or totally unbiased picture.[10]

Among overseas radio stations, the BBC (43%) is followed closely by Radio Australia (39%) in popularity.[11] When questioned on the relative superiority of overseas programming via satellite, those surveyed expressed in high numbers that overseas programming was neither superior nor more interesting than local programming. There is an interesting suggestion from commentators that the presence of foreign competition may improve local programming.[12]

Information About Programming

This data shows that the family is the main source of information about parabola. It suggests a possible link between oral culture and television culture in the determination of the cultural values of television. This has been suggested by cultural theorists of media but rarely demonstrated by empirical data.

Australia Television/Radio Australia

We nested specific questions about Australia Television and Radio Australia---the ABC's satellite service to Asia---in our study. Our interest in these services allowed us to test assumptions made about these services in Australia.[13] It also focussed attention on specific cases of cross-cultural communication and the extent to which the relationship between Australia and Indonesia could be said to be "mediated' by Australia Television and Radio Australia's programs.

Most of the sample reported watching less than 1 hour of ATV programming in a week (59%). 26% reported watching between 1 and 2 hours a week. The reported reason for watching ATV was Australian programming (31%) while 20% reported watching ATV in order to learn or improve English language skills. The preferred Australian genre of programs were entertainment (31%) with news at 16%. In focus group discussions however, Australia Television news was more highly valued than entertainment programming. While entertainment programming was often seen as lacking on a number of fronts, respondents were attracted to the news because they received news from ATV that they do not receive locally.

Most respondents (44%) did not find ATV broadcasts upsetting which conflicts to some extent with highly publicised accounts in Australia of "inappropriate" programming by ATV for "Asian" audiences. By the same token, many (48%) respondents did not find that ATV catered to them better than other overseas stations. This suggests that popular discourses which attempt to isolate something called an "Asian" audience is doomed to reductive and simplistic accounts of television consumption. Our survey suggests that Indonesian viewers are critical viewers of news and current affairs and do not subscribe to blanket acceptance of news reportage.

Responses were mixed in relation to a question regarding "accuracy" in the depiction of Australia. But, as to whether Australia could be considered an "Asian" nation the response was solidly negative (68%). This is contrary to the popular discourses in Australia. The considerable public discussion of Australia's "strategic inroads to Asia" may have failed to admit only a modest impact on the perception of Australia as an Asian nation.

Conclusion to the Survey

Despite the limited nature of the study as defined from the outset (as a pilot study), we believe significant insights and questions have resulted as a consequence of this study. The use of satellite television is strongly tied to the convergence of other communication technologies available to wealthy Indonesians. The expansion of the middle class, its use of these new technologies (internet, mobile telephones) may foreshadow tensions between this class of Indonesians and the information constraints placed on Indonesians generally by the government.

Audiences see the advantages related to being in touch globally even if the constraints on access through local media suggest contradictory values of participation in the media. The balance of media use is affected by satellite television with the lessening use of radio though not as significantly as has been predicted. Magazines and newspapers appear to be used in a complementary relationship to television.

The benchmark study in 1982 suggested that satellite narrowed the gap between rich and poor. The study concluded that satellite television was a democratising medium (Chu, Alfian & Schramm, 1991). Our contemporary account of satellite corroborates the findings of other recent studies in that it showed a definite leaning to middle and upperclass access suggesting the opposite trend in contemporary Indonesia to that of the 1982 study (Center for Research and Development of Information Media, 1994).

Preliminary discussions with professional and occasional viewers of satellite television reveals a willingness to discuss and debate the advantages and foibles of the mass media. The sense of an active and vibrant "critical" television culture suggests that television is examined carefully by its Indonesian audience with considerable scepticism as to the cultural values attributed to it. This pilot study has shown contradictions present in the stated preferences for particular genres of television. It has also shown a substantial interest in the capacity for satellite television to connect its audience to the presentation of foreign and domestic current events.

Conclusion

To complete the sense of what values are put into play by satellite television in Indonesia is to consider a country transformed by anti-colonial struggle and then a raft of emotional changes wrought by the uncertainties of new relationships with Western values---a world of riches held at arms-length or further. It is a narrative of progress that is not to be disturbed by visions of social division, fragmentation and dissent. Second, is the ascent of technology-based media. Literary work is increasingly translated into the language of the mass media. *Wayang Kulit*, the traditional Javanese shadow puppet theatre is a regularly televised event. The question remains whether this translation of the literary by electronic media has destroyed the "aura" of these works. Or has television permitted a continuity of storytelling and therefore the possibility of the communalising experiences of the word, at times provocative and violating of sacred norms? Our research demonstrates the ironies of new and old media as they jostle beside one another in the context of a transforming world. No sense can be made of these competing media without reference to local cultural preferences for the programs these audiences enjoy. No understanding of policy regulation can be developed without an accounting of the political values which continue to dominate Indonesia and the responses these practices engender. In this regard our largely quantitative study has been useful in framing more general qualitative questions. These questions concern the speed and direction of technological change with respect to the new media; they concern the commercialisation of media in its re-fashioning of culture; they concern the relationship between commercial values, political values and social change. The media, both local and global, continue to both mediate and not mediate, to both confirm and deny cultural continuities and discontinuities for communities as they are opened to forces not seen before---or presented with all too familiar scenes from a not so distant past.

Further research with control groups may reveal the extent to which satellite television makes a difference to the economic and social structure of Indonesian society. Other regional studies may open up comparisons in the differences that regional influence exert on media use. In-depth focus group discussion may provide a better account of the contradictions that surface in program preferences. They may also reveal the further tensions evident in the co-existence of sometimes incompatible televisual cultural values in the local/global nexus of satellite television.

Notes

[1]This collaborative project involved five researchers: Dr. Hart Cohen, Dr. Brian Shoesmith, Mr. Neville Petersen, Drs Basis Susilo, and Drs Andarini Sani. It was supported by grants from UWS, Nepean, Edith Cowan University, Australia Television and with support from AMIC, Singapore and the Universitas Airlangga, Surabaya, Indonesia.

[2]Summaries of preliminary focus group sessions are available with the authors. Since this study was completed, a longer more intensive focus group study was executed.

[3]Tracey, M., International Television Flows: *The Broad Picture*, p. 2.

[4]Subsequent studies have suggested that local cultures "read" *Dallas* in terms of their social and cultural traditions making *Dallas* less an example of media imperialism and more an example of media syncretism. See Ang, I., (1983) *Watching Dallas*, London: Methuen.; Liebes, T., & Katz, E., (1993), *The Export of Meaning*, Cambridge: Polity.

[5]"...The Archibald paradox is simply the paradox of being colonial...To know enough of the metropolitan world, colonials must in limited ways at least, move and think internationally; to resist it strongly enough in order to cease to be colonial and become its own place, they must become nationalists.", (Lawson, Sylvia, (1987) The Archibald Paradox: A Strange Case of Authorship, Ringwood, p. ix quoted in Willemen, P., "The National", in *Fields of Vision*, Devereaux and Hillman, eds., (1995) U. of California Press, Berkeley, p. 21).

[6]"The British Empire, which gained from a fusion of Roman law traditions and common-law traditions, has been exposed to the effects of increasing nationalization, based to an important extent on language under the influence of mechanization of the printed and spoken word, as in the case of the French in Canada, the Dutch in South Africa and the languages of India and Pakistan, and the attempt to revive the Irish language in Eire. The common-law tradition tends to become more powerful and to reflect the influence of elements which have been decentralizing in character. 'Under democratic control England must abandon all idea of influence upon the world's affairs' (Lord Salisbury). " Innis, H., (1950, 1986) *Empire and Communications*, Press Porcépic, Victoria, BC, p. 168.

[7]"...By local television then, the Institute means a television service related to an area that is the focus of administrative, cultural, economic and /or social interest for the viewers. In other words, local television covers a social and geographical territory which is broadly familiar to the viewer, an area within which news is generated, where broader national and international news stories are likely to have a specific interpretation and is an area comprising a social and economic culture with which the viewer identifies..." Rushton, D., (ed.), (1993) "Channel 5 and Local Television", in *Citizen Television*, John Libbey, London, 193-194.

[8]The life of Tirto Adi Suryo is exemplary in this regard. Tirto was publisher and editor of the first native-owned daily newspaper in Indonesia, instigated the first legal aid service, helped found the first modern Indonesian political organisation, co-published the first magazine for women and pioneered indigenous publishing in the Indonesian language. It is not surprising that the

author of a biography of Tirto Adi Suryo and an anthology of his journalism and fiction is currently banned in Indonesia.

[9]This is borne out by our current follow-up studies in Surabaya and Medan.

[10]Cohen, Hart, "Satellite Television in Suarbaya, East Java," Research Report, Part 2,unpublished. This report summarises qualitiative research conducted in 1996 utilising a focus group approach. It was submitted to the Australian Senate inquiry into Australia television and Radio Australia.

[11]In a follow-up study in Medan in North Sumatra, Radio Australia's programming in Bahasa Indonesia equalled that of the BBC.

[12]John Zubryzski, interview, Australian Broadcasting Corporation, Radio National, Media Report, Thursday, 28th December 1995.

[13]With the current Australian government intent on selling off and/or closing down these services, our research provides critical information about their viability and the potential consequences for the region in terminating them.

References

Ang, I. (1983). *Watching Dallas*. London: Methuen.

Center for Research and Development of Information Media. (1994). Reception of news and information programs from foreign television stations through parabolic antenna, Board of Research and Development of Information, Ministry of Information of the Republic of Indonesia (in cooperation with the Japan International Cooperation Agency), Jakarta.

Chapman, G. (1992, January-February). TV: The world next door? *Intermedia, 20* (1).

Chu, G., Alfian & W. Schramm (1991). *Social impact of satellite television in rural Indonesia*. Singapore: AMIC.

Collins, R. (1990). *Satellite TV in Western Europe*. London and Paris: John Libbey.

Dennis, E. (1992, January-February). The global news agenda. *Intermedia 20* (1),

Fell, L. (1995, March/April). Ambassador class. *Cable & Satellite Asia*, 40.

Goonasekera, A. (1993). Media technology and social imperatives: An examination of communication policies in selected Asian countries, *Media Asia, 20* (4).

Goonasekera, A. (1995). Asian viewers do not see Western programs as corrupting their culture, *Media Asia, 22* (4).

Holaday, D. (1996). The social impact of satellite TV in Indonesia: A view from the ground. *Media Asia, 23* (2).

Innis, H. (1950, 1986). *Empire and communications*. Victoria, BC: Press Porcépic.

Innis, H.(1951, 1994). *The bias of communication*. University of Toronto Press.

Liebes, T., & Katz, E. (1993). *The export of meaning*. Cambridge: Polity.

Paterson, R. (1982) *Brazilian TV in context*. London: BFI.

Rushton, D. (1993). Channel 5 and local television. In D. Rushton (Ed.), *Citizen television: A local dimension to public service broadcasting* (pp. 193-194). London: John Libby.

Shoesmith, B. (1993). Technology transfer or technology dialogue: Rethinking Western communication values. *Media Asia, 20* (3).

Sreberny-Mohammadi, A. (1996, June). *Preserving national sovereignty in a global village*. Paper presented at the AMIC conference, Singapore.

Tickell, P. (1993). *Free from what? Responsible to whom? The problem of democracy and the Indonesian press*. Paper presented at the Indonesia and Democracy Conference, Monash University, Australia.

Tracey, M. (No date). International television flows: The broad picture, unpublished.

Wang, G. (1993). Satellite television and the future of broadcast television in Asia-Pacific. *Media Asia,* 20(3).

Zubryzski, J. (1995, December 28). Interview, Australian Broadcasting Corporation, Radio National, *Media Report.*

Chapter 13

Cultural Transcendence as an Alternative to Cultural Imperialism: Role of Pro-Social Entertainment Television Programs in Developing Countries[1]

Arvind Singhal
Peer J. Svenkerud
Rita L. Rahoi-Gilchrest

With the proliferation of communication satellites, global syndication networks, cable television, and multi-lingual dubbing centers, McLuhan's "Global Village" is now a reality. Entertainment media programs, rock music, popular magazines, and other information-based products now freely cross the borders of developed and developing countries, bringing new opportunities as well as problems. Here we consider the promises and problems associated with one such global media strategy illustrated by the following examples:

> In 1969, the popular Peruvian television soap opera *Simplemente Maria* told the rags-to-riches story of Maria, a rural-urban migrant to the city from the Andes Mountains. The series earned average viewer ratings of 85 percent in Peru, and broke audience ratings records in several other Latin American countries where it was subsequently broadcast. Inspired by Maria's character,

young women in Peru and other countries enrolled in adult literacy and sewing classes (Singhal, Obregon & Rogers, 1994).

In 1983, the popular Japanese *asadora* (morning drama), *Oshin*, earned record audience ratings (up to 65 percent) in Japan. It told the story of a seven year old girl, Oshin, who survived many personal hardships to become a successful businesswoman. By 1997, *Oshin* had been broadcast in 53 other countries (see Table 13.1), including such culturally-diverse countries as Thailand, Belgium, Iran, Peru, India, and Cuba, where it met with tremendous audience success (Mowlana, 1991; Svenkerud, Rahoi, & Singhal, 1995; Singhal & Udornpim, 1997).

In Zimbabwe, in the late 1980s, John Riber, a talented film-maker, produced the movie *Consequences*, depicting problems associated with teenage pregnancy, and urging greater sexual responsibility. This film became the most popular movie of all time in Zimbabwe. By 1994, *Consequences* had been dubbed in five languages, and seen by more than 40 million young people in more than 65 countries (Singhal & Svenkerud, 1994).

The above three examples demonstrate the potential of entertainment media products to transcend cultural boundaries. They were popular with audiences not just locally, but in a broader cultural and geographic context. More importantly, all the above programs were "pro-social" texts, that is promoting socially desirable values among their audiences. The definition of "pro-social" programs is necessarily problematic given the value-laden nature of the term. What may represent pro-social for some, may not be for others. Here, in our chapter, we refer to "pro-social" programs as those that can help a majority of the audience members live happier, healthier, and safer lives. In this sense, pro-social programs tend to focus on such "problem" areas in society as illiteracy, gender inequality, teenage pregnancy, HIV/AIDS, and others.

The purpose of this chapter is to investigate the potential of pro-social entertainment television programs that can transcend cultural boundaries in developing country contexts. We analyze past trends in the worldwide flow of entertainment television programs, noting the historic propensity of cultural imperialism, and some recent shifts in worldwide television flows. We analyze the factors that influence the ability of pro-social entertainment television programs to transcend cultural boundaries. We then investigate the special promise of soap operas, as a television genre, in carrying culturally-transcendent pro-social messages, drawing upon our analysis of the Japanese soap opera *Oshin*. We conclude by identifying problems associated with the use of culturally-transcendent, pro-social entertainment television programming, and provide suggestions to overcome some of these problems.

Recent Trends in World Television Flows

The paradigm that shaped the scientific discussion about the role of communication in development, particularly between 1945 and 1965, sought to explain how traditional societies could achieve modernity (Lerner, 1958; Rogers, 1962; Schramm, 1964), and equated development with modernization. In this world view, modernity was defined as a participatory life-style (Mowlana & Wilson, 1990, p. 16). The mass media were viewed as being particularly important in the modernization process of "traditional" societies, where their primary role was to expose indigenous audiences to the outside world (Schramm, 1964).

Critics of this modernization paradigm argued that excessive contacts with industrialized capitalist media were increasing the development gap in developing countries. They claimed that the ideological bias of the modernization paradigm, coupled with international aid programs initiated by western industrialized countries, resulted in a primarily *one-way* flow of media technology and programming from the developed countries of the West to developing countries (Beltran, 1975; Nordenstreng & Varis, 1974; Schiller, 1971). This one-sided flow of media programs was referred to as a type of media-led cultural imperialism, creating situations where a center-nation (typically Western and industrialized) exercised control over a periphery nation (a developing country), leading to a disharmony of interests between the two (Beltran, 1975; Galtung, 1971; Oliveira, 1986; Schnitman, 1984; Warne & Tillinghast, 1994).

Several studies conducted in the 1970's and early 1980's on the topic of worldwide television flows (Lee, 1980; Murdock, 1982; Nordenstreng & Varis, 1974; Salinas & Paldan, 1979; Varis, 1984) noted serious imbalances in the flow of media programs. These studies claimed that various cultural, economic, and political factors determined the direction of television flows, and that Western-produced programs were often highly insensitive to local cultural values (Hoskins & Mirus, 1988; McAnany, 1984; Pool, 1977; Varis, 1984).

In recent years, however, the nature of worldwide television flows has been changing. Many development scholars now emphasize the importance of producing socio-culturally relevant television programming in developing countries. Increasingly, the emphasis is on the use of alternative concepts that are more sensitive and compatible with indigenous cultural values (Huesca & Dervin, 1994; Oliveira, 1986; Rogers & Antola, 1985; Warne & Tillinghast, 1994). There is a growing recognition that audiences in developing countries are not simply passive or fatalistic. Instead, they actively interpret mass media, and selectively resist what is not in their interest by creating their own popular culture out of the elements of a mass culture (Rogers, 1976). Today, the first preference of audiences is to view locally-produced television programs, followed by a preference for regional productions, all of which are relatively more culturally-proximate (or similar), than television imports (Straubhaar, 1992). This is not merely a theoretical paradigm shift; various studies have indicated that this change in worldwide television flows is already a reality (McAnany, 1984; Oliveira, 1990; Pool, 1977; Rogers & Antola, 1985; Straubhaar, 1992; Straubhaar, 1991; Straubhaar & Viscacillas, 1991; Singhal & Svenkerud, 1994).

The rise of various regional television production and export centers, such as Mexico and Brazil (Latin America), Egypt (the Middle East), and Hong Kong (Southeast Asia), has altered in some ways the dominant one-way flow of media programming from the West. This allows viewers in developing countries to consume television programming that is more culturally proximate (Singhal & Svenkerud, 1994). Cultural proximity is defined as the active preferential choice made by an individual in the audience to view international, national, or regional television programs, a choice that typically favors the latter two (when available) because of their greater cultural relevance for the audience member (Straubhaar, 1991). For example, Rogers and Antola (1985) concluded that indigenously-produced Brazilian, Mexican, and Venezuelan programs could compete successfully in Latin American countries against imported American television programming. Moreover, television programs produced in Brazil, Mexico, and Venezuela often displaced

US imports in neighboring Latin American countries (Oliveira, 1990; Rogers & Antola, 1985; Straubhaar, 1991). This shift in television flow is a phenomenon that is not just unique to Latin America. In Europe, more than 40 percent of imported television programs in Western and Eastern European countries now originate in other countries of those regions (Varis, 1984). The increase in regional exchange is also notable among Arab countries, where approximately one-third of all imported programs come from other countries (such as Egypt) within the region (Varis, 1984).

In sum, the development of indigenous cultural industries and popular genres, coupled with lower production costs, provides developing countries with the opportunity to substitute *foreign* television programming imports with more culturally proximate television programming (Oliveira, 1990; Straubhaar & Viscasillas, 1991; Waterman & Rogers, 1994). Media industries in developing countries also have the potential to create pro-social entertainment television programs that can transcend cultural boundaries. However, it is important to recognize that all culturally-proximate programming is not "pro-social" and vice versa.

Role of Entertainment Television in Promoting Pro-Social Change

Entertainment television programs can be effective in disseminating pro-social messages to audiences in various countries (Church & Geller, 1989; Head, 1985; Kincaid, Rimon, Piotrow & Coleman, 1992; Lozano & Singhal, 1993; Lull, 1990; McAnany, 1993; Nariman, 1993; Singhal, Rogers & Brown, 1993; Singhal & Svenkerud, 1994; Singhal & Udornpim, 1997). On a theoretical level, the creation of pro-social entertainment television programs draws upon Bandura's (1977) concept of social learning, postulating that people can model their behavior after observing role models in the mass media. Bandura's concept of role-modeling posits an "active" audience member, who can self-regulate one's behavior, i.e. determine whether or not to model a desired/undesired behavior depicted by a television model based on his/her observation of the consequences faced by the model for performing the given behavior. For instance, an audience member may actively decide to practice family planning by observing the socio-economic hardships suffered by a media role model for having a large family.

More specific analysis of pro-social entertainment television programs indicates that they are (1) *popular*, because people like to be entertained; (2) *pervasive*, because they have a wide and growing reach; (3) *personal*, since audiences are moved to share the experiences of the media characters; (4) *persuasive*, because they can encourage viewers to change their attitudes and behaviors regarding a pro-social issue; (5) *passionate*, because they can stir strong audience emotions about a pro-social issue, (6) *profitable*, because they can attract the support of commercial advertisers; and (7) *practical*, because they are feasible to produce (Kincaid et al. 1992; Piotrow, Meyer & Zulu, 1992; Singhal, Rogers & Brown, 1993).

Using entertainment television programs to promote pro-social messages maximizes audience exposure, liking, and recall of messages in ways that might not be achievable through the use of straight-forward didactic messages (Kincaid et al., 1992; Nariman, 1993). This is in opposition to purely entertainment-oriented television programs, which are generally ratings-driven and targeted to more affluent audience segments.

Pro-social entertainment television programs can be targeted to the oppressed and less empowered segments in a given audience, and can strike a balance between production-centered and people-centered programming (Singhal, Rogers & Brown, 1993; Singhal & Svenkerud, 1994). Whereas the creation of pro-social television programming might represent a great budget expense for a national government, pro-social entertainment television programs can be profitable and might potentially represent a win-win situation for purveyors of social change (Brown & Singhal, 1993; Kincaid et al. 1992; Nariman, 1993).

Why Produce Pro-Social Entertainment Programs That Transcend Cultural Boundaries?

Before we provide greater detail on the strategies, problems, and promises of designing culturally transcendent pro-social entertainment television programs, we first must examine the arguments in favor of the development of such programs.

The Need

First, the literature points generally to a significant interest on the part of developing countries to broadcast culturally-proximate television programs, especially when such programs are available.

A second more compelling argument for the production of culturally-transcendent television programming is that developing countries have a significant need for programs of a pro-social nature. Why? Development is the top priority of national governments in every developing country (Singhal & Rogers, 1989). Pro-social programs attempt to fulfill this priority by depicting cognitive, affective, or behavioral activities considered to be socially desirable for the intended audience (Brown & Singhal, 1990, p. 268). Examples of pro-social messages that aid in development range from adoption of family planning methods, to the promotion of adult literacy, to raising the status of women, or any number of combinations thereof.

Despite this need, the dominant entertainment fare offered by television systems in most developing countries serves little useful function in bringing about pro-social changes. The dominant domestically produced fare consists of mostly dull educational programming, or entertainment programs of dubious value. These television systems are often riddled with imported television programs that are far removed from the socio-cultural realities of indigenous television audiences. So, a strong argument for the development of culturally-proximate pro-social television programming is to counteract the pervasiveness of non-useful imported television programs, and to provide a more desirable alternative to existing domestic productions.

The Rationale

There are a number of reasons why national governments and private broadcasters in developing countries should consider the production of pro-social entertainment television programs that transcend cultural boundaries. These reasons can be explained as follows:

1. The idea of producing pro-social entertainment television programs that transcend cultural boundaries is consistent with recent advances in communication technologies. These have led to an increased outflow of US television programming to developing countries. Alternately, as in the case of certain developing countries

(such as Brazil, Mexico, Hong Kong, and China), these technological advances have also made feasible an increase in local and regional television productions (Singhal & Svenkerud, 1994; Waterman & Rogers, 1994).

2. Recent research suggests that economic obstacles facing many developing countries often determines the television menu for developing countries (Waterman & Rogers, 1994). Programming with high production values is expensive and requires artists, technicians, and facilities that individual countries might not be able to afford. This problem could be overcome if broadcasters in several developing countries agreed to pool talent and resources to produce programs of a pro-social nature (Singhal & Svenkerud, 1994). The quantitative and qualitative contributions of the various participating agencies may differ however, depending on their ability to mobilize human and material resources.

3. Developing countries might be able to overcome the limitations of broadcasting culturally-irrelevant imported television programming (Chan, 1994).

4. Developing countries might be able to reduce their dependence on global programming merchants, and instead move toward more regional and local interdependence.

5. Developing countries might be able to more effectively address common problems. The dissemination of AIDS prevention messages in various countries of Africa is an example.

6. Developing countries might be able to achieve higher production quality at a relatively lower production cost.

7. Developing countries might be able to tap into Diaspora markets outside the country of origin. For instance, television producers in Hong Kong can produce programs for domestic consumption, and also tap the larger and more profitable audience markets in China and in other countries of the Far-East, Europe, and North America, where expatriate Chinese reside (Singhal & Svenkerud, 1994).

The Possibility

To some extent, all human societies share common human traits, myths, and values; this makes cultural transcendence of pro-social entertainment television programming possible. The concept of cultural proximity is an important determinant of the extent to which cultural transcendence is possible. The notion of cultural proximity refers to the active choice made by audience members to consume (or not to consume) television programs based on the various social, cultural, historical, geographic, political, economic, and linguistic dimensions of the television program being broadcast (Singhal & Svenkerud, 1994). Creators of culturally- transcendent media programs therefore need to pay careful attention to the grassroots construction of meaning by individual audience members. For instance, the generation and utilization of common cultural symbols such as the use of myth and archetype might allow room for viewers in different cultures to relate to a message being portrayed in a particular media program (Svenkerud, Rahoi & Singhal, 1995). This strategy, then, can be useful in creating pro-social entertainment programs that transcend cultural boundaries.

Cultural Transcendence: The Case Of Oshin

In the previous section, we discussed the many possibilities for cultural transcendence offered by pro-social entertainment television programming. Among the entertainment television genres, the genre of melodramatic soap operas has emerged as most promising in terms of its ability to transcend cultural boundaries (Lozano & Singhal, 1992). The suitability of this genre for carrying pro-social messages in various cultural contexts is due to several unique features of the melodrama, including (1) the widespread popularity of the soap opera format; (2) the ability of the melodrama to depict the conflict between pro-and anti-social behavior; (3) the ability of melodrama to utilize myth and archetypes, and (4) its long-running, repetitive nature, which can help reinforce an educational message without causing boredom (Head, 1985; Lull, 1990; McAnany, 1993; Nariman, 1993; Rogers & Antola, 1985; Singhal & Svenkerud, 1994; Svenkerud, Rahoi & Singhal, 1995).

To illustrate our point, we analyze the case of the Japanese soap opera *Oshin*, which has been well received by viewers of 53 countries, hailing from diverse socio-cultural backgrounds (Singhal & Udornpim, 1997). The 1983 Japanese television program *Oshin* traced the life of the central character Oshin, documenting the difficulties she faced, and overcame, in moving from poverty to prosperity (Svenkerud, Rahoi & Singhal, 1995). The series followed the life of Oshin from the age of seven, when she was exchanged for a bale of rice to feed her poor family. She started working at a timber merchant's home, where she was ill-treated and falsely accused of stealing. In her youth, she fell in love with a handsome young man, only to find that he was in love with her best friend. Eventually, she married a wealthy farmer's son, whose mother treated her very poorly. During the outbreak of World War II, Oshin's son died during fighting and her husband committed suicide. She lost her house, but fought to re-establish a profitable family business of supermarkets. Her ability to transcend tragedy came from her personal strength, intelligence, and aggressiveness in looking out for the well-being of her family (Lull, 1990).

In November 1983, *Oshin* was viewed by about 65 percent of Japanese audiences. What rendered this soap opera as unique was its ability to transcend cultural boundaries. Consider the following audience reactions to *Oshin* from cultures across the world:

> In the Indonesian capital city Jakarta, where *Oshin* was initially aired in the late afternoon, the tremendous popularity of the series forced the television station to change the air time after complaints from viewers flooded in. A number of families wrote letters to the television station requesting a time change; they were tired of having supper served late because their maids were busy watching *Oshin* (Ylstra, 1991).

> In Belgium, where viewership during *Oshin* broadcasts was estimated at over 17 percent of the total television audience, a group of nuns regularly rescheduled their prayer time in order to avoid missing their favorite program (Ylstra, 1991).

> In China, the saying went that as soon as the broadcast of *Oshin* began each day, the streets cleared. An experimental survey of program ratings revealed viewership as high as 90 percent in some regions of the country (NHK, 1991).

> In Indonesia and Japan, it was reported that women, in particular, were often so moved by the perseverance and endurance of the central character Oshin that they broke into tears during the broadcast of the series.

To date, *Oshin* is recorded as the most popular Japanese entertainment television program of all time, both in and outside of

Japan. *Oshin* was broadcast in a number of culturally-proximate and (seemingly) culturally-diverse settings in the Eastern/Western and North/South part of the world (see Table 13.1).

Table 13.1 International Broadcasts of Oshin

Country	Year Broadcast	Country	Year Broadcast
1. Japan	1983	28. Bolivia	1991
2. Singapore	1984	29. Panama	1991
3. Thailand	1984	30. Nepal	1991
4. USA	1984	31. Guatemala	1992
5. Australia	1984	32. Nicaragua	1992
6. China	1985	33. Egypt	1992
7. Poland	1985	34. India	1992
8. Hong Kong	1985	35. Romania	1993
9. Macao	1985	36. Chile	1993
10. Brazil	1985	37. Uruguay	1993
11. Belgium	1985	38. Jamaica	1993
12. Canada	1985	39. Ghana	1993
13. Malaysia	1986	40. Honduras	1993
14. Indonesia	1986	41. Cuba	1993
15. Iran	1986	42. Vietnam	1994
16. Sri Lanka	1987	43. Taiwan	1994
17. Saudi Arabia	1987	44. Myanmar	1995
18. Brunei	1988	45. Paraguay	1995
19. Mexico	1988	46. Laos	1995
20. Qatar	1988	47. Mongolia	1995
21. Bahrain	1989	48. Costa Rica	1995
22. Syria	1990	49. Cambodia	1996
23. Philippines	1990	50. Sudan	1996
24. Dominica	1990	51. Turkey	1996
25. Bangladesh	1990	52. Bulgaria	1996
26. Peru	1990	53. Macedonia	1997
27. Pakistan	1991		

(Source: NHK International, 1991; Singhal et.al, 1997).

What were the reasons for *Oshin*'s amazing ability to transcend cultural boundaries and achieve such a high level of ratings among diverse audiences? Kobayashi (1990) argued that the actual broadcasts of *Oshin* were particularly effective because each culture in which the program was broadcast was allowed to rely on its own particular beliefs and ways of being as viewers of the melodrama. Viewers in different settings could freely translate, interpret, and decide how events and characters were intended to be conveyed. Other researchers (Svenkerud, Rahoi & Singhal, 1995) have discussed this as an exemplar of the use of the concept of "strategic ambiguity" developed by Eric Eisenberg (1984).

Eisenberg, drawing a distinction between *ambiguity perceived by a receiver* and *ambiguity utilized for a specific purpose*, noted that ambiguity could serve as a potential problem-solving strategy (a point also discussed in Eisenberg & Goodall, 1993; Eisenberg & Witten, 1987; Martin & Meyerson, 1988). This claim is strengthened further by recent studies of *Oshin*'s popularity, such as Takahashi's (1991) investigation into the pervasiveness of the series across varied audiences.

The series' success was not only due to its allowance for difference in interpreting, but can also be attributed in part to its focus on values (such as perseverance and endurance) that held meaning across a wide variety of cultures. Mowlana (1991), for example, concluded that the social and human appeal of *Oshin* was a key determinant in the popularity of the series. A number of examples would appear to bear witness to this theory.

In Belgium, for example, the tremendous success of *Oshin* was considered a factor of the many similarities between Belgian and Japanese lifestyles a century ago---the time period in which *Oshin* was set (Ylstra, 1991). Studies of *Oshin* conducted in Indonesia demonstrated that viewers were moved by Oshin's heroic struggle for her own life and well-being, and by the same qualities of perseverance and endurance that resonated with Japanese viewers (Takahashi, 1991). When the program was shown in Iran under the extreme economic and physical strife resulting from the debilitating Iran-Iraq War, 72 percent of the viewers observed that they found the setting and storyline of *Oshin* extremely similar to their own situation (Mowlana, 1991).

Amaralilit (1991) delineated several important reasons for the enormous popularity of *Oshin* in Thailand. The suffering and hunger experienced by Oshin in the time of Meiji Japan, for instance, was very similar to the prevailing problems faced by many contemporary farmers in Northern Thailand. Furthermore, *Oshin* called attention to the fact that many young girls of ages 12 to 16 routinely were (and still are today) sent to Bangkok from the Northern Province so that they can earn money to send to their families (as Oshin did in the television series).

Despite the tremendous cultural differences between Japan, the host culture developing *Oshin*, and the cultures/countries in which it was popular, we can conclude that certain modes of behavior, cultural expectations, and values were perceived as similar among these nations. This appears particularly true in reference to appropriate responses to, and possible reasons for, human tragedy and suffering (Svenkerud, Rahoi & Singhal, 1995).

A third reason why *Oshin* might have gained such a strong following in such a variety of cultural contexts is its use of culturally-embedded archetypes. Drawing on the work of Carl Jung, Lozano and Singhal (1993) defined archetypes as forms and images that comprise part of a universal and collective memory, often manifested through symbols, prototypes, and myths. Archetypes are a powerful venue for instruction (Lozano, 1992), and at least three come into play in Oshin; the *self seeking individual*; the *disobedient female*; and the *heroic struggle* (Svenkerud, Rahoi & Singhal, 1995). Using imagery that resonated deeply in a number of cultural contexts, *Oshin* was a classic---and effective---example of the use of archetype in an entertainment television program (Singhal & Udornpim, 1997).

Li (1991) offered a fourth possible reason for this melodrama's ability to broadcast pro-social messages across cultural boundaries, theorizing that the popularity of *Oshin* in China could be attributed to the sense of realism that the series conveyed. Since the Chinese realist literary tradition emphasized the naturalistic depiction of characters, the well-developed personalities and actions of featured players in the *Oshin* series fit right into the Chinese cultural tradition (Li, 1991, p. 57). Kato (1991) added that this was a potential key determinant in the program's success, noting: "*Oshin* was very simple and direct, and you didn't have to be knowledgeable about the entire history of Japan to be able to understand [it]" (p. 51).

Oshin discussed "real-world" problems of the kind its many viewers face daily. *Oshin's* messages appealed to diverse audience groups because the program portrayed messages that were born out of the shared experiences of diverse audience groups (Surkhamad, 1991). Clearly, the more deeply *Oshin* touched human emotions, the more the program's embedded messages were accepted (Svenkerud, Rahoi & Singhal, 1995; Singhal & Udornpim, 1997).

We have seen, then, that *Oshin* is a useful case study in determining the viability of utilizing the television soap opera genre for carrying pro-social entertainment messages. *Oshin's* allowance of ambiguity in interpretation, its focus on values, its reference to established archetypes, and its realism combined to create a pro-social force that transcended cultural boundaries and achieved popularity among culturally diverse audience groups. So, for both theoretical and practical reasons, we believe it is worthwhile to explore the potential of pro-social entertainment television programs to transcend cultural boundaries. Yet, this promising media strategy is not without its limitations; these will be delineated and discussed in the following section.

Limitations

Pro-social entertainment television programs that can transcend cultural boundaries have certain limitations:

1. Their having an exactly equivalent effect on all audience groups is unlikely;
2. They might lack a specific focus appropriate to, or desirable for, the specific problems of a target audience in a regional or linguistic group;
3. They are more likely to engender multiple audience readings, given the heterogeneity that is present even in culturally-proximate audience groups (Ram, Rahoi & Svenkerud, 1994);
4. They run the risk of eroding the cultural identity of individual audience groups in a much larger culturally-proximate group (Singhal & Rogers, 1989). Homogenization of cultural values, the dominance of one group's worldview on others, and the like might represent potentially undesirable outcomes of television programs that transcend cultural boundaries. However, this is mitigated to a great extent by an

active audience interpreting the mass media content selectively and resisting what is not in their interest;

5. They are not value free. What constitutes pro-social to one audience segment might be perceived differently in another group (Rushton, 1982) and so, face several ethical dilemmas. For instance, the ethical dilemma manifest in the question: Who is to determine what is right for whom? (Brown & Singhal, 1990). We must also consider the issue of unintended, unanticipated, and undesirable consequences of pro-social entertainment television programs that transcend cultural boundaries (Brown & Singhal, 1990; Rogers, 1995);

6. Striking a balance between pro-social content and entertainment can be a challenge;

7. Many logistical challenges exist to creating, maintaining, and implementing pro-social entertainment television programs that transcend cultural boundaries. The paths, minds, and interests of government policy-makers, commercial sponsors, creative producers, development officials, and broadcasters seldom converge. Even if they did, other challenges abound: For instance, finding a talented scriptwriter to create a pro-social program that appeals to different audience groups can be a difficult task (Singhal & Svenkerud, 1994).

These problems should not be ignored if we are to explore the full potential of entertainment television programming in disseminating pro-social messages that transcend cultural boundaries. Obviously, the best way to handle such issues is on a case-by-case basis. Given that we do not always operate in the best of all possible worlds, however, the following are potential solutions that offer guidance for problem-solving across the board:

1. The use of formative research to assess the needs of culturally-proximate (or similar) groups, focusing on the nuances of their differences.

2. Enlightened political leadership that can put the weight of its position behind the idea of creating pro-social entertainment television programming in order to transcend cultural boundaries.

3. Activation of consensus-building among policymakers, broadcasters, the creative community at large, development officials, advertisers, and audiences.

4. Effective creation, maintenance, and sharing of pro-social entertainment television programs through co-production, syndication, and distribution networks.

Conclusions

In this analysis, we investigated the potential of pro-social entertainment television programs in transcending cultural boundaries. We argued that the media strategy of "cultural transcendence" might represent a viable conceptual alternative to the notion of media-led cultural imperialism. We reviewed the reasons for developing countries in particular to consider producing pro-social entertainment television programs that can transcend cultural boundaries. Such programs have the potential to serve a useful development function in society, and can provide a more desirable alternative to culturally-irrelevant imported foreign programming. Creation of programs that appeal to a wider range of audiences can help developing countries pool resources, fight common development problems, reduce their dependence on imported programming, and promote regional and local interdependence.

This review also pointed out that certain specific genres of entertainment television, such as the melodramatic soap opera, offer advantages in transcending pro-social messages across cultural boundaries. The widespread popularity of the soap opera format, the ability of the melodrama to depict the tussle between pro-social and anti-social behaviors, the effective utilization of such factors as myth and archetype, and the repetitive, long run of these programs makes the soap opera genre especially suited for carrying pro-social messages across cultural boundaries.

As we have also established, pro-social entertainment television programs seeking to transcend cultural boundaries have their limitations and problems. A certain degree of message dilution invariably accompanies the quest for message diffusion. Targeting specific problems in specific audience groups is difficult. The identity of a relatively small homogenous group can be threatened in a larger culturally proximate group. The value-laden nature of pro-social content can be problematic, as is the ethical dilemma associated with the question of who is to determine the right course of action for others.

As mass media systems in developing countries expand, media programming becomes a crucial factor in determining whether or not the media would serve pro-social or anti-social objectives. Another issue is the choice to fulfill global or local interests. In any case, given the promise and problems of pro-social entertainment television programming that can transcend cultural boundaries, *Oshin* is an exciting case study of a viable alternative to present-day programming options in developing countries. With subsequent study, however, *Oshin* may represent a programming prototype to drive social change in developing countries.

Notes

[1] This chapter draws upon Singhal and Svenkerud (1994) and Svenkerud, Rahoi, and Singhal (1995).

266   *International Satellite Broadcasting in South Asia*

References

Amaralilit, T. (1991). *Thailand. A land without snow.* Proceedings
rom the International Symposium: The world's view of Japan
hrough *Oshin. Japanese TV programs in the world media market*
(pp. 39-42). Tokyo: NHK International.

Bandura, A. (1977). *Social learning theory.* Englewood Cliffs, NJ:
Prentice-Hall.

Beltran, L. R. (1975, Spring). Research ideologies in conflict.
Journal of Communication, 187-193.

Brown, W. J., & Singhal, A. (1990). Ethical dilemmas of pro-social
television. *Communication Quarterly, 38,* 268-280.

Brown, W. J., & Singhal, A. (1993). Entertainment-education
edia: An opportunity for enhancing Japan's leadership role in
hird World development. *Keio Communication Review, 15,* 81-
101.

Chan, J. M. (1994). The media internationalization in China:
Processes and tensions. *Journal of Communication, 44(3),* 70- 88.

Church, C., & Geller, J. (1989). "Lights, cameras, action!".
Population Reports, 38, 1-31.

Eisenberg, E. (1984). Ambiguity as strategy in organizational
communication. *Communication Monographs, 51,* 227-242.

Eisenberg, E. M., & Goodall, H.L. (1993). *Organizational
communication: Balancing creativity and constraint.* New York:
St. Martins Press.

Eisenberg, E. M., & Witten, M. G. (1987). Reconsidering openness
in organizational communication. *Academy of Management
Review, 12* (3), 418-426,

Galtung, J. (1971). A structural theory of imperialism. *Journal of
Peace Research, 2,* 81-117.

Hamelink, C. J. (1983). *Cultural autonomy in global
communications: Planning national information policy.* White
Plains, NY: Longman.

Head, S. W. (1985). *World broadcasting systems: A comparative
analysis.* Belmont, CA: Wadsworth.

Hoskins, C., & Mirus, R. (1988). Reasons for the US dominance of the international trade in television programs. *Media, Culture and Society*, 499-515.

Huesca, R., & Dervin, B. (1994). Theory and practice in Latin American alternative communication research. *Journal of Communication, 44*, 53-73.

Kato, H. (1991). *International appeal of visual products*. Proceedings from the International Symposium: The world's view of Japan through *Oshin*. Japanese TV programs in the world media market (pp. 49-103). Tokyo: NHK International.

Kincaid, D. L., Rimon, J. G, Piotrow, P. T., & Coleman, P. L. (1992, April). The enter-educate approach: Using entertainment to change health behavior. Paper presented at the   Population Association of America, Denver, CO.

Kobayashi, Y. (1990). *Oshin --Why so popular*. Proceedings from the International Symposium: The world's view of Japan through *Oshin*. Japanese television programs in the world media market (pp. 57-77). Tokyo: NHK International.

Lee, C. (1980). *Media imperialism reconsidered*. Beverly Hills, CA: Sage.

Lerner, D. (1958). *The passing of traditional society*. New York: Free Press.

Li, D. (1991). *Oshin does not belong only to Japan*. Proceedings from the International Symposium: The world's view of Japan through *Oshin*. Japanese television programs in the world media market (pp. 57-59). Tokyo: NHK International.

Lozano, E., & Singhal, A. (1993). Melodramatic television serials: mythical narratives for education. *The European Journal of Communication, 18* (1), 115-127.

Lull, J. (1990). *China turned on: Television, reform, and resistance*. New York: Routledge.

Martin, J., & Meyerson, D. (1988). Organizational cultures and the denial, channeling and acknowledgment of ambiguity. In L. R. Pondy, R. J. Boland, Jr., & H. Thomas (Eds.), *Managing ambiguity and change* (pp. 93-126). Chichester: John Wiley & Sons.

McAnany, E. G. (1984). The logic of cultural industries in Latin America: The television industry in Brazil. In V. Mosco & J. Wasko (Eds.), *The Critical Communication Review,* 11 (pp. 185-207). New Jersey: Ablex.

McAnany, E. G. (1993). The telenovela and social change. In A. Fadul (Ed.), *Serial fiction in TV; The Latin American telenovelas.* School of Communication and Arts, Sao Paulo, Brazil.

Mowlana, H. (1991). *The spirit of fighting against oppression.* Proceedings from the international symposium: The world's view of Japan through *Oshin.* Japanese television programs in the world media market (pp. 31-39). Tokyo, Japan: NHK International.

Mowlana, H., & Wilson, L. J. (1990). *The passing of modernity: Communication and the transformation of society.* New York: Longman.

Murdock, G. (1992). Large corporations and the control of the communications industries. In M. Gurevitch, T. Bennett, J. Curran, & J. Woollacott (Eds.)., *Culture, society and the media.* New York: Methuen.

Nariman, H. (1993). *Soap operas for social change.* Westport, CT: Praeger.

NHK International (1991). *The word's view of Japan through Oshin. Japanese TV programs in the world media market.* Tokyo: NHK International.

Nordenstreng, K., & Varis, T. (1974). *Television traffic-A one way street.* Paris: UNESCO.

Oliveira, O. S. (1986). Satellite TV and dependency: An empirical approach. *Gazette, 38,* 127-145.

Oliveira, O. S. (1990, June). Brazilian soaps outshine Hollywood: Is cultural imperialism fading out. Paper presented at the International Communication Association, Dublin, Ireland.

Piotrow, P. T., Meyer, R. C., & Zulu, B. A. (1992). AIDS and mass persuasion. In J. Mann &   others (Eds.), *AIDS in the World* (pp. 733-759). Cambridge, MA: Harvard University   Press.

Pool, I. (1977, Spring). The changing flow of television. *Journal of Communication,* 139-149.

Ram, A., Rahoi, R. L., & Svenkerud, P. J. (1994, June). Deciding who wears the white hat: More effectively using myths and archetype in pro-social entertainment-education programming --- Lessons to be learned from *Hum Rahi*. Paper presented at the annual meeting of the International Communication Association, Sydney, Australia.

Rogers, E. M. (1962). *Diffusion of innovations* (1st edition). New York: Free Press.

Rogers, E. M. (1976). The passing of a dominant paradigm. In E. M. Rogers (Ed.), *Communication and development*. (pp.121-133). Beverly Hills: Sage.

Rogers, E. M. (1995). *Diffusion of innovations* (4th edition). New York: Free Press.

Rogers, E. M., & Antola, L. (1985, Autumn). Telenovelas: A Latin American success story. *Journal of Communication*, 24-35.

Rushton, J. P. (1982). Television and pro-social behavior. In D. Pearl, L. Boutilet, & J. Lazar (Eds.), *Television and behavior: Ten years of scientific progress and implications for the eighties, 2*, 248-258.

Salinas, R., & Peldan, L. (1979). Culture in the process of dependent development: Theoretical   perspectives. In K. Nordenstreng & H. I. Schiller (Eds.), *National sovereignty and international communications*. Norwood, NJ: Ablex.

Schiller, H. I. (1971). *Mass communication and the American empire*. Boston: Beacon.

Schnitman, J. A. (1984). *Film industries in Latin America -- Dependency and development*. Norwood, NJ: Ablex.

Schramm, W. (1964). *Mass media and national development: The role of information in the developing countries*. Stanford, CA: Stanford University Press.

Singhal, A., Obregon, R., & Rogers, E. M. (1994). Reconstructing the history of *Simplemente Maria*, the most popular telenovela in Latin America of all time. *Gazette, 54(1)*, 1-18.

Singhal, A., & Rogers, E. M. (1989). *India's information revolution*. New Delhi: Sage.

Singhal, A., Rogers, E. M., & Brown, W. J. (1993). Harnessing the potential of entertainment-education telenovelas. *Gazette, 51*, 1-18.

Singhal, A., & Svenkerud, P. (1994). Pro-socially shareable entertainment television programs: A programming alternative in developing countries. *The Journal of Development Communication, 5(2)*, 17-30.

Singhal, A., & Udornpim, K. (1997). Cultural shareability, archetypes, and television soaps: 'Oshindrome' in Thailand. *Gazette*, 59 (3): 171-188.

Straubhaar, J. (1991). Beyond media imperialism: Asymmetrical interdependence and cultural proximity. *Critical Studies in Mass Communication, 8*, 39-59.

Straubhaar, J. (1992). Asymmetrical interdependence and cultural proximity: A critical review on the international flow of television programs. A paper presented for the symposium, Television study: A cultural/critical view, Taipei.

Straubhaar, J., & Viscacillas, G. M. (1991). Class, genre and the regionalization of television programming in the Dominican Republic. *Journal of Communication, 41*, 53-74.

Surkhamad, W. (1991). *Entertainment and education: Two separate entities?* Proceedings from the International Symposium: The world's view of Japan through *Oshin*. Japanese TV programs in the world media market. (pp. 93- 98). Tokyo: NHK International.

Svenkerud, P., Rahoi R. L., & Singhal, A. (1995). Incorporating ambiguity and archetypes in entertainment-education programming: Lessons learned from Oshin. *Gazette, 55* (3), 147-168.

Takahashi, K. (1991). *An international "Oshin".* Proceedings from the International Symposium: The world's view of Japan through *Oshin*. Japanese television programs in the world media market (pp. 23-30). Tokyo: NHK International.

Varis, T. (1984). The international flow of television programs. *Journal of Communication, 34*, 143-152.

Warne, J., & Tillinghast, D. S. (1994, July). TV viewing in Baranquilla, Colombia: A question of cultural imperialism? Paper presented at the International Communication Association, Sydney, Australia.

Waterman, D., & Rogers, E. M. (1994). The economics of television program production and trade in Far East Asia. *Journal of Communication, 44*, 89-111.

Ylstra, Y. (1991). *Oshin in Belgium and Holland*. Proceedings from the International Symposium: The world's view of Japan through *Oshin*. Japanese television programs in the world media market (pp. 107-113). Tokyo: NHK International.

Chapter 14

A Critical Examination of a UNESCO Study on Television Flows in Europe and Asia

Jan Servaes
Patchanee Malikhao

The growth in communication activities is directly reflected in the growth and spread of television and radio in countries all over the world. National governments and private companies are investing large amounts of money to expand and upgrade the broadcasting facilities to capture ever larger segments of the population. Local programme production capacities cannot keep pace with the expansion of television-time, resulting in the importation of ever larger amounts of foreign programme material usually from the developed Western countries, particularly the United States. In addition, satellite-based national and regional television transmissions are becoming more numerous. Therefore, spill-over television programmes or regional and international satellite-based television receptions are becoming increasingly important and causing worry to national and local authorities.

Any study of the international flow of television material needs to take these developments into consideration and design research methodologies and instruments that are capable of capturing the rapidly changing media scene. Such a study must begin with a re-examination of the earlier methodologies and theories before proceeding to the development of new ones.

The international flow of television programmes has been the subject of several studies by Unesco, including *Television Traffic -- A One-Way Street?* (Nordenstreng & Varis, 1974), its sequel *International Flow of Television Programmes* (Varis, 1985), and *Import/Export: International Flow of Television Fiction* (Larsen, 1990). In addition, a general summary of research on international information flows appeared in *International Flow of Information: A Global Report and Analysis* (Mowlana, 1985). In 1994, the Unesco report *TV Transnationalization: Europe and Asia* was published from edited and abridged reports prepared by Preben Sepstrup (1992) and Anura Goonasekera (1993). This report commissioned by Unesco presents two exploratory studies which examine the international flow of television programmes both in terms of its supply and its actual consumption in five European (Bulgaria, the Netherlands, Hungary, Italy, and Sweden) and four Asia-Pacific (Australia, India, the Philippines and South Korea) countries.

This chapter summarizes and comments upon the 1994 Unesco report and raises a number of questions related to this kind of research.

Rationale for a New Approach

In the past, empirical research on communication flows concentrated mainly on the study of the supply characteristics of national television only (see for instance, Nordenstreng & Varis, 1974; Varis, 1985). One analyzed how much of the output on national channels was imported and from which countries this import originated. The underlying assumption of most studies in international television flows between and among countries has been that they have cultural and economic effects in specific countries or among specific groups of viewers. Together with concepts from media imperialism or dependency theories, this assumption has been the dominant theory that guided most data collection. These theories argued that a few countries, particularly the U.S., dominate the content of international media to such an extent that they impose their culture, values and ideologies on the recipient nations (see for instance, Boyd-Barrett, 1977, 1982; Fejes, 1981; Lee, 1980; Mattelart, 1983; McPhail, 1981). In these early studies of the international flow of television programmes, attention was focused on imports and exports of media material---not consumption of imported programmes and effects of consumption. It was assumed that if there is supply, there is consumption and the effect of consumption is the adoption of foreign, generally U.S., values and life-styles.

Unesco felt the need to improve on the methodology used for this particular type of research. Of late, the total output of television results from national channels, spill-over channels from neighbouring countries, and satellite channels. The main objective of the Unesco project was to develop a methodology which could cope with the above mentioned changes and problems. In other words, the study aimed at examining a number of methodological issues in order to develop a methodology for an individual country which could cope with all three categories of television supply (i.e. national, spill-over, and satellite). Unesco also felt that it was important to include the analysis of viewer consumption with regard to the country of reception, instead of studying only the sources of television flows.

Theoretical Framework

The theoretical framework proposed for the empirical study of the Unesco report by Sepstrup (1990) and Goonasekera (1993) is illustrated in Figure 14.1. The international flow of television programmes between country 1 and n is the first independent variable which determines the dependent variable "transnationalization in television supply in a certain country" or the *first level of effects.* The amount of foreign programming available in a certain country (the transnationalization of total supply) influences consumption of transnationalized television programmes in the country (*second level effects*). In this relationship, transnationalized supply is the independent variable, and consumption of transnationalized television programmes or transnationalization of consumption the dependent variable. Figure 14.1 shows that the consumed amount of foreign programming (total consumption of transnationalized television programmes) may lead to cultural effects (*third level effects*).

In this last relationship, "consumption of transnationalized television programmes" is the independent variable, and the "potential cultural effects" the dependent variable. Cultural effects is used in a broad sense and includes (substantial) effects which are relevant from a cultural, economic, or consumer point of view, such as the formation of values, impact on the national language(s), lifestyle, national production of television programmes, conditions for national broadcasting, or consumption patterns.

Consumption of transnationalized television programmes has not been included in any previously executed study of international television flows. An analysis of the consumption of transnationalized television programmes is necessary to understand the potential substantial effects of the increasing amount of international television flows. Therefore, the study focused on both the first and second levels of effects in Figure 14.1 (i.e. transnationalization of supply and

**Figure 14.1 Basic Framework for the
1994 Unesco Study**

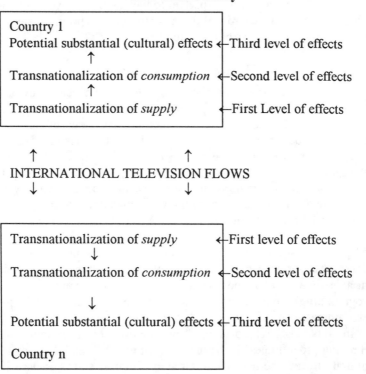

consumption of transnationalized television programmes). In some ways, one may say that the description of these effects of international television flows is a rather tedious exercise. That is perhaps why there are so many attempts to circumvent it and go straight from observations of the international flows to predictions of the third level of effects.

Information on transnationalized supply and consumption of transnationalized television programmes is relevant and interesting. Since the mid-1980s, audience studies on reception (for an overview, see Bilitereyst, 1996) have quickly grown into quite a popular approach treating a wide range of topics such as the social functioning and understanding of specific media genres, their ways of mediating specific social issues, the determining influence of contextual factors on understanding media reception, and of demographic typologies. A number of studies have been focusing on the issue of the reception of foreign, and more specifically U.S., fiction programmes by non-American audiences. Arguments on the encoding, the textual characteristics and the inherent appeal mostly point in the direction of the openness, the universality and the highly polysemic character of transnational/U.S. (fiction) programmes.

In the theoretical approach to this study, transnationalization of supply and consumption of transnationalized television programmes are variables related to specific areas or subjects; such as a group of countries, a country in particular, or specific groups of television viewers in a particular country. In other words, this means that transnationalization is regarded as a *national* phenomenon which is a consequence of international television flows.

Two earlier Unesco studies on international television flows (Nordenstreng and Varis, 1974; Varis, 1985) concentrated on only one source of supply for programming, namely, the national channels which at the time of these studies almost totally dominated television supply. But, as already mentioned, in the current circumstances it is necessary to distinguish between three sources (or dimensions) of supply. These sources are: nationally-distributed, bilaterally-distributed, and multilaterally-distributed television[1] and are identified as 'national television' (television supplied on strictly national channels), 'spill-over television' (television signals which are distributed terrestrially, in general from neighbouring countries) and 'satellite television' respectively. Therefore, this study concentrated on

Table 14.1 Summary of Measurements
of Transnationalization

Object	Total transnational- ization in countries or social groups	Dimension of transnationalization		
		Multilaterally- distributed or *satellite* television	Bilaterally- distributed or *spill-over* television	Nationally- distributed or *national* television
Supply	T-S	T_m-S T_m-S/CO	T_b-S T_b-S/CO	T_n-S T_n-S/CO
Consum- ption	T-C	T_m-C T_m-C/CO	T_b-C T_b-C/CO	T_n-C T_n-C/CO

Reprinted with permission from *TV Transnationalization: Europe and Asia,* Papers on Mass Communication, No. 109. © UNESCO, 1994.

T-S: The total transnationalization of supply in a specific country. It also applies to a group of countries or a specific group of viewers; **T_m-S**: The supply of multilaterally-distributed or satellite television in a specific country. It also applies to a group of countries or specific groups of viewers; **T_m-S/CO**: The supply of multilaterally-distributed or satellite television in a specific country from a designated country of origin. It also applies to a group of countries or specific groups of viewers; **T_b-S**: The supply of bilaterally-distributed or spill-over television in a specific country. It also applies to a group of countries or specific groups of viewers; **T_b-S/CO**: The supply of bilaterally-distributed or spill-over television in a specific country from a designated country of origin. It has two elements: domestic production from the country of origin and imported programmes. It also applies to a group of countries or specific groups of viewers; **T_n-S**: The supply of nationally-distributed television in a specific country which has been produced outside the country concerned. It also applies to a group of countries or specific groups of viewers; **T_n-S/CO**: The supply of nationally-distributed television in a specific country which has been imported from a designated country of origin. It also applies to a group of countries or specific groups of viewers. **T-C**: The total transnationalization of consumption in a specific country. It also applies to a group of countries or specific groups of viewers; **T_m-C**: The consumption of multilaterally-distributed television in a specific country. It also applies to a group of countries or specific groups of viewers; **T_m-C/CO**: The consumption of multilaterally-distributed television in a specific country from a designated country of origin. It also applies to a group of countries or specific groups of viewers; **T_b-C**: The consumption of bilaterally-distributed television in a specific country. It also applies to a group of countries or specific groups of viewers; **T_b-C/CO**: The consumption of bilaterally-distributed television in a specific country from a designated country of origin. It also applies to a group of countries or specific groups of viewers; **T_n-C**: The consumption of nationally-distributed television in a specific country which has been produced outside the country concerned; **T_n-C/CO**: The consumption of nationally-distributed television in a specific country which has been imported from a designated country of origin. It also applies to a group of countries/groups of viewers.

relating transnationalization of supply and consumption of television programmes across the three dimensions.

The technological development and increasing use of satellites and cable-networks have increased the importance of satellite and spill-over signals for the transnationalization of television supply and consumption of transnationalized television programmes. Thus, the proposed three main sources for transnationalization are useful for economic, technological, and cultural media policy decisions.[2]

Based on this framework, Table 14.1 summarizes the measurements of transnationalization used in the Unesco study.

Theory and Praxis

The Unesco study looks at both supply and consumption analyzed in terms of a large number of variables, including the type of transmission (national, bilateral, multilateral), programmes, demographics of the audience, and consumption patterns. It measures consumption as a ratio of supply.

Although initially it was intended that the same theoretical framework and methodology would be applied to both the European and Asian case studies, it became obvious very early that this objective could not be met. Therefore, each team adopted research instruments and definitions more suitable for its respective region and country.

To illustrate this, the major methodological characteristics of each regional study are outlined below.

Methodology of the European Study

This study involved 15 national channels, 20 spill-over channels and 36 satellite channels from 17 different countries. The actual number of satellite channels under study was 18. At the time of study (1991) there were 753 terrestrial local channels, two regional channels and 15 national channels operating.

In the 13 empirical studies discussed in Sepstrup (1990)[3], the two-week period from March 11, 1991 (Monday at 5 a.m.) to March 25, 1991 (Monday at 5 a.m.) was selected for data collection. The research team did not claim that this two-week period constituted a representative sample. Consequently, the results cannot be generalized to represent some specific (longer) period.

Each participating country completed a 18 page-form of tables and definitions with basic information on television and video hardware, software and consumption patterns. The outline of this form was similar to the structure of the report. The report was organized with sections on supply, consumption and utilization of television programmes for each country. Within the subcategories of supply, consumption, and utilization, specific information was sought at three levels: national, spill-over from neighboring countries, and satellite (Unesco, 1994).

An adequate number of countries had to be involved to establish the necessary heterogeneity, and that exactly the same methodology and measurements be implemented across countries. Finally, it meant that all countries on the globe be coded as potential countries of origin, and all television channels operating at the time of the study be identified as potential suppliers to viewers in the five countries under study.

Methodology of the Asian Study

This study involved five television stations in Australia, two in India, five in the Republic of South Korea, and five in the Philippines. The data were collected during different time frames between 1990 and the beginning of 1992.

In Australia, the background data pertaining to the television landscape were obtained from a number of sources, including the Australian Broadcasting Tribunal and their publications. Data related to the national origins and nature of programmes over the audience survey period were derived from weekly television programme guides appearing in magazines and newspapers.

The empirical data on television consumption were purchased from the national ratings company, Nielson. Two sets of ratings (derived from so-called 'people meters') were obtained as follows: (a) Two weekly reports for the population of Sydney, covering the period from June 2 to June 15, 1991, with a sample size of 406 households; and (b) Two weekly reports for the population of Melbourne covering the period from July 7 to July 20, 1991, with a sample size of 404 households.

The ratings encompassed five major networks; three of them were commercial broadcasters, namely The Seven Network, The Nine

Network, and Network Ten; and the remaining two were government television services which were known as ABC and SBS.

In India, a sample survey was conducted in four regions of the country covering four television centres, namely, Ahmedabad, Delhi, Lucknow and Chennai. The sample group consisted of 483 respondents.

In the Republic of South Korea, a sample of 845 respondents (from 200 households) was drawn from the main metropolitan areas in Seoul, the capital city. Data collected were derived from the people meters developed by the Korean Survey Polls, Ltd., affiliated with Gallup International.

In the Philippines, the study adopted four research methods: a sample survey, a content analysis, interviews and documentary research. Empirical data pertaining to the viewing habits and demographic data were obtained through a survey of 1,247 respondents from Metro Manila, Baguio City and Trinidad Valley in Benguet Province. Random sampling was used to choose the study areas, while cluster sampling was used to select the actual respondents. The content analysis was conducted to gather data about television programmes by using the categories of programmes prepared by Unesco. The interview method was used in order to gather background data on the video landscape from knowledgeable people from the five television stations, the National Telecommunication Network, and advertising and video agencies. Related secondary data was also collected from library material.

Summary of Major Findings

Europe

Supply

There were a few similarities found among the five countries under study. These could be divided into three groups: (1) two Eastern European countries, (2) two smaller West European countries, and (3) one big West European country.

Most of the cultures of the world were not presented to viewers in the five countries during the study period. Most of the imported programmes came from a few Western countries. Thus, the traditional fear of foreign cultural influence from imported television programming in general was not borne out. The only two programme categories which contained a high share of transnationalized supply were drama and movies. Most of the imported drama came from the U.S. The U.S. was the only country which contributed significantly to the transnationalization on national channels. Its market share of imports to Europe was high, but its share in the total supply was normally below ten percent. The major European countries did not substantially influence the supply to the five countries. The findings indicate that there was no tendency that any (group) of the European countries imported each other's programmes.

Consumption

National circumstances, the national situation, the environment for television viewing, cultural factors, programme schedules, perhaps economic development and degree of commercialization of the channel, were stronger determinants of the transnationalization of consumption than demographic characteristics. Therefore, one should not generalize the effects of international television flows among Western European countries or the role of American television in Western Europe.

Also when it came to transnationalization of consumption of programme categories, the most obvious conclusion was that there were no similarities among the countries. This said, it may be possible to identify three common features: (1) drama had a large, dominating share of consumption, and the largest degree of transnationalization; (2) other programme categories with a high transnationalization of consumption had a low share of total consumption; and (3) except for drama, transnationalization was low in programme categories with high shares of total consumption.

The national background for the transnationalization of consumption was even more one-sided than the one on supply. The viewers in the five countries had a chance to experience only one foreign culture (that is, U.S. programmes) and the consumption was characterized as almost nationalistic. However, it is difficult to conclude that, on the basis of the findings of the study, the share of U.S. programmes of consumption was perceived as a cultural problem.

Consumption of transnationalized programmes on national channels was very small when analyzed by gender, during certain time-spans, and in specific programme categories. A slightly higher transnationalization among females was found. This was probably due to the consumption of drama and light entertainment.

Asia

Australia

Supply. The amount of foreign content broadcast by Australian commercial television was regulated by the government. In 1990, the draft standard set by the Australian Broadcasting Tribunal (ABT) stated that Australian content must occupy 35 percent of the 6 pm to 12 pm time period, and it is to increase by five percent each year until 50 percent is reached. In 1992, the commercial channels exceeded the ABT's 50% demand.

The national television programming supply of Australia was 45.85 percent of the total domestic supply. The largest area of national supply fell within the category of light entertainment, followed by information, sports, news, education and drama. Over half of the foreign supply fell into the category of drama. Second came light entertainment and third was education. During prime time, there were more new nationally produced broadcasts than other categories. Ninety seven percent of the national programmes and only five percent of the imported programmes were first transmitted during prime time. More repeated transmissions from both national and foreign origins were shown outside prime time than in prime time during the study period.

The study showed that there were no less than 24 countries which supplied programmes to Australia. Great Britain, the U.S. and Australia itself were the three largest programme suppliers in Australia, comprising over 95 percent of the overall consumption. Programmes from other countries were scarce.

India

Supply. The most significant characteristic of Indian television was its self-reliance of software supply. It was found that Indian television had more than 95 percent of its programmes produced within the country with very little input from foreign sources (only about four percent). Another distinguishing feature was that very few programmes broadcasted were repeated.

As development and education were the main goals of Indian television, there was a high proportion of educational programmes broadcasted for about 150 minutes every day. In spite of this regular broadcast of educational programmes, which was 12 percent of the supply time, it should be noted that the viewership of these programmes was only four percent of the total consumption.

Philippines

Supply. Two-thirds of the programmes broadcasted were of national origin and the remaining were of foreign origin. During prime time, the proportion of foreign programmes increased to 47 percent of the total supply and most of them were series. The programmes with national origin mostly fell within the categories of variety shows, humour, and satire which took up 16 percent of the total broadcasting time. The largest area of foreign programmes by far fell into the categories of series and cartoons, each comprising 14 percent and 13 percent of the total broadcasting hours respectively.

Generally, the U.S. dominated the share of the foreign programming supply in almost every category. The U.S. alone accounted for 92 percent of the total foreign programme broadcasting time to the Philippines. The most popular programming was television series which accounted for 15 percent of the total American supply. This was followed by the action/adventure movies. It was estimated that 94 percent of the movies shown on television in the Philippines were of American origin. Also a substantial amount of the cartoons, information, religious and games programmes were supplied by the US.

Next to the U.S., but further down, was Japan which accounted for four percent of the foreign programmes. All of its supply fell under the light entertainment category. Taiwan was the third biggest programme supplier. Its supply was mostly movies, followed by series, variety and information. Only 0.2 percent of the total foreign programmes was supplied by Canada. Countries in Europe accounted for a very low proportion (only 120 minutes of Italian programmes were shown during the study period).

Asia

Australia

Consumption. An average Australian watched over three hours a day. The elderly were by far the heaviest consumers, watching an average of over four hours a day. Females were inclined to watch more television compared to males. In terms of education, those with higher education spent less time watching television than those with lower education. Both children and youth spent approximately half of their total daily viewing time watching programmes that were broadcasted during prime time. During the time of the study, females were the heavier consumers of television series, serials and imported programmes.

Local content accounted for over 60 percent of consumption during the time of study. However, it should be noted that, what was classified as local content by the Australian Broadcasting Tribunal (ABT) and the researchers, included the 'shell programmes', in which broadcast material from overseas is repackaged and presented as a locally produced programme. Thus, although they were classified as Australian, the foreign content may have been more than 95 percent of the total content.

The most consumed programme categories were drama and movies (37 percent of consumption) in which foreign productions accounted for the vast majority of consumption. Ranked second was light entertainment (22 percent of consumption). This category was dominated by local content. A prevalent pattern from the findings of this study shows that despite the substantial local content available in the national network's programming, they primarily rely on foreign productions to construct the drama content.

India

Consumption. From the study, average daily viewing was about an hour and a half. However, the actual viewing time varied from 45 minutes on weekdays to four and a half hours on Sunday.

Though the viewing habit among various age, gender and educational groups did not vary much, the young and educated viewers living in metropolitan areas seemed to be heavier consumers than others. Similarly, females were also likely to watch more television than males.

There were only a few foreign programmes. The exposure to foreign programmes was comparatively higher among males than females, among the young as opposed to the elderly, and among urban residents than rural people. It is also noteworthy that out of the total number of foreign programmes viewed, three-fourths of them were sports programmes.

Most people watched television for entertainment. Cinema/movies were the most frequently watched programmes among all categories (38 percent), followed by series (28 percent) and news. Cinema/movies and series alone made up for over half of the consumption time.

Korea

Consumption. The study shows that the average viewing time per day was one hour and twenty minutes. Only 34 percent of this total viewing time was devoted to the evening prime time programmes from 8 p.m. to 10.30 p.m.

Koreans spent very little time watching foreign programmes. Only 5 percent of their total consumption was devoted to foreign programmes. In contrast, national programmes dominated the total viewing time, especially drama and movies. This category achieved the highest rating during the time of the study. On average, approximately 27 percent of the viewing time was spent on drama/movies 89 percent of which was of national origin. The second ranking went to television series (with 24.4 percent of the total consumption). National programmes accounted for 91 percent of the series consumed, while foreign programmes occupied only a small portion of total consumption.

Philippines

Consumption. The average viewing time of the Philippinos ranged from three to five hours a day. Children appeared to be viewing the most, followed by the elderly, the adults and the young. Females had higher viewing rates than males. In terms of education, the highly educated individuals viewed more television during prime time. Rural viewers were the biggest consumers of all non-prime time shows. In prime time, urban groups seemed to outnumber others.

Sports was the most popular programme among the locally produced shows; among foreign programmes, American drama/movies were the most preferred. Japanese programmes, mainly falling into the light entertainment category, had large viewership especially among children and young viewers. However, Taiwanese programmes were frequently watched by adults and the elderly. Canadian educational programmes had the lowest consumption.

Conclusion

Australian programmes were influenced by the American program material. The influence was manifested in the style and content of the local commercial channels. Some influence from the U.K. was also evident in Australian television, especially on the ABC station. The evolution of the national ABC, based on the British BBC, is the result of historical factors.

Also Philippine television was highly influenced by American programmes. The ongoing supply of programmes from the US were necessary due to the fact that purchasing a package programme was cheaper than producing it locally.

India appeared to be unaffected by the influence of American programmes. However, reports from India show that the government and the media persons are still concerned about "cultural invasion" from satellite channels.

Koreans consumed very few foreign programmes; national programmes seemed to be more popular. However, it should be noted that the data collected were not adequate for a detailed analysis.

Observations and Recommendations for Future Research

The over-all picture presented by these case studies points to the fact that the actual viewership of programmes compared to the supply is quite small. This holds for both domestic and foreign programmes. This raises a fundamental question. What is the point in increasing the load of television fare, particularly foreign fare, when the reception is limited to a low percentage of what is available? Is it possible to speak of a saturation point in television consumption? Are we on the road to reaching this point? What implications do these findings have for theories of cultural imperialism and cultural synchronization? Does this study offer any direction or guidelines for policy makers? Studies along these lines should be continued, encompassing more countries. Only then can one elucidate the process of international television flow and its effect on transnationalization.

This study has demonstrated that the flow and consumption of international television differs from country to country, and that the findings, in some ways, are interesting for researchers and decision makers in each of the participating countries. The importance of this kind of study depends very much on the actual accessibility to cable and satellite reception (among many other factors) in each country.

But this study also proved to be difficult and took an enormous amount of energy, time and money. The problems encountered had to do with the difficulties in 'streamlining' a comparative and international research. Since the definitions of age, levels of education, and level of urbanization differed for each country, the comparison between countries in order to reach a generalization was often not reliable.

This kind of study should not be left to broadcasters' own procedures for the collection of national or international statistics or responses to questionnaires; the data may not be comparable or may be too difficult to control. This implies that the funding of comparative research must encourage studies that measure consumption in countries where it is not yet done on a routine basis. This research could be supervised centrally but has to be carried out nationally.

There is a need for an international agreement for more consumption-oriented definitions for programme categories and country of origin in order to establish an international routine for statistics on key data that can describe the development of transnationalization of television. Since it was found that 10 to 15 programme categories are enough for future research, it is necessary and possible to establish standard procedures for its reporting, so that the broadcasters can easily contribute the necessary data for the above-mentioned categories.

There is also a need for theoretical clarity on the topic. The findings in this report clearly question the idea of 'Americanization' when the U.S. imports are related to total supply and not to total imports. Though the share of American television programmes on European and Asian prime-time screens is not negligible, one knows little about the possible effect on the national, social and cultural context from exposure to U.S. television programmes. Consequently, some may believe that national and cultural identities are being eroded, while others may contend that the central historical element of national cultures will be resistant to external and/or alien forces (see Biltereyst, 1996; Sinclair, Jacka & Cunningham, 1996; Skovmand & Schroder, 1992).

Therefore, Servaes (1989, 1991) and Hamelink (1989), among others, claim that cultural identity has become a crucial concept in the debates on international communication. This problem of cultural identity is a complex one. It goes beyond mere linguistic differences and traditional values. Undoubtedly, proficiency in other languages and familiarity with other cultures are a way to bridge cultural barriers. But communities are also separated by what Dallas Smythe (1981) referred to as cultural screens.

The term cultural identity refers to two complementary phenomena: on the one hand, an inward sense of association or identification with a specific culture or subculture; on the other hand, an outward tendency within a specific culture to share a sense of what it has in common with other cultures and of what distinguishes it from other cultures. Like all social processes, these processes are not purely rational or preplanned events. Thus culture must be seen as the unintended result of an interweaving of the behavior of a group of people who interrelate and interact with each other.

Finally, it is easier to say what is necessary and possible in principle than to carry out such an empirical investigation in a real situation. Since it was found from this study that very few countries are important for transnationalization of both supply and consumption (and that transnationalization is concentrated in a few programme categories) it should be possible to keep the international and comparative statistics relatively simple, and it should be possible (though not ideal) to establish a data production unit for any given number of interested countries.

Though a number of relevant circumstances vary from country to country, it is evident that: (1) transnationalization of consumption generally must be included in studies of international television flows; (2) spill-over and satellite channels must be included in future studies; and (3) the inclusion of transnationalization of consumption is even more important when supply from spill-over and satellite channels have become important.

In conclusion, the climate in which television consumption takes place, and other factors such as the scheduling of programmes, the culture, and socio-economic development may be stronger determinants of transnationalization of television consumption, than demographic criteria such as gender, age, education or urbanization.

Notes

[1] See Sepstrup (1990) for detailed definitions.

[2] For further discussion of the relevance for third level effects of distinguishing between the three sources of television supply, see Sepstrup (1990), chapter 2.

[3] Nordenstreng and Varis (1974); Chapman et al (1986), Pragnell (1985); Varis (1985); "Television Programming in Europe" (1987,1988); EBU Statistics (1989); Larsen (1990): Krugger (1988); Kjellmore and Svedberg (1990); Jensen and Qvortrup (1990); Westrell (1987)

References

Biltereyst, D. (1996). The cultural imperialism thesis and qualitative audience research--more than revisions and cultural populism? *Communicatio, 22* (2), 2-13.

Boyd-Barrett, J.(1977). Media imperialism: Towards an international framework for the analysis of media systems. In J. Curran, M. Gurevitch, & J. Woollacott (Eds.), *Mass communication and society,* pp. 116-141. London: Edward Arnold.

Boyd-Barrett, J. (1982). Cultural dependency and the mass media. In M. Gurevitch, J. Bennett, J. Curran, & J. Woollacott (Eds), *Culture, society and the media,* pp. 17-195. London: Methuen.

Chapman, G et al. (1986). *International television flow in West Europe.* (Vols. 1-5). Cambridge: Development Policy Ltd.

EBU Statistics (1989), vol. 10, part 3, Origin of Television Programmes.

Fejes, F. (1981). Media imperialism: An assessment. In *Media, Culture and Society, 3,* 281-289.

Goonasekera, A. (Ed.). (1993). *A survey of transnationalization of television in four Asian countries.* Report submitted to Unesco, Paris. Singapore: AMIC

Hamelink, C. (1989). The relationship between cultural identity and modes of communication. In J. Anderson (Ed.), *Communication Yearbook 12* (pp. 417-426). Newbury Park: Sage.

Jensen, N. J., & Qvortrup, L. (1990). *Programvalg og seervaner i Grenaa Byantenne.* Grenaa: Grenaa Kommune.

Kjellmore, S., & S. Svedberg. (1990). *Satellit-tv:s publik. Vad händer när man far satellit-tv?* Report 4. Stockholm: SR/PUB Swedish 's Radio.

Krüger, U. M. (1988). Infos-infotainment-entertainment. Programanalyse 1988. *Media Perspektiven, 10,* 367-663

Larsen, P. (Ed). (1990). *Import/export: International flow of television fiction.* Reports and papers on Mass Communication, No 104. Paris: Unesco.

Lee, C. C. (1980). *Media imperialism reconsidered: The homogenizing of television culture.* London: Sage.

Mattelart, A. (1983). *Transnationals and the Third World: The struggle for culture.* South Hadley: Bergin & Garvey.

McPhail, T. (1981). *Electronic colonialism: The future of international broadcasting and communication.* Beverly Hills, CA: Sage.

Mowlana, H. (1985): *International flow of information: A global report and analysis.* Reports and Papers on Mass Communication, No. 99, Unesco, Paris.

Mowlana, H. (1986). *Global information and world communication.* New York and London: Longman.

Nordenstreng, K., & Varis, T. (1974). *Television Traffic - A one-way street? A survey and analysis of the international flow of television programme material.* Reports and Papers on Mass Communication, No. 70, Unesco, Paris.

Pragnell, A. (1985). *Television in Europe: Quality and values in a time of change.* The European Institute for the Media, Media Monograph No. 5. Manchester.

Rubin, B. (1993, January-February). Asia survey: New technologies breach the five barriers of media control. *Intermedia, 21* (1), 22-28

Sepstrup, P. (1990). *Transnationalization of television in Western Europe.* Acamedia Research Monograph 5, John Libbey, London.

Sepstrup, P.. (1992). *Transnationalization of television in five European countries.* Report submitted to Unesco, Paris.

Servaes, J. (1989). Cultural identity and modes of communication. In J. Anderson (Ed.), *Communication Yearbook 12,* (pp. 383- 416). Newbury Park: Sage.

Servaes, J. (Ed.). (1991). Europe 1992: Impact on the communications environment. *Telematics and Informatics (special issue),* 8 (3). Oxford: Pergamon Press.

Sinclair, J., Jacka, E., & Cunningham, S. (Eds.). (1996). *New patterns in global television. Peripheral vision.* Oxford: Oxford University Press.

Skovmand, M., & Schroder, K. M. (Eds.). (1992). *Media cultures: Reappraising transnational media.* London: Routledge.

Smythe, D. W. (1981*). Dependency road: Communications, capitalism, consciousness,and Canada.* NJ: Ablex.

Unesco (1989). *World communication report.* Paris: Unesco.

Unesco (1994). *TV transnationalization: Europe and Asia.* Papers on Mass Communication, No. 109. Edited and abridged from reports by P. Sepstrup and A. Goonasekara. Paris: Unesco.

Varis, T. (1985). *International flows of television programmes.* Reports and Papers on Mass Communication, No 100. Paris: Unesco.

Westrell, C. (1987). *Satellit-tv:s publik.* Report No 13. Stockholm: PUB/SR Swedish Radio.

Chapter 15

International Satellite Broadcasting in India and other Areas: A Critical Summary

Ewart C. Skinner
Krishna P. Kandath

STAR TV serves here as a catalyst for fleshing-out a range of ideas on the nature and impact of globalization, and a site for discussing its substantive impact on Indian society. STAR is a *fait accompli* rather than a retractable proposition. It is now a key feature of India's media system, an acknowledgment of the inexorable power of the global media corporation.

In this volume, the congeries of observations on STAR and related cultural and political-economic epiphenomena, if only through their diversity of attack, assault long-standing presumptions of international media influence. Their underlying commonality is in their closeness to Smith's thesis (1981) that much international media research is---as is the concept of cultural imperialism---"formulistic and reductionist"; "formulistic in the sense that it seeks to specify universal laws or processes in blatant disregard of the singular or idiosyncratic ... and reductionist, because it forces the particular case to express its identity solely in terms provided by the general category." (p. 78).

Therefore, these contributors want to attribute vital agency to state actors and institutions. No pride of place is given to theory by dint of tradition. The interest is in the here and now, the disposition of actors acting within the new, primarily Indian, media environment. Expansion of theoretical possibilities rather than a reduction to predictable premises is the goal. The exercise is a search---apart from theory---for reasonableness of explanations sacrificing neither tough questions nor difficult-to-digest answers.

Though disparate in approach, recurrent themes pulse through the essays: interpretations on global justice and civil society, state-media relationships, the institutional status of Doordarshan and its place in a "modernized" India, the cultural politics of language, globalized media and class structure, and the appropriateness of research methods and adequacy of theory. Although some of these essays touch on nations beyond the sub-continent and take on peripheral matters, it must be remembered that the core of the volume is on the heuristic value of STAR as it impacts on the Indian television system.

One can note from the outset that by honing in exclusively on the national dynamics, the contributors beg several significant questions which they so competently identify. The instinct to withdraw to the Indian nation for answers seems compelling theoretically. But more than Indian *status quo*, STAR is a phenomenon of global representativeness. What it implies for India, an erstwhile socialist democracy controlling a government-owned broadcasting media until recently, also applies to Asia and the rest of the Third World.

Reflecting on the chapters in this volume, two positions are taken in this summary: (1) that the STAR phenomenon can be appreciated more keenly as an international system and (2) one can take into account particularistic aspects of the Indian nation without violating prescriptions of international cultural political theory.

None of these authors would deny the preponderant influence of capitalism in the globalization process, nor India's emblematic status for the Third World in postcolonial survivability. They all would surely recognize that the muted potential of India's (and other Third World powers') cultural-political voice (at the level of news flow, for example) on the international stage is due in great measure to the crowding-in of global information brokers such as STAR. Yet, there is an implied ideological concurrence in the text which works at exciting what arguably, could be seen as a tiresome redundancy in much of the cultural imperialism debate. For example, Petras (1993), whose views resonate the cultural imperialism thesis, asserts:

"Cultural terrorism," by preying on the psychological weakness and deep anxieties of vulnerable third world peoples, particularly their sense of being "backward," "traditional" and "oppressed," projects new images of "mobility" and free expression," destroying old bonds to family and community, while fastening new chains of arbitrary authority linked to corporate power and commercial markets. (p. 142)

There are problems with this type of analysis. For example, what if there were a willing collaboration with the international community, the authors ask in this volume. How would this change the nature of the discourse, the research program, and ideological perspectives on the meaning of globalization? Even for those who approvingly follow the cultural imperialism thesis, Petras' views seems too pat an answer and too confident a knowledge of the psychological susceptibilities of Third World people.

But why the compulsion to balance the theoretical ledger, to reassess historical processes, to re-determine how international forces are to be reckoned? Surely, the fundamentals cannot be refuted: the rule of the British Empire, its centripetal suction of economies, its centrifugal impulsion of culture. Much of history supports this view. The implied answer is that Indian intelligence is shortchanged. It is untenable that one-half century after independence, many old propositions still hold, colonial imperial formations are still binding, and post-colonial India in some ways is a cultural and economic pastiche entirely of the Anglo-American imagination. In other words, Third World institutions offer little toward their own liberation. The answer these chapters offer is to restore some local aptitude where policy makers and audiences command at least some degree of agency.

Much of the discourse in this volume crashes back on the primal issue of "development." Its history coincides neatly with the discourse on media in the Third World. This hasn't changed much in the world of global television. Third World communication theory is still as much about theory of development as it is about the attributes and effects of communication systems. A change in the former (Third World communication theory) implies a change in the philosophy of development. Theoretical discourse itself charts a program for development with implied relationships in economics, sociology, politics and culture.

Narratives in both history and theory are claims for turf and legitimacy with practical implications for the system in question. There is such an example in this text, particular to our concerns. As Kumar posits, when Doordarshan bureaucrats write that organization's history endorsing their *modus operandi,* they in effect are legitimating a set of practices; and their discourse affects the system. This discourse reinforces systematic stasis, or institutional inertia (Rajagopal 1993, p. 93) we can read into. In so doing, Doordarshan's bureaucrats engage in the management of the ideas, if not ideology, of development. The essays in this volume shift the focus of international media effects— broadly conceived—from international to national analysis. These narratives are therefore extremely important in directing the trajectory of these debates. And, understandably, they begin from the points of least resistance: the modes of analysis of international research, the adequacy of macro theory, the significance of conclusions of global theorists, and the definitions of the terms of the discourse, such as nationalism and identity.

Following Smith's (1981) earlier mentioned criticisms it is easy to point out inadequacies of extant approaches. The question is where, how and on what basis do we look for new frameworks and concepts. These chapters answer by calling for: a move away from media-centeredness, a focus on nations' internal dynamics, a reconsideration of the nature and attributes of the audience, and a revisitation of the issue of identity. Some of the perspectives and approaches to these issues deserve critical reflection.

Shields' paper cogently summarizes the foregoing concerns. He argues from two core positions: (1) that media centeredness in cultural imperialism research diverts attention from more central sociological variables such as the meaning of identity and (2) such a divergence shifts attention away from important underlying concerns such as involvement of the state in media control, and the emergence of civil society and democratic outcomes. But what precisely is meant by media centeredness is unclear. And if there is a crisis in India pertaining to state-owned media and civil society, it may well be centered in the idea of development rather than the idea of democracy.

We know that the media themselves are vested in conditions of the state and its mode of operation, they are not mere epiphenomena. If a shift in subject is called for, it should be in its ontological, not disciplinary status: a shift regarding the nature of media and how we view it rather than a shift in   sociological perspective.   While allowing for disciplinary enlightenment, shifts in disciplinary focus merely postpone the difficult media issues substantive of our field.

For example, we can agree with the book's collective accusation that Doordarshan works in the interest of the state and for the elite, thereby marginalizing rural, traditional India, and at the same time endorse the centrality of the media demand side, i.e. middle class media consumption, in instigating cultural disparities between rural and urban India. Therefore, media *per se* is also seen as a locus of sociological substance. The disagreement, if there is one, has to do with different perspectives on the media. One view places emphasis on the commodification of information and the other stresses information as a public good. A third perspective dwells on what weight to place on these kinds of analyses when thinking about 'development' or 'democracy.' This is essentially a difference in media quality and value; a disagreement which inspires an insight into how we look at the constituent power of information *per se* to sustain its own need in the minds of individuals and groups. The latter is essentially a media dependency perspective, discussed by DeFleur and Ball-Rokeach (1989). It is the media (as media) which in many ways signal a shift from traditional industrial to service and electronic industries. It is the optimism of this new economics associated with the allure of modern television which sustains the hopes of those aspiring, institutionally and symbolically, to the middle class.

It is noteworthy that the audience-centered research in this volume, for the most part, study the emergent middle class, not the lower class. Melkote et al., Cohen, Das and others *ipso facto*, acknowledge the shift in emphasis and affect of this class on the new global communication process. The presumption is that the middle class audience is pivotal in the strategic supply/demand equation of both local and global information offerings.

The acknowledgment of the middle class by scholars underscores, *ipso facto,* a new development strategy. Today, a prerequisite for entry to the global economy is the establishment and maintenance of a vital, consuming middle class. The demand side of the media equation is of ultimate interest from a mediacentric point of view. Its correspondence with the development of the global market, attitudes and consumption patterns in turn can directly impale traditional development projects on the stake of global consumption. One example is that of Doordarshan jettisoning (more and more) its public service function as it competes with STAR and other private networks for advertising revenue. If there is a "crisis of institutions" in India it certainly follows from this latter day "revolution of rising expectations."

It is in this light that one can interpret what Pathania calls India's reluctant liberalization. The allure of global capital such as new markets and foreign investment, arguably not only made India a reluctant participant but a compliant one which has conceded its hand in determining terms of the cultural direction of the country. The question unresolved here is how are we to assess state's rights in establishing its own set of democratic parameters, and determine the limits of emergent civil society in the context of global media. The obverse would assume that STAR is better suited to judge democratic outcomes within India than is the Indian government itself.

The flourishing of regional Indian media is often quoted as a possible democratic spin-off of the STAR movement. Impressive growth in regional media then becomes an endorsement of the democratic potential of global forces as well as a catalyst for giddy indigenization of Indian media culture. It is easy to draw from this result the satisfaction that globalized media act as democratizing agents in the Third World, as promoters of civil society. This mind set puts a new spin on the modernization paradigm (Lerner, 1958, Schramm, 1964), the "rebirth of hope" in the communication sector (Stevenson, 1994, p. 165), and the triumph of liberal democracy (Fukuyama, 1992). It discredits or ignores an entire body of literature in the 1970s and the 1980s relating to the New World Information and Communication Order. In effect, this view separates media industries from other types of global firms (manufacturing and industrial) and isolates them from critical theories of global capitalism. Furthermore, these media firms are credited with salutary outcomes of participatory democracy (see Stevenson, 1994). However, it is possible to see the push for states' cultural rights and the concomitant political undercurrents as "a continuing response and challenge to, rather than a divergence from, increasing economic marginalization and impoverishment manifest in the world capitalist system" (Scrase, 1995, p. 156).

The triumph of liberal democracy has much to do with the Western concept of the middle class. Given the transparent reasons for its growth, obvious sponsorship by government for example, there is surprisingly little questioning of what constitutes this middle class, or to the underlying premises of its emergence. Is there a question of ethics if a government shifts its attention from the lower to the middle classes? Can investment in the middle class be consistent with traditional development goals? In most of these essays, the prior question of the composition and cohesiveness of the middle class across language and regional and state boundaries remains opaque. Its motives, priorities, predispositions *vis a vis* other classes are taken propitiously, and for granted. We are only informed of its acts and predispositions, not about how it is constituted. What we can observe is an economic/cultural exchange as members of the middle class take up their global identities through this newly acquired civic privilege. As Scrase (1995) points out, the Indian middle classes seek to maintain their cultural hegemony by precisely adopting the cultural logic of globalization to their advantage (for example, that English is a significant global language and must be taught), and so ultimately preserve a hierarchical social order in India (p. 78). Thus, the logic that globalization can lead to a form of personal liberation in this particular case is inverted in the sense that the possibility for "justice" (essentially a bigger slice of the economic cake) is monopolized by the middle classes (Scrase, 1995, p. 156). But how important are those aspects of tradition which fall away as this class joins the global bourgeoisie? Audience-centered research should be able to tell us more about this exchange, because it is precisely at this juncture that development, media, national policy and questions of identity meet.

Das, Cohen, Sinclair, Woodfield and Singhal et al. broach language, identity and cultural issues. The optimism of the latter two pieces offer salutary advice on language equity and international programming issues, but too easily bypass some of the more intractable problems of implementation. Woodfield insists that the matter of language equity can be solved by the state---by adopting a normative rather than a political framework. Similarly, Singhal et al.'s "cultural transcendence" is proposed to address, and solve in some cases, the cultural imperialism problem. However, the irony is that given their assumption of the active audience, these approaches must assume out of existence the possibility of cultural imperialism; so, there is nothing to counter. The optimism of Woodfield and Singhal et al., takes precedence over political reality. For Woodfield's well-formulated perspective to take hold, Indian media must first be "unshackled," the autonomy of Doordarshan and AIR established and the politics of language divorced from the politics of media. A daunting task indeed. Apart from their "limitations," Singhal et al ignore or make light of crucial aspects of programming including the politics of funding, and of representation. As they themselves hint, as "cultural transcendence" becomes accepted, its representativeness will become politicized.   For example, which type of program would then "represent" India, etc. in the global market?   Would "culturally transcendent" programming lead ultimately to homogenized programming?   These issues may well be moot since successful traffic in global television programs have more to do with the enigma of aesthetic and appeal than with the proscriptions of social science, from which perspective the authors write.   It is doubtful that successful transcultural programs of *social value* could be routinely produced, and upon demand. Sensibly, Singhal et al point out a number of "limitations" which draw the reader back to the hard reality of cross national television marketing.

Das' media personnel interviews seek to "ferret out underlying assumptions about the nature of national identity and its relationship to national unity, impingement on formulations of nation state, national fragmentation, etc." She illustrates well that there are problems with the notion that "Indian identity can be easily disembedded from (their) local moorings and tied into supra-national levels of affiliation."   A more critical view would have seen that while it is true that there are global identities being developed, this community remains by and large, "imagined."   The self-other construct imposed by imperialism is still a defining form in inter-national relations (Ashcroft et al, 1989). This construct refers to a significant identity gap between the colonizer (other) and the colonized (self).   As a mechanism of post-Bretton Woods control, it remains functional and fundamental today as the self-other distinctions are used in carrying out projects at the International Governmental Organization (IGO), USAID, international banks and other commercial firms.   Thus, it is difficult to agree with Das that "national and other collective identities have little existence outside meanings they are given by those who experience and articulate them."   That is clearly not true. Identity is a phenomenon that emerges from the dialectic between individual and society (Berger and Luckmann, 1966).   Global identities are at best partial formulations.   However, Das concedes that there is still much to be understood about identity insofar as it is accounted for among the Indian middle class and media elites; and one might add, there is much to learn about identity and the politics of race and ethnicity as well.

Several authors look at the question of language and the hegemony of Hindi.   This is an issue with tremendous resonance at the local level.   Its impetus comes from more or less atavistic impulses, bound up, particularly in the south, with those emerging states' attempt to preserve the traditions and history of the region. But expression of regional identity is not peculiar to India. The current crisis of language and cultural balkanization in India can be seen as a global movement---as regional groups fight for political/cultural autonomy world wide. There is spectacular example of this in stable Western democracies such as Spain and France and to some extent in the United Kingdom though in this case language is not the dominant factor. The politics of language may well continue to fragment identities in India, but not necessarily because of Hindi hegemony.

Cohen is very informative on the way countries struggle politically to ensure that their sense of nation survive in spite of international pressures. We are reminded that as nations came out of colonialism, an abiding theme was for national unification and guided development. In most of the Third World, the mandate of independence was national preservation, unification and development.   National unification was the abiding principle.   Late twentieth century reality inverts the model: global accomodation has replaced national unification as the operational principle. There was no other reasonable option then and there seems to be no other reasonable option now.   So it is with the choice of national languages. Hindi was the choice of the Indian Constituent Assembly after India's independence.   Would Tamil, Bengali or Telugu have been acceptable, or have averted the current problem in language hegemony? Certainly a multiple language option would not have sufficed in 1947.

The focus on the local is not without its sociological precedents, neither is it a perspective without substance.   Tony Smith (1981) has long suggested that writing preoccupied with the international system is a "chief methodological error which deprives local histories of their integrity and specificity, making local actors little more than pawns of outside forces" (p 77). He further argues that "political organization of social life on the periphery emerges as the single most important variable to grasp if we would understand the history of these peoples" (p. 79). It is this spirit which underlies most of the essays in this volume. But is this a reasonable proposition? Is there historical or current justification to "go local" in international media analysis? India certainly commands the material, cultural and structural resources to implement a seriously indigenous sub-continent-wide media program. But since its formal organization in 1934, Indian broadcasting media have balanced between local and non-local policy weights, whether the 1960s rural radio forums with Canadian and UNESCO support (Masani, 1981) or Indo-US collaboration on the SITE project in the 1970s (Acharya, 1987). Connors (1993) posits:

SITE was but one of a number of satellite projects in which India was involved during the late 1970s and early 1980s. All of these projects drew on widespread international co-operation: the Satellite Telecommunications Experiment Project (STEP) was conducted between 1977 and 1979 using Franco-German Symphonie satellite; Bhaskara 1 & 2, India's first remote-sensing satellites were launched by Soviet vehicles in 1979 and 1981. (p. 32)

Arguably, broadcasting media have never been truly indigenized, except in the sense that "political personages regarded media (AIR/Doordarshan) as a tool for *their* publicity and propaganda (Masani, 1981). Therefore, the local integrity of the media has been compromised since its conception. Today, Indian broadcasting media policy functions primarily as a response to international satellite broadcasting.

While one can isolate issues which are particularistic, it is hard to imagine that such an intrinsically global matter as satellite television can be considered in a primarily local perspective. Such a view would only serve to spare the sentiments of those who eschew the cultural imperialism perspective. However, it would lose at the very least, the wonderful heuristic that the cultural imperialism approach offers. Even if language policy *per se* can be seen as a local matter, government initiative in media policy is hardly an exclusively local matter. The internationalization of culture and global capitalism are tightly linked. The question remains: How are we to acknowledge political potency within nations without understating the impact of global capitalism in the Third World? To paraphrase Smith (1981) to our own device, "we can do so if we can draw attention to the interconnectedness of economic and political processes and events in a global manner, but are willing to grant [some] autonomy, [some] specificity, [some] particularity [to national issues] independent of its membership as a whole" (Smith 1981, p. 78, parenthesis added).

The problem is to distinguish those problems which are primarily local from those which are primarily international, if indeed that distinction can be made. Indeed, some social processes register equally on both local and international accounts. The double role of the middle class and its economic/cultural role in the globalization process has been addressed by post-imperialist theories. Using this theory as a sounding board, it is possible to put into relief some aspects of the global idea without denying a measure of autonomy to local actors. Although coming from the field of political economy, the theory can elucidate some heretofore opaque issues regarding the use of media within nations, satellite television and globalization of culture.

Post-Imperialist Sounding Board

Post-imperialist theory as a concept grew out of "political theories of the modern business corporation and class analysis of political power in the Third World" (Becker & Sklar, 1987b, p. ix). This perspective is "an intellectual response to two empirical findings that contradict standard theories of capitalist imperialism ...the growing separation of national interest from the interests of the dominant classes in the industrial capitalist countries and, a growing congruence of national interests and dominant class interests in the Third World" (p. ix). Becker et al (1987b) argue that research findings are

> incompatible with the belief that capitalism drives nation-states to dominate and exploit one another" but consistent with the evident spread of industrialization to all regions of the world and with the coalescence of dominant social classes across national and continental frontiers. Every where, dominant classes embrace supranational and global values while subordinate classes are relatively more nationalistic. (Becker et al. 1987b, p. ix).

According to Becker et al (1987a), the "post-imperialism thesis is specifically class analytic. It propounds the idea of transnational class formations based upon the coalescence of dominant class elements across national boundaries..... and neither cultural nor ideological barriers have prevented the formation of business partnerships between dominant class elements on a transnational basis" (p. 9-10). Post-imperialist thinkers affirm that business corporations are non-statist political institutions which "rival and check statist political power both within national societies and, increasingly in world politics." (Becker et al, 1987a). One does not have to agree with all, nor the major part of these two hypotheses nor their corollaries, to acknowledge their utility in terms of understanding the transnational media situation. Merely by describing aspects of STAR's involvement in Asia, one finds intact a few core principles of the postimperialism thesis: its oligopolistic structure, its association with elites, the domicility of national rules and forms, etc.

The STAR institution, one must believe, does its tailoring through the seams of class theory. The expectations must be that provident audiences would comprise of an emerging transnational bourgeoisie---a group functioning across regions of India---English speaking, well educated, culturally aware, politically conscious, economically well-off and aware, socially positioned but nevertheless traditionally sensitive. As we have seen, such is the case in Asia (Indonesia in this volume) and such is also the case in Latin America (Becker, 1987a; 1987b).

These class factors interplay with media consumption at the sector at which the need for theory is most important: in the international/national/local meeting point, its impact on national audience pools and politics, and on national policy. But the wider context in which STAR emerged is just the heuristic ground needed for probing the applicability of the post-imperialist theory.

STAR's Post-Imperialist Context

The essential characteristics of STAR's viability is the "assertive pragmatism" (Becker et al, 1987, p.112) currently in vogue in Asian cultural economics. While not willing to cede its cultural space entirely to Anglo-American products, the Indian government has undertaken to build relationships with Murdoch and others in order to take advantage of economic development and the creation of resources generated through capitalist initiative in an opening up of global opportunities. STAR came about in an advantageous competitive environment in Asia, particularly in China and India. The following factors were crucial in its development: its early alliances and integration with ancillary media, its underwritten support from well-established transnational media personalities, its leverage with entrenched political regimes, its technologically sophisticated leadership, its monopoly of channel space, naiveté of its audiences (Westlake, 1991; Kraar, 1992), and the corporate media sophistication of its developers.

STAR's structure, laid out initially by Hong Kong billionaire Li Ka-shing demonstrates the sophistication of Asian media oligarchies in accommodating transnational capital and bringing them into regional importance. Ka-Shing's alliances and collaboration with HutchVision, Cable & Wireless, China International Trust & Investment Corp, is further evidence of alliances between international capital and Third World political leadership. (Kraar, 1992, p. 109).

Not surprisingly, the Asian government sponsors and STAR TV both had first options on Asiasat's transponders. "In fact, more than half of Asiasat's transponders [were] rented out by Asian governments for the use of local TV and phone services" (Kraar, 1992, p. 109). This duopoly, rather "congruence between national interests and dominant class interests" existed for a critical period in STAR's development. "Asiasat was the only satellite available for the next two or three years for full broadcast coverage within the Asian region" (Westlake, 1991, p. 60) and by reserving 10 of Asiasat's 24 transponders---"the remainder of them reserved for individual countries' telecommunications services or TV relay use by various countries"---allowed STAR effectively to block any other pan-Asian TV service" (Westlake, 1991, p. 60) from developing at the time.

Doordarshan, more than other Asian media systems was impacted significantly by STAR because it underestimated STAR's potential and because of its own "ambivalent" mandate. Shortly after STAR TV started to program to India, Doordarshan had its monopoly broken (Westlake, 1991, p. 61). It underestimated the importance of the sub-regional language issue, the embrace of global values by the Indian consumer class, and by the openness of Indian entrepreneurial classes to media capitalism. Doordarshan's policy makers thought that English language programming, and the cost of buying a large expensive satellite dish would narrow STAR's profitability. Doordarshan's bureaucrats did not envision the capitalistic ingenuity of its own constituency, the Indian middle class attachment to Western programming, and the emergence of a new, informal, cable system---reaching 12 million homes initially---to develop in support of STAR (Westlake, 1991, p. 61).

The content of STAR's channels that ranged from MTV Asia, BBC World Service News, Primetime Sports, and STAR Entertainment further ensued a coalescence of global values and appreciation. With the launching of Asiasat2, STAR gained a much expanded channel capacity---of 100 channels---and a footprint that spanned from east Asia to western Europe ("STAR TV Rising," 1993).

In mid-1993 when, Rupert Murdoch, paid $500 million for sixty-four percent share of STAR TV, the system entered its truly transnational phase ("Murdoch's Asian Bet," 1993, p. 13). Asian audiences, it was thought, suffered from a qualitative media disadvantage with their Western counterparts. It was widely believed that Americans and Europeans had access to about 25 channels, while in Asia, including Japan, the average was 2.4 channels with "most of them government-controlled and filled with boring propaganda" (Kraar, 1992, p. 109). Viewers within the Asian region were either dissatisfied with the programming available or were seeking global supplements. Tanzer (1991) sees the very high VCR penetration in Asia--- 70% in Hong Kong, for example---"as an indication of the dissatisfaction with TV programming" (p. 59).

Apparently, STAR's managers understood the implications of projections that in terms of audience needs, size (60% of the world by 2005) and economic growth, in Asia---meaning the parts of that vast continent east of Iran but outside the ex-Soviet empire---STAR's success would be guaranteed ("Murdoch's Asian Bet," 1993, p. 13). In fact, reports have shown that "Asia's share of gross world product is closer to 20% rather than 7% projected in the 1990s" ("Murdoch's Asian Bet," 1993, p. 13). The fast rise in Asian economies of the past 20 years represents an increasingly large Asian middle class, a potential audience which it is claimed welcome membership in the international video world and a consumption pattern based on what is called the "firecracker effect" ("Murdoch's Asian Bet," 1993, p. 13) which implies that as family income doubles, their consumption of goods and services will also double, particularly in the area of information.

STAR's programming and audience draw had an immediate effect on India's Doordarshan but with repercussions on other regional media configurations. Doordarshan moved from broadcasting programs based upon Hindu scriptures to showcasing Disney programs. By early 1992, they were broadcasting old reruns of "Dallas" taking a programming turn that propelled them into the orbit of the "Big Five" or "The Gang of Five," then STAR's leading competitor. These sources included CNN, Discovery, the Australian Corp., and Viacom Cable (Kraar, 1992) which launched a PALAPA B2P satellite covering much of south east Asia (Tanzer, 1991, p. 59). Among the groups that have joined PALAPA are ESPN, HBO (a division of Time/Warner), Television Broadcasting Ltd. (TVD), and the Asia Business News (Dow Jones Industrial) (Kraar, 1994). Both PALAPA and STAR operate on the C-band section of the C-band radio spectrum which offers immense geographical coverage but a weak signal requiring a large (eight feet in diameter) dish for signal reception (Tanzer, 1992, p. 60). These conditions inspired a noticeable, nascent petty industry in local cable, tolerated reluctantly by the Indian government, presenting a perplexing problem for Doordarshan which:

toyed with the idea of five new private channels, but politicians thought this a bad idea. Indian governments have always regarded television as part of the state propaganda machine. So Doordarshan decided that another government outfit, the National Film Development Corporation, would take charge of the new channels [Gang of Five], none of which would be allowed to broadcast news, and whose current affairs programs would be controlled (Kraar, 1994 p. 101).

Star TV Asia: The Post-Imperialist Evidence

Institutionally (or structurally) STAR is but one aspect of a worldwide economic free market liberalism in which cultural and political fragmentation and reformulation are now *de rigueur*, and in which economic and political philosophies face constant refurbishment with accompanying repercussions in socio-cultural and geo-political relations. It represents a techno-globalized age in which a technological consciousness, driven by key words such as "deregulation, globalization, synergy and convergence" (Dyson and Humphreys, 1990) implacably impress the social and cultural sectors of metropolitan institutions on "Third World" consciousness.

As the chapters in this book show, since its inception STAR has had to account for the fragmentation of national media networks in India leading to the ascendance of regional media; reassertion of the rights of the individual to receive information in a variety of competing discourses and languages; creation of a *de facto* competitive media environment across several information sectors including advertising, production and distribution of media products; creation and acknowledgment of a consciousness of globalization and a privileging of the global involvement by the middle classes' which propels them into the ranks of the transnational bourgeoisie. One can draw from this that STAR serves as a force for cultural understanding and cultural interchange. For us, at least, the discourse on satellite broadcasting can be seen as reinvigorating the academic/scholarly discourse on the democratizing influence of new technologies, the "global village" and civil society.

STAR's detractors argue that as a system of the transnational media, it is opposed to the fundamental principles of national development, it intensifies the competition for audiences by lowering the national cultural fare and highlighting foreign programming, it interferes with national policy making apparatus of the Indian media establishment, it encourages the trend toward oligopolistic control in the global community and media concentration in the home regions, it marginalizes the least wealthy, it creates a false transnational middle class, it creates alliances with foreign media powers and national political institutions, and it is motivated by a philosophy dictated by right wing, arch conservative industry leaders.

The problematic in the foregoing chapters has been to understand the role STAR TV plays in Indian broadcasting media, and to interpret STAR's relationship to media institution such as Doordarshan, and its impact upon the Indian media-consuming public. Since the late 1960s, both analytical instinct and organized theory have leaned toward the view that an impact such as STAR's would inevitably be negative in a Third World context. Much research based upon the cultural imperialism perspective has supported that line of argument.

The foregoing chapters plead, by force of argument, for a view that is more sensitive to the maturity of national responses to international cultural institutions. Therefore, much of the work and thought represented here is from or about the potential of local, i.e. national agencies and agents, or their constraints vis a vis other national agents or agencies. And the edge of the collective argument is its critique of the cultural imperialism line and with it, a suspicion of international theory as a whole.

While analytical focus on the national level is enlightening, neglect of international theory is unwarranted. Approaching the problematic, principally for its heuristic value, this final chapter asks whether there can be an accommodation between both insights, the national and the international. This chapter proposes that the postimperialism theory of Becker et el (1987a) is a way to look at some of these matters because it acknowledges, on the one hand, the power and influence at the national level of bureaucratic parastatal organizations and the burgeoning technocratic-industrial elite, and on the other hand, accepts that global corporations work to domicile themselves and adapt to Third World conditions out of economic self interest.

The aim here was neither to develop, argue, nor propose postimperialist theory but to identify it as one heuristic in the game of interpretation. By all accounts, the role of emergent bourgeoisie classes, of international corporate domicility, pragmatic adaptation of indigenous institutions are all aspects of the incursion of global media institutions in the Third World. Without sacrificing too much of the arguments of these chapters, postimperialist theory brings the global back to the local and hence becomes a useful reflection on the relations between endogenous and exogenous actors in international media. What is still left out, however and what the postimperialist theory cannot provide is the cultural ramifications of these relationships.

Conclusion

Thus, STAR's drive for its mass audience brings it into a matrix of political and cultural concerns vis-à-vis Asian governments and their broadcasting authorities. Of course, STAR's principal motive is return on capital generated through audiences throughout Asia. Cost efficiencies would dictate that advertisers send the same message, in some cases, to thirty-nine countries (Kraar, 1994 p. 100) which extends the political cultural issues across regional borders. Kraar (1994) explains:

Programming that works splendidly in the US and Europe may not fly in Asia. More than audiences anywhere else in the world, Asians are segmented by a broad spectrum of languages, religions, and social systems. Though US reruns work in India, which has a large English-speaking population, they don't fare as well elsewhere in the region (p. 100).

However, the fragmentation of the Indian audience by state and language has proven costly and economically inefficient for STAR. What post-imperialist theorists have not envisioned is the resistance and change from subordinate groups, an adjustment more intractable than the ideological doctrine of domicile could accomplish (see Becker at al., 1987a). This resistance has caused STAR itself to reshuffle its programming in order to accommodate to three aspects of the Asian environment: a) the complex cultural and language demands of audiences, b) competition from indigenous media operators and c) the emerging national policy. STAR's motive for change is not principally for the benefit of these constituencies *per se*, nor a safe haven of domicile but is part of a constant adjustment to the competition in the Asian cultural and economic environment, with the potential of wrecking many a global ship.

In this regard, one must also be aware of India's legacy. Within its complexity of circumstances, India remains the world's largest democracy; it has incorporated both cultural and institutional aspects of the West with remarkable success. It has colonized Westminster politics as surely as it has colonized cricket. Both have been subverted by local institutions and adapted to local needs through local nuances, regardless of their seeming exoticism. In the end, it may colonize STAR TV too. Meanwhile STAR's global leverage remains the most important factor in India and DD's adjustment to the prerequisites of modernization and the global media corporation.

References

Acharya, Rabi Narayan (1987). *Television in India*. Delhi: Manas Publications.

Aschroft, Bill, Griffiths, Gareth, Tiffin, Helen (1989). *The empire writes back: theory and practice in post-colonial literatures.* New York: Routledge.

De Fleur, M. L, and Ball-Rokeach, S. (1989). Media system dependency theory. In De Fleur and Ball-Rokeach (Eds.). *Theories of mass communication,* (pp. 297-327). New York: Longman.

Becker, David G., Friedan, J., Schatz, Sayre P., and Sklar, Richard L. (Eds.). (1987). *Postimperialism: international capitalism and development in the late twentieth century.* Boulder, Colorado: Lynne Rienne Publishers.

Becker David G., and Sklar, Richard (1987a). Why postimperialism In Becker, David G; Friedan, J.; Schatz, Sayre P.; and Sklar, Richard L.(Eds.). (1987). *Postimperialism: international capitalism and development in the late twentieth century.* (pp. 1-18). Boulder, Colorado: Lynne Rienne Publishers.

Becker David G., and Sklar, Richard (1987b). Preface. In Becker, David G; Friedan, J.; Schatz, Sayre P.; and Sklar, Richard L.(Eds.). (1987). *Postimperialism: international capitalism and development in the late twentieth century.* (pp. ix-x). Boulder, Colorado: Lynne Rienne Publishers.

Becker David G. (1987a). Development, democracy, and dependency in Latin America: a post imperialist view. In Becker, David ,G; Friedan, J.; Schatz, Sayre P.; and Sklar, Richard L.(Eds.). (1987). *Postimperialism: international capitalism and development in the late twentieth century.* (pp. 41-62). Boulder, Colorado: Lynne Rienne Publishers.

Becker David G. (1987b). "Bonanza Development" and the "New Bourgeoisie": Peru under military rule. In Becker, David, G; Friedan, J.; Schatz, Sayre P.; and Sklar, Richard L.(Eds.). (1987). *Postimperialism: international capitalism and development in the late twentieth century.* (pp. 63-106). Boulder, Colorado: Lynne Rienne Publishers.

Berger, Peter L. and Luckmann, Thomas (1966*). The social construction of reality: a treatise in the sociology of knowledge.* New York: Anchor Books - Doubleday.

Connors, Michael (1993). *The race to the intelligent state: Towards the Global economy of 2005.* Cambridge, MA: Blackwell Business.

Dyson, K. and Humphreys, P. (1990). Introduction: politics, markets and communication policies. In Kenneth Dyson and Peter Humphreys (Eds.). *The political economy of communications: international and European dimensions.* (pp. 1-32). New York: Routledge.

Fukuyama, Francis (1992). *The end of history and the last man.* New York: Free Press.

Kothari, R. (1989). *State against democracy: In search of humane governance.* New York: New Horizons.

Kraar, L. (1992 ,July 13). A billionaire's global strategy. *Fortune.* pp. 106-109.

Kraar, L. (1994, Jan 24th). TV is exploding all over Asia. *Fortune.* pp. 98-101.

Lerner, D. (1958). *The Passing of the Traditional Society: Modernizing the Middle East.* New York: Free Press.

Masani, Mehra (1981). Broadcasting in India. In William E. McCavitt (Ed.). *Broadcasting around the world.* (pp. 207-219). Blue Ridge Summit, PA.: TAB Books.

Murdoch's Asian bet (1993, July 31st). *The Economist.* pp. 13 - 14.

Petras, James (1993). Cultural Imperialism in the late 20th century. *Journal of Contemporary Asia.* Vol 23 No 2. pp. 139 - 149.

Rajagopal, A. (1993). The rise of national programming: The case of Indian television. *Media, Culture and Society.* 15: 91-111.

Schramm, W. (1964). *Mass Media and National Development.* California: Stanford University Press.

Scrase, Timothy J. (1995). Globalization, India and the struggle for justice. In a new world order? In David A. Smith and Joseph Borocz (Eds.). *Global transformation in the late twentieth century.* (pp. 147-161). Westport, Conn.: Greenwood Press.

Scrase, Timothy J. (1993). *Image, ideology and inequality: cultural domination, hegemony and schooling in India.* New Delhi: Sage.

Schatz, Sayre P. (1987) Assertive pragmatism and the multinational enterprise. In Becker, David G; Friedan, J.; Schatz, Sayre P.; and Sklar, Richard L. (Eds.). (1987). *Postimperialism: international capitalism and development in the late twentieth century.* (pp. 107-129). Boulder, Colorado: Lynne Rienne Publishers.

Smith, Tony (1981). *The pattern of imperialism: The United States, Great Britain, and the late- industrializing world since 1815.* Cambridge: Cambridge University Press.

STAR TV Rising. (1993, April 17). *The Economist..* pp. 66-67.

Stevenson, Robert Louis. (1994). *Global communication in the twenty-first century.* New York: Longman.

Tanzer, A. (1991, November 11) The Asian Village. *Forbes,* pp. 58-60.

Westlake, M. (1991, May 30th). Reach for the STARs. *Far Eastern Economic Review,* pp. 60-61.

Index

About the Editors and Contributors

Binod C. Agrawal is Director of TALEEM Research Foundation in Ahmedabad, India. His work includes development communication, instructional communication, transactional and alternative learning for emancipation and empowerment.

Syed Amjad Ahmed is Reader and Head of the Department of Mass Communication in the University of Calicut in Calicut, India.

Hart Cohen is Senior Lecturer in the School of Communication and Media, University of Western Sydney in Nepean, Australia. His research interests are in the global media.

Shobha Das recently completed her doctoral work from the Open University, Milton Keynes, United Kingdom. She works as a caseworker in Support Against Racist Incidents in Bristol, United Kingdom.

Krishna Kandath is a doctoral candidate in the School of Interpersonal Communication in the College of Communications at Ohio University, Athens, Ohio.

Keval J. Kumar is Reader in the Department of Communication and Journalism at the University of Poona in Pune, India. He is also the Director of the Resource Centre for Media Education and Research. He is the author of *Mass Communication in India* (Jaico Paperbacks), and *Media Education, Communications and Public Policy: An Indian Perspective* (Himalaya Publishers).

Patchanee Malikhao is Senior Consultant in Communication and Graphic Arts in Brussels, Belgium.

Srinivas R. Melkote is Professor of Telecommunications and Associate Dean in the Graduate College at Bowling Green State University in Bowling Green, Ohio. His research and teaching interests are in development communication, quantitative research methods, mass communication theory and health communication. He is the author of *Communication for Development in the Third World: Theory and Practice* (Sage Publications, 1991).

Sundeep R. Muppidi is a doctoral fellow in Mass Communication at Bowling Green State University in Bowling Green, Ohio. His research and teaching interests include development communication, health communication, media theory and video production.

Geetika Pathania is a doctoral candidate in the Department of Radio-Television-Film at the University of Texas in Austin, Texas.

Rita Rahoi-Gilchrest earned her doctoral degree in communication from Ohio University and now works in a corporate setting.

Sandhya Rao is Associate Professor in the Department of Mass Communication at Southwest Texas State University in San Marcos, Texas.

B. P. Sanjay is Professor of Communication and Dean of the S.N. School of Communication and Performing Arts at the University of Hyderabad in India.

Jan Servaes is Dean of the Faculty of Political and Social Sciences and Professor of Communication at the Katholieke Universiteit Brussel in Belgium.

Peter Shields is Assistant Professor of Telecommunications at Bowling Green State University in Bowling Green, Ohio. His research and teaching interests include media and policy issues, and social implications of communication technology.

John Sinclair is Professor in the Department of Communication, Language and Cultural Studies at Victoria University of Technology in Melbourne, Australia.

Arvind Singhal is an Associate Professor in the School of Interpersonal Communication in the College of Communication at Ohio University.

Ewart Skinner is Associate Professor of Telecommunications at Bowling Green State University in Bowling Green, Ohio. His research and teaching interests include international communications, qualitative research methods, media theory and effects.

Peer Svenkerud earned his doctoral degree in communications from Ohio University and now works in a corporate setting.

Andrew Woodfield is Reader in Philosophy and Director of the Center for Theories of Language and Learning at the University of Bristol in the United Kingdom. He is a member of the executive committee of the Foundation for Endangered Languages.